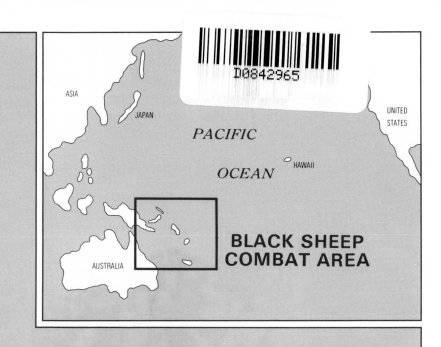

PACIFIC

OCEAN

ASIA

JAPAN

HAWAII

UNITED
STATES

AUSTRALIA

**BLACK SHEEP
COMBAT AREA**

I C

O C E A N

PIRITU
SANTO

MALEKULA

**NEW
HEBRIDES
ISLANDS**

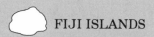

FIJI ISLANDS

Noumea

ONCE
THEY
WERE
EAGLES

ONCE THEY WERE EAGLES

The Men of the Black Sheep Squadron

FRANK E. WALTON

THE UNIVERSITY PRESS OF KENTUCKY

The University Press of Kentucky
Scholarly publisher for the Commonwealth,
serving Bellarmine College, Berea College, Centre
College of Kentucky, Eastern Kentucky University,
The Filson Club, Georgetown College, Kentucky
Historical Society, Kentucky State University,
Morehead State University, Murray State University,
Northern Kentucky University, Transylvania University,
University of Kentucky, University of Louisville,
and Western Kentucky University.

Editorial and Sales Offices: Lexington, Kentucky 40506-0024

Library of Congress Cataloging-in-Publication Data

Walton, Frank E., 1909-
  Once they were eagles.

  Includes index.
  1. World War, 1939-1945—Aerial operations,
American. 2. World War, 1939-1945—Campaigns—Pacific
Ocean. 3. World War, 1939-1945—Regimental histories—
United States. 4. United States. Marine Fighter
Squadron 214—History. I. Title.
D790.W32   1986   940.54′4973   85-29447
ISBN 0-8131-1579-5

To the Black Sheep

those young eagles who forged a blazing path across the skies
of the South Pacific, and especially to those Black
Sheep who did not return to the fold:

Robert A. Alexander • George M. Ashmun • Harry R. Bartl
James E. Brubaker • Pierre Carnagey • J. Cameron Dustin
Robert T. Ewing • Bruce Ffoulkes • Walter R. Harris
Donald J. Moore • Virgil G. Ray

They shall not grow old, as we that are left grow old:
Age shall not weary them, nor the years condemn.
At the going down of the sun and in the morning—
We will remember them.

Lawrence Binyon, "For the Fallen"

Contents

Foreword

This is the exciting story of eighty-four days in the life of a famous Marine Corps fighting squadron during the battle with the Japanese for control of the South Pacific. It is an account of a group of fifty-one men commanded by a very unusual but talented combat ace, who in a very short time destroyed twenty-eight enemy planes and in turn was finally shot down himself to become a prisoner of war for twenty months and to win the Congressional Medal of Honor.

When Frank Walton called me from Honolulu to tell me about this book, I recalled my first conversation with him in Saigon about writing the story of Pappy Boyington and his Black Sheep. Knowing Colonel Walton's colorful background as deputy commander of the Los Angeles police force, his career as a foreign service officer in Southeast Asia, and his wartime adventures as a marine with Colonel Boyington and VMF 214, I told him that with this background and his skill as a writer he should surely produce a book. This story is the result.

Greatly interested, I asked Colonel Walton to send me a copy. A few days later a package of manuscript arrived. I opened it expecting to find another well-written story of marines in combat—this time in the air. What I did find was an intensely interesting and superbly written narrative, which I could not let go until I had finished.

The book is unique in that it not only vividly describes the life-and-death battles fought by the young marine pilots of the Black Sheep Squadron in the skies over the South Pacific, but follows up this story in the second portion of the account with personal interviews, extending over a two-year-period, with squadron survivors giving their recollections of the Great War and telling what has happened to each of them since.

Walton was air combat intelligence officer for his squadron and bases his story on his personal war diaries of the time, which he illuminates with a vivid memory and a great writing talent. It is a moving account of war and tells of men's loyalties to one another in the great tradition of the U.S. Marine Corps.

WALLACE M. GREENE, JR.
General, U.S. Marine Corps (Retired)
23rd Commandant

Preface

In 1976, a television show appeared entitled *Baa, Baa Black Sheep*, allegedly based on the World War II exploits of the famed VMF 214—the Black Sheep Squadron of Marine fighter pilots. It was a hoked-up, phony, typical Hollywood-type production depicting the Black Sheep as a bunch of brawling bums who were fugitives from courts-martial. Even the squadron commander, ace flyer Gregory "Pappy" Boyington himself, who was billed as "technical adviser" for the series, claimed that he'd recruited the squadron pilots by giving them the choice of standing trial for various unspecified misdeeds or joining him in the Black Sheep Squadron.

Not only was nothing further from the facts (no Black Sheep pilot had ever been charged with a court-martial offense), but such false allegations had a detrimental effect on the professional careers of a number of the former Black Sheep. These lawyers, college professors, businessmen, government officials, artists, and engineers did not appreciate the label of bums and misfits. Nor, certainly, did the widows, mothers, fathers, and children of those Black Sheep who had given their lives in the service of their country.

As intelligence officer of the original Black Sheep Squadron, I knew how false the picture was. I had retired in Hawaii—after 27 years of service with the Marine Corps, the Los Angeles Police Department, and the State Department's foreign service—when I was approached by some former Black Sheep to try to arrange a reunion.

After all those years, locating men from 23 states was a formidable job, but the search was a labor of love. I started with the 33-year-old addresses listed in my War Diaries. Leads from these gave me more addresses.

I found that some had not lived to return to the States. Bill Crocker had been lost on a mission out of Green Island on 25 March 1944. Bill Hobbs had been lost over New Ireland on 30 March 1944.

Paul Mullen had returned to the States and then gone out to Japan, where he'd been lost in a midair collision in Kikuma on 12 February 1946. Stan Bailey had gone on to command the new VMF 214 on a carrier assignment; he'd then returned to Hawaii, where he'd been lost on a night flying mission on 5 April 1948.

Bob Bragdon and John Brown had died of natural causes after the war.

Including the 11 we'd lost during our two combat tours, a total of 17 had gone to the Valhalla for fighter pilots, leaving 34 survivors from the original 51 Black Sheep. It took two years, several hundred letters and long distance telephone calls, and the resources of Marine Corps headquarters, hometown newspapers, local police, and in some cases the FBI to locate them all. Would they be interested in coming to Hawaii for a reunion? Many of them were and 17 did, 15 with their wives.

It was an exhilarating experience for all of us. We held a luau; we dredged the words of old songs from our collective memories; we met with the young pilots from the squadron stationed at the Kaneohe Marine Corps Air Station and marveled at the fact that even the *helmets* fighter pilots now wear cost $20,000! The Black Sheep pilots' helmets had cost something like a dollar and a half.

The reunion whetted our appetites to try for a repeat performance, and that opportunity came in the 1980 invitation to participate in the "induction" of a Corsair into the Smithsonian Institution. Greg Tucker, lawyer son of Black Sheep Burney Tucker, worked out the details with the National Air and Space Museum of the Smithsonian. I supplied the addresses of all the surviving Black Sheep. Eighteen of us attended the ceremony.

That was when I decided to tell the story of these young eagles who flew and fought in the South Pacific some 40 years ago, and of what happened to them in the decades that followed.

 # ONE

The Black Sheep
Squadron in Combat

Born of the sun they travelled a short while toward the
  sun
And left the vivid air signed with their honor.
    Stephen Spender, "I Think Continually of Those"

1 | Recollection

It is five minutes of five on a black tropical morning. The darkness is relieved at infrequent intervals by brief flashes of lightning, which momentarily bathe our air-field in blue-white light. Even at this hour the air is warm, moist. A smell of decaying vegetation drifts out of the thick jungle that presses in against the airstrip. All around me are deep shadows of the high dirt revetments along the taxiways lined by tall coconut palms. I can hear the cough and rumble of the engines on our fighting planes; I can see the spitting blue flames of their exhausts.

Last night at ten o'clock I had briefed the whole flight. The target is Rabaul—last Japanese South Pacific stronghold.

Breakfast was at 0415: hamburger, onions, fruit juice, toast, coffee. At 0430 we were in the trucks and on our way down to the strip, the beam from our headlights getting scant welcome from the jungle hovering over the winding road. Down a steep hill, a turn to the left, and we were rolling along the coral taxiway.

Already the mechanics had some of the planes idling over in the revetments, waiting for the Black Sheep pilots to bring them to life as the blazing "whistling death" of the skies. One by one we dropped off each pilot at the plane assigned him: Pappy, Blot, Oli, Mat, Quill, Rope, Notebook, Long Tom . . .

Conversation was sparse; just a quiet "good luck."

With their helmets, goggles, throat microphones, yellow Mae West life jackets, jungle survival backpacks, parachutes, and rubber boat packs, they resembled strange monsters as they waddled to their planes, scrambled up on the wings, and were helped into the cockpits.

Now I sit, with Flight Surgeon Jim Reames, high on the bank beside the tent that serves as office and ready room.

It is five minutes of five, and our slumbering moths have come to life. They hesitate as though testing their wings and then roll haltingly out of their cocoonlike stalls and onto the taxiway. They fall into a long, wavering, awkward line and lumber out onto the strip. Only their small red and green wingtip lights, their taillights, and their exhaust flames are visible as they reach the end of the runway and prepare to take off.

With his brakes set, Pappy revs up his engine in a rising crescendo for a final check and then lets it return to idling speed. Swinging the tail around to square with the runway, he waits for the "go" signal from the control tower. Down the strip, in front of him, the small yellow lights that outline its edges converge in the distance. Beyond that—nothing. Everything else is black in this darkest hour before dawn.

So each pilot sits, alone with his thoughts in the sultry tropical morning on the lonely South Pacific island of Vella Lavella, waiting for the signal that will send him spinning down the runway on his 15,000-pound blue steed.

Then it comes—just a flick of a switch, and a green light stares at him saying, in its impersonal way: "You're next." The engine takes a deeper tone; the plane moves down the runway faster and faster and then hurtles along, barely skimming the hard-packed coral. The streamlined, gull-winged craft lifts free and gives a final *blaaat* as it climbs away, only the blinking lights and exhaust flames marking its path.

One after the other, Pappy's Black Sheep roar past us, and I mentally tick them off. They flash by, climb, and circle away in the darkness. The last one is gone and the roar fades to a drone, then to a hum. Then the morning is still. Doc and I sit quietly, wondering how many of these kids are going to come back. Last night they were happy; joking. This morning they were tense, grouchy, like football players before the big game.

But this is a deadly game.

And I wonder what motivated them, volunteers all, to come out to this remote part of the world and put their lives on the line. We realize that it is right to fight and even to die 10,000 miles from home in order to protect our homes and our families. Nevertheless, I sit saddened, knowing that not all of our eagles will always make it back to the nest.

This is the loneliest time of the day for Doc and me. We sit quietly in the dark. Doc has looked over each pilot to make sure he is fit to fly. I've briefed them as completely as possible. Now each is strapped in the cockpit of his seven-ton plane, surrounded by instruments, dials, switches, maps, notes—and the darkness. Below him are the lukewarm waters of the Solomon Sea. Ahead, enemy fighters are waiting to challenge him in deadly duel for the airspace.

Each pilot must rely on his own skill and initiative to handle this complex array of problems. He must draw from somewhere out of his background—his education, training, experience, and briefing—the right flash of thought to meet each situation instantly as it presents itself. Even so, instead of winging back and bouncing once more on our runway, his plane might join others that have spun down and crashed in the water or the tangled jungles.

"Well, I've got to get to these reports," I mumble, and Doc and I get up and walk into our tent. I light the gasoline lantern and we sit down at the rough table. The hiss of the lantern and the scratch of my pen are the only sounds as I busy myself with the paperwork. Though often condemned, it is really the bottom line of our activity. From such reports, information is gleaned that leads to changes in tactics, ordnance, training, equipment, conditioning, organization. Here are facts on the actual combat performance of aircraft and the men who fly them. Range, speed, fuel consumption, power settings, ammunition effectiveness, performance characteristics, physiological effects of flying are all shown here—and these, added to similar reports from other squadrons, present a picture to the men who build our planes and equipment, train our pilots, and run our war.

Those who study our reports find them impersonal; they're looking for facts. But to Doc and me, sitting in the dim little tent, they are part of our hearts as we write how Alex got his or how Junior bailed out or how Harpo almost spun in when he had an attack of vertigo or how Don just never came back.

As the time draws near for our Black Sheep to return, Doc and I listen for the sound of engines. After many false alarms we're finally sure, and we go back to our perch to watch the planes come in. It is daylight now, and I check them off as they break up their formations and swing into the traffic circle. We can always tell whether they've been in action. If not, they maintain their tight formation, break up smoothly, and land with precision. But when they straggle in and bounce their landings, then we know they've been into some shooting.

The time drags slowly between the landing of the first plane and the arrival of the truck at our ready tent with the first load of pilots. The boys are noisy, full of horseplay. They're talking excitedly, waving their arms as they hang up their chutes and backpacks.

They crowd around my desk to give me the word on the mission. The field telephone begins to ring; Operations wants to know what's happened on the flight: how many planes? any losses? important observations? sightings?

Doc Reames, a broad grin on his face, is passing out small shots of brandy to calm down some of the most excited.

Gradually, I get my story straight, gather all the facts and data for my reports.

Then a truck hauls the Black Sheep away for showers, lunch, and rest.

One more mission completed.

2 | The Time, the Place, the People, and the Plane

The Black Sheep Squadron sprang into being almost overnight, like Minerva from the skull of Jupiter. Almost overnight, too, they became a legend in the annals of Marine Corps history: youth-suddenly-become-men who blazed a brilliant arc across the skies of the South Pacific.

"There is a tide in the affairs of men," said Shakespeare, "which taken at the flood leads on to fortune." The military situation, the development of a combat plane capable of meeting the Japanese Zero on equal or better terms, the fortuitous availability of a mix of combat-experienced and fresh new pilots, and the presence of a leader who could mold them into the toughest combat squadron in existence at the exact time that it was needed all combined to form just such a tide.

The Japanese campaign had devastated everything before it across China, Hong Kong, Malaya, Indochina, Thailand, Burma, Singapore, Indonesia, the Philippines, the Marianas, the Carolines, and the Solomons. The Japanese had seized some three million square miles of Oceania in six months and had only been stopped by the Marines in bloody fighting on Guadalcanal.

Admiral William Halsey, in his characteristic manner, termed the Guadalcanal landing "Operation Shoestring": shortly after the initial assault, Japanese bombers drove the supply ships from the beachhead before they could fully unload, leaving the Marines stranded for days. Half-starved, disease-ridden, fighting a fanatic foe, these few sweating men advanced slowly toward the airstrip. Securing the airfield, they knew, would bring other Marines who, at their rear bases, were sweating out each painful inch of the way with them.

That the operation was a frayed shoestring may be seen from this excerpt from the January 1943 official logbook of the Marine Aviation Unit that moved into Guadalcanal's Henderson Field right behind the Marine ground troops: "Heavy bombers all gone, medium bombers all busted, dive bombers got no props, fighters got no tanks, torpedo bombers bogged down, airstrip out of commission, pilots all sick, am sending dispatch requesting instructions."

Cost to our Navy was high, too: two aircraft carriers, ten cruisers, and ten destroyers. But things got better after Operation Shoestring.

By August 1943, Guadalcanal had become a rear area, subjected only to nightly bombing raids. Marines had landed on the Russell Islands, Rendova, and Munda and were eyeing Bougainville, 300 miles north of Guadalcanal. From Bougainville our fighters could reach the Japanese stronghold at Rabaul.

Marine aviators had kept pace with their brothers on the ground, covering their landings, blasting ground installations, and knocking enemy fighters out of the sky. But these airmen, carrying too heavy a load on their shoulders, were beginning to show signs of strain. They flew daily from before daylight till after dark with only brief halts for refueling and rearming. During their catch-as-catch-can rest periods on the ground, they were subjected to nightly air raids. All through the night, Japanese bombers throbbed across the sky and sowed their deadly explosives. Their unsynchronized engines gave them an easily identifiable sound; the Marines called them "Washing Machine Charlies."

The route from Guadalcanal to Tokyo was blocked by many obstacles; major ones were Bougainville and Rabaul. Rather than carry on a costly, time-consuming island-by-island campaign, the Joint Chiefs of Staff settled on a plan to capture some of the islands and neutralize and bypass others.

It was in this climate that Admiral Halsey decided to press forward up the Solomon Islands slot toward Tokyo. He was poised for an assault on Bougainville which would give him an air base from which he could reach the Japanese-held Rabaul, at the northern end of the Solomon Islands—the Japanese Pearl Harbor. At that time (mid-1943), Rabaul's four airfields contained 400 aircraft; 100,000 Japanese troops were massed on the island of New Britain, where Rabaul is located. The Japanese considered the base impregnable. They did not intend to give up Rabaul.

While the U.S. had no plans to seize it, Rabaul had to be neutralized if the drive toward Tokyo was to move forward. But Bougainville came first. Bougainville was protected not only by thousands of Japanese troops but also by five airfields, the most important of which was Kahili, on its southern tip. Off that tip was the island of Ballale, an airdrome surrounded by bristling antiaircraft guns. Obviously, air power was needed: bombers to demolish ground installations, fighters to protect the bombers while they did their job, fighters to take on the Japanese Zeros head to head.

Halsey reviewed his requirements. One was a fighter plane that could hold its own against the Japanese Zero. He had it in the gull-winged F-4-U Corsairs recently developed by the Chance-Vought Aircraft Corporation. They had started arriving in the Solomons in February 1943. By August, enough had been delivered to the combat theater to equip the Marine squadrons. Ironically, they were available to the Marines only because the Navy had turned them down as unsuitable for carrier operations.

The Corsair was a clean, sleek aircraft with a 2,000-horsepower engine. Its rated speed of 415 miles per hour at sea level made it the fastest aircraft in the theater at that time. The Corsair carried six 50-caliber machine guns, three in each wing.

Halsey had his fighter planes. Next, he needed pilots to fly them and a commander to lead.

3 | The Squadron Commander

Normally, a Marine fighter squadron was formed in the States, given organizational and operational training as a unit, and then shipped overseas intact with its administrative staff and maintenance sections as well as its aircraft, flight echelon, and equipment.

But Halsey needed another Marine squadron right now, and no organized unit was available.

The solution was suggested by Major General James Moore, Assistant Commanding General of the First Marine Air Wing. The Wing was based at Espiritu Santo in the New Hebrides, some 600 miles south of Guadalcanal. A Marine fighting squadron, VMF 214, had just completed a combat tour during which its commanding officer had been killed. Its pilots were off to Australia for R and R (rest and recreation) and were to be scattered to other assignments. For that reason, the squadron number was available. Why not staff the number with new people and send them into combat at once?

A sufficient number of replacement pilots fresh from the States and several combat-experienced casuals were available to man the squadron. Still required were a commanding officer, an executive officer, a flight surgeon, and an intelligence officer.

The key position was the commanding officer.

Major Gregory Boyington, a hard-drinking former Flying Tiger, was causing a furor around the fighter base on the other side of the island, demanding an assignment as a squadron commander.

Boyington was born at Coeur d'Alene, Idaho. His parents had been divorced when he was a year old, and his mother had married E.J. Hallenbeck when Greg was three. The boy had thought Hallenbeck was his father.

Greg "Hallenbeck" graduated from the University of Washington, where he was a middleweight wrestler. By 1935 he was married and bogged down in a dull job as a draftsman at Boeing Aircraft. Marine Aviation offered him a way out of his doldrums. The only problem was that Marine Aviation would not take a married man. It was at this time that Boyington learned that his natural father was Boyington, not Hallenbeck.

So it was as Gregory Boyington, an "unmarried person," that he signed up for the Marine Corps. All through his training period he had kept his family hidden. In doing so, he managed to acquire sizable debts, as a young lieutenant would who was trying to maintain two residences, one at the base Officers' Club and one off-base for his wife and children.

By mid-1941 his marriage was failing; he was deeply in debt and in danger of being cashiered by the Marine Corps.

Then he was offered a solution to his situation. General Claire Chennault was forming an aviation unit to be called the American Volunteer Group, whose members would fly as mercenaries for the Republic of China against the invading Japanese. The pilots were to be paid what was a handsome salary at that time: $500 per month plus $500 for each Japanese plane they shot down.

These were the Flying Tigers.

The recruiter assured the prospective candidates that the plan had the full approval of the U.S. government, including President Roosevelt. Their papers would be kept in Washington. Upon their return, they would be reinstated in their respective services without loss of rank or precedence.

Along with a number of other Marine, Navy, and Army pilots, Boyington signed up.

Many people think that the Flying Tigers were shooting down Japanese planes before the United States entered the war, but the fact is that they never got into action until after Pearl Harbor.

Boyington claimed six Japanese planes between December 1941 and June 1942 during his service with the Flying Tigers. Becoming disenchanted with Chennault (some say the disenchantment was mutual), Boyington returned to the States.

There he ran into a bureaucratic foulup: he couldn't get back into the Marine Corps! While the U.S. desperately needed trained pilots, it appeared that no one could find his records. He took a job as a parking lot attendant while he was awaiting action.

In desperation, he sent a long telegram to the Secretary of the Navy, Frank Knox, spelling out the whole situation, including the details of the secret agreement between the U.S. Government and the Republic of China for the Flying Tigers. This telegram got results. He was reinstated in the Marine Corps and sent to San Diego. On 5 January 1943, Boyington was one of a group of 19 pilots ordered to "duty beyond the seas."

He served one tour as executive officer of VMF 122 at Guadalcanal in April 1943 but saw no combat action. At a rear base after his tour, he'd broken his leg in a barroom incident and been shipped to New Zealand to recuperate. Now he was back at Espiritu Santo, looking for an assignment.

Major Boyington was the right rank for a squadron commander; he was an experienced combat pilot; he was available; and the need was great. These assets overcame such reservations as the general may have had about his personal problems.

General Moore made the decision.

"We need an aggressive combat leader. We'll go with Boyington," he said.

The squadron had its commander.

4 | The Intelligence Officer

I became a member of the Black Sheep by a circuitous route. As sergeant in charge of War Traffic Control Planning for the Los Angeles Police Department, I was draft exempt. But by mid-1942, as I read of the Japanese advances in the South Pacific, it was obvious that the war was already the biggest show on earth and destined to get bigger. I believed that the place for every able-bodied man was in the service. My wife, Carol—not one of those weeping "don't leave me" types—was fully in agreement.

Volunteering for service, I was appointed a first lieutenant in the U.S. Marine Corps and ordered to proceed to Camp Lejeune, New River, North Carolina, for duty.

Camp Lejeune had been hacked out of the wilderness and swamps of the coast of North Carolina. It was said that an Army detail sent down there to look it over had reported that the place was not fit for human beings to live in, so it was turned over to the Marines.

I was one of 50 in an officer indoctrination course, all trying to sort out "Field Sanitation," "Arms and Ammunition," "Thompson Submachine Gun," "First Aid," "Map Reading," "Scouting and Patroling," "Identification of Ships," "Navy Firepower," "Military Gases," "Defense against Air Attack," and a hundred other topics—interspersed with calisthenics, close-order drill, long-range hikes, field maneuvers, overnight bivouacs, command practice, marksmanship (rifle, machine gun, and pistol), and regular turns as Officer of the Day.

All this and more was crowded into us in 35 days.

I had a pleasant home leave, then reported to Camp Elliott near San Diego and was assigned to the 22nd Replacement Battalion. On 1 July 1943 came orders for "permanent duty beyond the seas." I was a little concerned about the word "permanent." I knew that a lot of Marines had found permanent resting places in the South Pacific.

My wife came down to San Diego to see me off. We had a stiff-upper-lip farewell, and then I boarded the former Dutch ship *Bloemfontaine* along with some 2,300 men, 250 officers, and a crew of 200. Carol returned to Los Angeles, applied for work at Lockheed, and spent the war as a rigger on combat aircraft.

Except for a submarine scare, which kept us at full alert for 24 hours, our trip was uneventful. We docked in Noumea, New Caledonia, on 24 July 1943.

On Monday, 16 August (my wedding anniversary was the next day), I was transferred to the First Marine Air Wing. I drove up to Tontouta (35 miles north of Noumea) and, with four other officers and about 500 bags of mail, loaded into a DC-3 cargo plane for the four-hour flight to Espiritu Santo in the New Hebrides.

I was assigned to the Wing Intelligence Office and immediately commenced an on-the-job training program in aircraft identification, reading Japanese documents, escape and evasion reports, survival information, and other documents that would be of assistance to the pilots when I was assigned to a squadron.

I had been undergoing the cram course in Air Intelligence duties only about two weeks when Captain Dave Decker, Wing Intelligence Officer, called me in one morning.

"You don't drink, do you, Frank?"

"Well," I said, "I enjoy a drink now and then, but I'm not a drunk."

"That's what I mean. They're forming a new squadron over at the fighter strip, and they need an intelligence officer. The CO is to be a man by the name of Boyington. He has a reputation for getting drunk, and when he gets drunk, he gets belligerent and wants to wrestle. We need someone with him who won't get drunk and who is big enough to handle him if he gets too mean. Your background and your size make you a logical candidate."

"Well, managing drunks was no big problem for me in the Los Angeles Police Department. I think I can handle him."

Captain Decker was a lttle vague as to exactly what else I was to do. It appeared that "Standing Operating Procedures" had not yet been developed for air combat intelligence officers. I was to help the pilots all I could with any information they might need and make detailed reports to the local Fighter Command, the Group Headquarters, Strike Command, and Wing Headquarters. Exactly what kinds of reports was not spelled out, just that they all wanted to know what was happening. As a result, my early reports of the Black Sheep Squadron combat actions were written in narrative style. The Wing reproduced them and distributed them throughout the South and Southwest Pacific under the title "Air Battle Notes from the South Pacific."

Later on, as was no doubt inevitable, forms were developed that required dry-as-dirt statistical data. The forms were more efficient, perhaps, but they lost considerably in readability.

On Tuesday, 7 September 1943, I was transferred to Marine Air Group Eleven to serve as intelligence officer for Marine Fighting Squadron 214. I drove through coconut groves, across the island, and checked in with Captain George Waite, Group Intelligence Officer.

"Your squadron is down at their ready room at the strip now, having their squadron photo taken. Go on down and report to Major Boyington."

I drove along a coral road and found a Dallas hut with a sign "VMF 214." Out in front, a group of pilots was lining up near a blue, inverted-gull-wing Chance-Vought Corsair. I looked around for a pair of gold maple leaves and spotted them on a slight, smartly turned-out Irishman who seemed to be directing activities.

"Major Boyington?" I said and saluted. "I'm Lieutenant Walton."

"I'm not Major Boyington. I'm Major Bailey, the Squadron Exec," he said. "You must be our intelligence officer."

"Yes sir, Captain Waite told me to report to Major Boyington."

"Come on, I'll introduce you."

We approached a thick-necked, slope-shouldered, stocky individual dressed in a baseball cap, rumpled khaki shirt open halfway down his chest, wrinkled trousers, and house slippers.

"This is Major Boyington," Bailey said.

Boyington gave me a wry grin and a firm handshake, shuffled his slippers, and put me in the lineup; I was a member of the squadron.

After the photos were over we had a short talk.

"Get as much intelligence dope as you can," he said. "You don't need to check with me. We'll be leaving for our combat tour in a few days, so you don't have much time. You spend all your time getting your equipment together.

"By the way, we're having a squadron party tonight at Fisher's hut. Come over and get acquainted with the boys."

I spent the rest of the day gathering maps and pamphlets, studying reports, and talking to Captain Waite, his assistant Captain Landauer, and other intelligence officers just out of the combat area.

An intelligence officer's job included dozens of written duties and just as many unwritten. First, of course, was gathering information for the pilots: area maps, reports on Japanese aerial tactics, survival information, locations of antiaircraft positions. Of these, survival information rated a high priority in the minds of the pilots: what they should do if they went down, what equipment to have with them, where to look for help, possible "safe" places if they should land on an island.

All the time there was the paperwork. Flash reports: brief, preliminary statements of results that required immediate action by higher authority, such as planes down, enemy ship sightings. Action reports: detailed narratives of the missions, including dates, time, target, participants, planes used, call signs, degree of success, friendly and enemy losses, ammunition expended. Special reports: locations of AA positions, sightings of special types of ordnance used by the enemy.

Once a month a War Diary was prepared. It listed all the squadron's activities during the month; number of missions flown by each pilot; the achievements of each; plane damage; casualties suffered.

As the oldest person in the squadron (four years older even than Boyington, who—at 30—had been dubbed "Pappy" by his men), I was a father figure to many of the pilots. I spent many hours talking one-on-one about the war, its meaning, its progress, and life in general. I scrounged cigarettes and canned fruit juice (pineapple juice was in great demand) for the pilots; acted as squadron censor for their mail (I was the most liberal); helped arrange billeting and transportation; drew their flight gear for them. My feeling was that *anything* I could do to help these young men in their missions, I would be willing to do.

I made it a point to get to know them individually; in private interviews I learned their home addresses, where they'd grown up and gone to school, what they'd majored in, and what activities they'd participated in, whether or not they were married. I found out when they'd joined the Marine Corps, where they'd trained, when they'd left to come overseas, what they'd been doing. As a result of these interviews, I knew more about their personal backgrounds than did anyone else.

This exercise was to pay off handsomely at Munda.

5 | The Pilots

That night the squadron gathered in the hut of Don "Mo" Fisher, a gentle, 240-pound giant of a lad who had interrupted his pre-med training at the University of Florida after three years in order to join the Marine Corps. Don always knew the ins and outs of the supply business. Out of nowhere he'd managed to round up ten cases of beer and plenty of hamburgers.

Mo was as lazy as they come. His hut looked as though a herd of hobos had lived in it for a month and moved out. Bottles and remnants of food were scattered about the deck; the bunks were unmade; clothing and miscellaneous gear dangled from clothes-lines straggling about the sides and from corner to corner of the hut. To solve the problem of empty bottles, a hole had been cut through the deck, and the empties were tossed into it to land on the ground some three feet below.

The pilots were sitting on the ground in front of the hut, their backs against coconut logs. The conversation was of combat flying, food, home, and women.

Late in the evening, as I had been warned, Boyington suddenly lurched to his feet and assumed a wrestler's ready stance, his body slightly forward, arms hanging loosely in front of him. He glared around the group and challenged, "I'll wrestle anybody in the crowd."

He paused and then added, "Except Walton."

And I knew I'd passed my first test.

As the pile of empty beer bottles rose and the conversation lulled, some of the boys began to sing. It was soon evident which men were to head the choral group. Mo Fisher was one of them, but George Ashmun, of Far Hills, New Jersey, was the acknowledged leader. Quiet most of the time, he'd round up the boys and get them going in a songfest. He was slender, reserved, with blond, curly hair. A 1941 Hobart College grad in economics, he'd been a flight instructor for six months in Jacksonville before coming overseas.

Mat Matheson—tall, dark, so handsome he could have been a leading man in the movies—was another of the singers. Mat was always at the ready with a neat phrase: on one occasion, when a well-endowed girl walked into the lobby of the Australia Hotel in Sydney with her most prominent features bouncing, he quipped, "She just washed them and can't do a thing with them."

Before he enlisted in the Marine Corps, Mat had had three years at the University of Illinois, where he had lettered in ice hockey.

Ed "Oli" Olander, another songster whom we called "Big Old Fat Old Ed," was the most prolific letter writer of the group. He was an Amherst grad with a major in history. Give Ed a cigar and a small jug of beer, and in ten minutes he'd have you spellbound with the wonders of Massachusetts and the glories of a nation in the hands of the Republicans. Mat was sure Oli would one day be governor of Massachusetts.

The final two members of the choral society were Sandy Sims and Moon Mullen, from Philadelphia and Pittsburgh, respectively. They each had a tour of combat duty at Guadalcanal with enemy planes to their credit, and their judgment as to aerial combat was respected. Sandy was a year short of graduating from the University of Pennsylvania.

Moon was a Notre Dame grad. He not only carried a smooth melody but also contributed a great deal to overseas squadron singing by writing the song "In a Rowboat at Rabaul," which, six months later, was being sung by Army, Navy, Marine, and New Zealand squadrons throughout the entire South Pacific.

These five men were the choral society. Whenever any three or more of them got together in the evening, it naturally turned into a songfest with the whole squadron joining in.

Flight Surgeon Jim "Happy Jack" or "Diamond Jim" Reames we called "King of the Yamheads" (southerners). At 26, he was a graduate of the University of Tennessee Medical School and the Pensacola Aviation Medical Course. He'd been flying as flight surgeon on hospital planes evacuating wounded Marines from Guadalcanal when he was tapped for service with our squadron, where he dispensed brandy, snakeoil, and various sorts of good cheer.

He was also able to pry into the boys' minds with his "puhsnal" questions and ferret out their aches and hangups. Jim's wife, Rosalita, was in Memphis.

Major Stan Bailey, the Exec, was the exact opposite of Boyington. A spit-and-polish type, competition equestrian, member of the military jumping team, he was one you'd expect to carry a swagger stick—and he did. He tried to maintain some sort of respect for rank on the ground but found it difficult because Boyington was as down to earth as an old shoe.

Twenty-six years old, he had interrupted his schooling, after three years at the University of Illinois, to join the Marine Corps and had sailed from San Diego on the same ship as Boyington. In two combat tours at Guadalcanal, he was credited with having downed two Japanese planes.

In addition to Boyington, Bailey, Mullen, and Sims, the squadron's nucleus of combat-seasoned veterans with enemy planes to their credit included five others.

Captain Robert "Rootsnoot" Ewing was the Flight Officer. A 23-year-old Hoosier, he had spent three years at Purdue University before enlisting in the Marine Corps. In his tour at Guadalcanal, his score was three enemy planes: two Zeros and one bomber.

Henry "Hank" McCartney was a tall drink of water from Long Island. At 25 and married, he was among the older pilots. He had earned his degree in engineering and sociology from Houghton College, New York, before joining the Marine Corps. As a veteran of two combat tours in Guadalcanal, he had three Japanese planes and two probables to his credit. Hank's wife, Evelyn, was following his career from their home in New York.

Next was Hank Bourgeois, called "Doctor Boo" by the squadron mates with whom he'd served his first two combat tours. Hank got hooked on flying early in life: his father had been instrumental in bringing air service to New Orleans and had a friend who owned a flying service in that area; as a result, young Henry had his first flight when he was seven, was in a crash at eleven, and soloed at thirteen.

Hank had been in his last year as an aeronautical engineering major at Louisiana State University when he went into the service. He had two combat tours at Guadalcanal and two Japanese planes to his credit when he joined the Black Sheep.

I asked him how he'd got the name "Dr. Boo." He told me he'd lost his communications after having been shot up on a mission and ended up flying in exactly the opposite direction when he attempted to return to base. He'd put his plane down in a lagoon in the center of a small island, where he'd been picked up by natives.

"Somehow they got the idea that I was the number one Marine," said Hank. "They took me to the chief and then to a leanto where an obviously pregnant native woman was lying on a mat.

" 'Baby no come,' they said.

"I got out my first aid kit and gave them all my sulfa pills, telling them to give her one twice a day. When I was picked up the next day by the flying boat, a Navy corpsman said they'd send down a doctor.

"The doctor reported back that the baby had been born O.K. and that the Chief was so happy they named the baby 'Boo Ja Wa,' which was as close as they could come to saying my name."

So it was "Doctor Boo" for Bourgeois from then on.

The other two combat-experienced veterans with Japanese planes to their credit were Bill Case and John Begert. Begert's education (he was a journalism major) had been interrupted after two years of college, one each at Kansas and Texas. He'd had two combat tours at Guadalcanal and had downed one Zero.

Case had completed two years at Oregon State University. He also had a Zero to his credit from his Guadalcanal combat tours. He had a wife, Ellen, waiting for him in Vancouver.

"Long Tom" Emrich, John "Blot" Bolt, and Ed "Harpo" Harper were called "the Quartermaster Kids." They were continually collecting souvenirs of all kinds and shipping them home by the crate. We were sure that their families were building warehouses to store the stuff.

Bolt, from the University of Florida, was the most energetic member of the squadron. In addition to his quartermaster activities, he was always turning up with a gunnysack full of fish he'd dynamited; he'd organize pig roasts and beer parties; he made Cook's Tours around the islands whenever he had time off. He thoroughly investigated and tested every new gadget or technique reported or developed.

Harpo was a serious, studious individual who learned a lesson from every experience and filed it in his memory for use as needed. He'd completed two years at the University of Idaho.

Long Tom was the squadron's Don Juan, with a head of rich, thick black hair that required his constant attention. His two years at Wentworth Military Academy also made him a walking encyclopedia on all the new military scoop, usually far fetched. "The Germans have a new plane that weighs 9,875 pounds with a speed of 782.5 miles per hour," he'd say. "Climbs 5,000 feet a minute . . . "

At 26, Bob "Meathead" Bragdon was one of the older men, having graduated from Princeton in 1939 as a psychology major. An all-round athlete, he'd been on the boxing, track, rugby, and baseball teams. We called him the "Princeton Steelworker." He was positive he'd never amount to a damn. He had a glib, facile manner of tossing away a phrase so carelessly that he'd be two paragraphs further along before the import hit you.

William "Junior" Heier had signed on in the fall of 1941 with the Royal Canadian Air Force because he'd lacked the two years of college required to join any of the U.S. air arms. He'd transferred to the Marine Corps in the spring of 1942. He was sure that nothing could stop the Army Air Corps but the weather. He was always there with a quick comeback.

Denmark Groover, Jr., born and raised in Quitman, Georgia, had had two years in pre-law at the University of Georgia. His accent was soft as butter, and we nominated him as First Vice-President of the

Yamheads. We originally called him "Boone" but changed it to "Quill" or "Quill Skull" because his hair stuck out from his scalp like the quills of a porcupine.

Burney "Tuck" Tucker was another southerner, born in Nashville, and another fine athlete; he'd lettered in football, track, and basketball during two and a half years at Tennessee State. As big men often are, he was softspoken and gentle, and spent much of his time keeping the Quartermaster Kids quiet.

We called Jim Hill the exception: he was a *quiet* Chicago boy. He'd had two years at Northwestern, his second year as an engineering major. He didn't have a lot to say but he was always in there in the formation where he belonged.

Virgil Ray, from Hallsboro, North Carolina, had earned his commission the hard way. He'd enlisted in the Marine Corps and gone to boot camp at Parris Island. He'd passed top man in a competitive examination to transfer to aviation, taken his flight training, and flown one combat tour at Guadalcanal as an enlisted pilot.

Bob Alexander was the typical all-American boy. In his nearly three years at Iowa State, he'd been a track man, a wrestler, and a gymnast. He'd also been Governor of Boy's State in 1939. A fine, strapping, crewcut lad, he could have posed for a Marine recruiting poster.

Tall, likable Walter "Red" Harris was in his last year as a zoology major at the University of Nebraska when he joined the Marine Corps. He'd been a member of the basketball team, the Thespians, and the Glee Club.

Rolland "Rollie" Rinabarger had majored in mechanical engineering during his two years at Oregon State. He'd also found time to letter on the boxing team, though he was tall and slender enough to have made a good basketball player.

Don "Deejay" Moore, from Amarillo, was the only Texan in our squadron. He was another who'd first joined the Royal Canadian Air Force, transferring to the Marine Corps after serving ten months there. He spent part of his spare time working on lessons for correspondence courses, and the rest he whiled away on the silver trombone he carted about with him.

Bob McClurg was a quarterback and a business administration grad from Westminster College in New Wilmington, Pennsylvania. He was said to have been rejected by other squadrons because he couldn't fly well enough. When Boyington heard this, he snorted, "If the boy can't fly well enough, it's up to me to teach him." And the CO proceeded to do just that.

Chris "Wild Man" or "Maggie" Magee was our free spirit. He

usually carried with him some thick tome on witchcraft or philosophy. He refused to wear boots; instead, he wore tennis shoes when he was flying. Utterly fearless, he usually took along a lapful of hand grenades, which he tossed over the side at various Japanese installations as he flew at hair-raisingly low levels. He always, and I mean *always*, wore blue nylon bathing trunks—we wondered if he ever took them off. A physical culture faddist, he could be seen in his spare time working out with his barbell, a blue kerchief tied on his head and his muscular body glistening in the sun.

No one, *no one*, messed with Maggie. One evening a group of Black Sheep were crowded into a weapons carrier after a night of celebration at a rear area officers' club. Boyington, well under the weather, got belligerent and began waving a bayonet around to the considerable discomfort of those who were crowded into the vehicle with him. Magee promptly took the bayonet away from him.

Magee had majored in journalism for a year at the University of Chicago, where he participated in track, boxing, and football. He was another who'd come to the Marine Corps via the Royal Canadian Air Force.

These, then, were the original Black Sheep: 28 pilots, the flight surgeon, and me. We were a microcosm of America: northeasterners with their broad As; southerners with accents soft as butter; Pennsylvanians and sharp-as-a-tack New Yorkers; rawboned midwesterners from the wheat and corn belts; men from the west coast and one from Texas. Some were seasoned veterans who'd already faced the enemy in aerial combat; others were fresh, green, eager.

The pilots who'd flown previous tours had a total of 14½ planes to their credit, and Boyington was already a legendary figure as a Flying Tiger. Several cuts above the usual basic training graduates as well were the three members of the squadron with RCAF experience and two who had been instructors.

It was a mix that jelled into a hard-hitting, battle-ready outfit.

6 | Going into Action

On 11 September 1943, Boyington called us together.

"We're leaving tomorrow for our first combat tour."

Everyone jabbered excitedly for a few moments and then quieted as he spoke again:

"We're going to Cactus (code name for Guadalcanal) and then on up to the Russell Islands. We'll fly 20 planes up. The rest of you will fly up on a SCAT (military transport) plane."

The remainder of the day was spent gathering final bits of equipment, packing our gear, and storing most of it with the Group Quartermaster. We were taking only a handbag each for a six-weeks combat tour. Transport space into the combat area was so limited that no room was available for luxuries. A couple of pairs of field shoes (boondockers, we called them), half a dozen pairs of socks, a few shirts, trousers, a minimum of toilet articles just about completed our load of personal gear.

We were up at 4:00 A.M., loaded into trucks, and hauled some 15 miles across the island to the bomber strip, where we were checked in and weighed in. After an hour's wait, we were trucked out to a brown two-engine Douglas transport plane, the workhorse of the South Pacific, and packed on top of what appeared to be several thousand pounds of aircraft parts, tools, medical supplies, and mail bags. The pile was so high our backs almost touched the ceiling.

Then the pilot and copilot climbed in and crawled over to us to the cockpit. A few minutes later the engines sputtered to life, the plane swung about, and we moved along the taxiway. The overloaded craft staggered off the ground, not lightly and smoothly, like a bird, but sluggishly and laboriously, straining and complaining and groaning, until we were at last airborne. We circled out over the water and then crossed the end of the island, its solid jungles looking like a carpet of broccoli.

Just before noon, Guadalcanal came into view. We could see the wrecked Japanese ships and troop barges on its shores and on the reefs about it. Entire jungle areas were masses of splinters; huge gouges showed in the deep green foliage.

At twelve o'clock we bounced heavily down onto Henderson Field, for which the Marines had paid such a high price. The name honored a Marine aviator who had lost his life at the Battle of Midway.

A truck hauled us over to the transient area past a complicated scene of destruction, rot, flies, and stench. We unloaded and had lunch: Spam and beans. At the Intelligence shack we learned that the pilots were to fly the 20 planes on to the Russell Islands that afternoon; the rest of us would fly up the next morning on the transport plane.

A couple of us borrowed a jeep and took a tour around the island. We saw the Lunga River, the Tenaru, Bloody Ridge—all scenes of gallant, costly Marine victories. We saw that the Army had been there, too. Even though they had come much later than the Marines, they'd had their share of fighting. Over one of the roads a sign read:

> KILL THE BASTARDS!
> On this road 20 wounded soldiers
> of the regiment "Queen of Battles"
> —being carried on litters—were
> bayoneted, stabbed and shot by the
> yellow bastards.
> KILL THE BASTARDS!

They were playing for keeps here.

The next morning we took off shortly after seven o'clock and landed in the beautiful Russell Islands some 30 minutes later. The Russell Islands could have been a Hollywood set for a tropical movie. The water was a clear, cobalt blue. The sand was clean and white. Tall coconut palms waved lazily in warm breezes scented with frangipani and other exotic flowers.

But as our truck began to climb a short hill to our quarters, we saw that this was no time for lazy contemplation and lolling on the beach. Beside the road was a sign: "Marine Air Group 21, where the extermination of Japs is a business, not a pastime."

Our squadron had been assigned Scramble Alert duty for the day. That meant that the pilots were to stand by, to take off at short notice to intercept any enemy planes that might come our way.

Boyington took advantage of the opportunity to give the pilots some instruction on tactics. He sat on his heels in the shade of the ready room, with the pilots gathered about him like players around their coach, and covered the crushed coral surface of the ground in front of him with diagrams.

"There's one thing you must always keep in mind," he said. "Carry out your mission. If you're covering bombers, cover them to the target and back. Don't take off some place to attack a couple of Zeros off to one side. I know you all want to shoot down planes. But our first job is the completion of the mission, whatever it is. Keep in mind that when you do get your opportunity, it'll just be a quick flash and your chance will be gone. Be prepared to take full advantage of it. When you get your chance, attack immediately and let him have it."

Boyington then went over the differences between the Zeros and our Corsairs.

"You're flying one of the sweetest fighters there is," he said. "But there are certain things a Corsair won't do. Don't try to loop with a Zero because the Zero is a lighter, more maneuverable plane and will loop inside you and he'll end up on your tail. The same goes for turning—don't try to turn with him. But your ship is faster; it will climb away from him in a shallow climb, and you can outdive anything they've got. So what does all this add up to? Just this: get above him; come in on him in a high stern pass; hold your fire till you're within good, close range; let him have it and watch him burn. When they're hit right they burn like celluloid.

"If you miss him, don't stick around to dogfight. Dive out—get the hell out of there—climb away and come back into the fight with some altitude and speed.

"Stay together if you can, particularly your two-plane section. Unless you're completely swamped on all sides, you're in good shape if you keep your section together.

"Depend on your plane; it's built to take a beating and still bring you home. And try to bring them back, men; they're all we have.

"Remember that fighter planes are built to fight. That's our primary general mission. Any time there are enemy planes in the air and we have fighters up, we should tangle with them if we can do so without leaving our own bombers or photo planes unprotected."

That was the essence of the Boyington system—aggression. He often advocated that our fighters be stripped of their camouflage coating and left their natural silver color; it would make it easier for a fight to begin, he said. With the camouflage on our planes, an enemy formation might not see us, and a chance for a fight would be lost.

As it turned out, the Black Sheep had plenty of opportunities to fight.

That night, we all gathered in our hut to talk over plans, to sing, and to enjoy a general gabfest.

"I think we should have a name for our squadron," someone suggested.

The idea was instantly accepted and we began to toss around one name after another. We agreed at once that we did *not* want one of the

Walt Disney bugs, bees, and bunnies types of names that were so prevalent. Then someone said:

"How about Boyington's Bastards?"

After all, our squadron had been slapped together from replacement and pool pilots. Our skipper had been told he'd never fly again. We'd had practically no training as a squadron. We'd been assigned ground and administrative echelons, but they'd been left at Espiritu Santo.

The name fit us perfectly.

The next day I told Jack DeChant, the Marine Corps public relations officer in the Island Group Headquarters, about our choice.

"That won't do," he said. "You'll have to find a more printable name." The press was considerably more straitlaced in those days than it is now.

When I reported this to the boys, we again got our heads together and came up with the name "Black Sheep." It told somewhat the same story.

Next, of course, we had to have an emblem, and after further discussion we worked out a heraldry shield with its top formed by the cowl and inverted gull-wings of the Corsair. Diagonally across the shield we put a bar sinister, the heraldry sign for bastard. In the upper left we had a woebegone, lopeared black sheep; in the lower right we put our squadron number—214—and finished off with a circle of stars in the center. Bill Case drew a preliminary draft, and then Pen Johnson, a Marine combat correspondent, produced a beautiful original for us. With a name and an emblem, we began to feel more like a unit.

The first combat flight for the newly named Black Sheep came on 14 September. Munda airstrip had been taken by the Marines, although fighting was still going on around it. The earlier Marine pilots had written a glorious page in aviation history for us to carry on: between 7 December 1941 and that date nearly two years later, Marine airmen had shot down more than half of all the aircraft destroyed in the entire Pacific area—more than the Army, Navy, and New Zealand Air forces combined.

So it was with a mixed feeling of anxiety and satisfaction that Doc Reames and I watched 24 of our Black Sheep (four of them in borrowed planes) take off on this first mission. They were to escort Army B-24s to bomb Kahili, strongest of the five Japanese airfields on Bougainville.

Shortly before noon, our planes began to come back and circle in the landing pattern. Then the boys were in the ready room, and I began to piece together the story of the flight. The B-24s had dropped most of their bombs in the water off the end of the strip; no enemy aircraft were encountered and very little antiaircraft fire.

The boys were a little disappointed.

7 | "Zeros Spilled Out of the Clouds"

At one o'clock in the afternoon of 16 September 1943, Pappy Boyington taxied to the end of the white coral runway, gunned his engine, and sped out over the blue waters of the bay off the Russell Islands. Twenty-three other Black Sheep followed in smooth order. The 24 planes got off the ground in just seven minutes.

This was to be a strike on Ballale, a strategically located island in the bay off southern Bougainville. Its airfield was operational, and the whole island was solid with antiaircraft positions. Black Sheep pilots were to act as high cover for Marine torpedo and dive bombers. They made their rendezvous with the bombers on schedule over Munda at 1:50 P.M.

The formation moved northward under a fleecy layer of clouds, the bombers at 13,000 feet and the Black Sheep at 21,000. Between them were a layer of New Zealand Warhawks at 15,000 and a layer of Navy Hellcats at 19,000 as intermediate cover.

As twenty-four-year-old John Begert reported, "Zeros spilled out of the clouds" onto them when the bombers started their dives on the target. Some 40 to 50 Zeros attacked the Black Sheep and started a fight that spread all over the sky for 200 square miles and lasted 30 minutes. It was a mad scramble, with 16 of the 24 Black Sheep seeing action for the first time.

Twenty-two-year-old Bob Alexander, one of the newcomers to combat, was flying wing on Major Bailey. The two Corsairs dived toward a circling hive of 20 Zeros, selected one, and came down on him in a quarter pass. The Zero rolled onto its back and dived. The two Black Sheep followed it down to 10,000 feet.

At this point Alexander saw a flight of three Zeros preparing to dive on them. He pulled up to keep them off his division leader's tail. Bailey stayed with his Zero, continuing to fire till it went into the clouds, smoking.

Bailey followed it into the clouds, went on instruments, circled, and pulled out into the clear. He saw a Zero coming down on him, firing, so he ducked back into the clouds. When he came out, the same thing happened again, and then three times more. Bailey decided this was not his day, so he stayed in the clouds and headed for home on instruments.

Coming out into the clear, he saw a pilot floating down in his chute with a Zero making passes at him, attempting to machine-gun him as he dangled there.

Bailey dived at the Zero. It pulled up in a tight loop and got on his tail. The Major dived out, circled back and then heard the thud of bullets on his plane. Three Zeros were on his tail. Convinced anew that this was not his day, Bailey dived out and nursed his bullet-scarred plane home.

Alexander, meanwhile, had attacked the three Zeros that had been preparing to dive on him and Bailey. They scattered, and Alexander was left momentarily alone in the sky.

He spotted two Zeros about a thousand feet below him. The wingman was trailing about a hundred feet to the right, slightly stepped down. Alexander dived on them, and leveled off, making a direct stern approach on the wingman. He closed till he could spot the red roundel, then opened fire at 150 yards. He saw his bullets sieve the cockpit, tail, and mid-fuselage. Bits of metal and fabric flew off, and the Zero began to smoke.

Alexander continued to fire as he closed and then pulled up and passed over the Zero's right wing within 50 feet of the enemy. Looking into the cockpit, he saw flames come up from under the instrument panel and immediately fill the whole cockpit.

"It looked just like they do it in the movies," Bob told me.

Alexander cut across in front of the flaming Zero and sighted in on the leader, who rolled over and dived down. Alexander spotted four Zeros above him with the leader peeling off for an overhead pass at him, so he nosed his Corsair over and dived out.

Seeing that his tail was clear, he began to climb again toward a 16-

plane melee above him—only to find that they were all Zeros, circling and slow-rolling among themselves. Realizing this was no place for a lone Corsair without altitude advantage, Alexander dived and headed for home.

Bill Case was leading a division of four Corsairs when he spotted seven Zeros attacking a flight below them. His division rolled over and dived on the Zeros. Their leader saw them coming and pulled up. All four Black Sheep got in short bursts, pulled up, rolled over, and went down on the Zeros in an overhead.

Case picked out one and corkscrewed down with him for two turns and then pulled out. By this time Case had lost his second section, but his wingman, Rollie Rinabarger, was still with him.

"Nine Zeros, nine o'clock and up," reported Rinabarger suddenly, and Case spotted them off to his left.

The two Corsairs spread out about 200 yards apart, flying a level parallel course with the enemy planes still at high nine o'clock.

In spite of their numerical superiority, the nine Zeros failed to press home the attack, making only short, ducking, ineffectual passes.

Case and Rinabarger gradually pulled away until they spotted four more Zeros attacking two Corsairs. As one of the Corsairs dived out of trouble, Case and his wingman dived on one of the Zeros. The Japanese plane smoked, pulled up sharply, and then rolled over and down, leaving a black trail.

Case rolled and spiraled down behind him, losing his wingman in the dive. Rinabarger had mistaken the other Corsair for Case and had joined with him.

Case, in turn, joined a Navy Hellcat, and the two started home. The Hellcat pilot spotted a straggler in trouble, waggled his wings, and turned to attack with Case following. The Hellcat pilot made a beam run, firing, but missed, and the Zero turned in toward Case. The two planes—Japanese and American—came at each other with guns firing. Four of Case's six guns quit, but he continued his head-on run.

It was the Zero that pulled out in a chandelle to the left. Case pulled sharply to the right and rolled over on him in an overhead pass. The Japanese pilot rolled over and spiraled down, Case staying with him even though only two of his guns were firing.

At 4,000 feet Case began his pullout, leveling off at 1,500 feet. The Zero had disappeared.

During the scramble Rinabarger saw a "daisy chain": a Corsair had a Zero on its tail, another Corsair was on the Zero's tail, and another

Zero was on the second Corsair's tail. Ronnie dived to make the fifth, but the last Zero pulled away as he did so.

John Begert was leading a division of Black Sheep when the skies rained Zeros.

"After a few violent maneuvers," he told me, "a Zero came across my bow, followed by a Corsair. The Zero slow-rolled to the right, rolled on his back, and pulled through too tightly for the Corsair to follow. I peeled off and got in a short burst at the Zero. He burst into flames from the underside of the engine and all along the belly. The pilot bailed out.

"Thirty seconds later the same thing happened. Another Zero, followed by another Corsair, pulled through so sharply the Corsair couldn't stay with him. I opened fire from about 50 yards and gave him a short burst. The Zero rolled over on his back, and I rolled with him, firing all the way through. He caught fire along the sides of the cowl as we were inverted, and then he spun down burning and crashed in the water."

Bob Ewing, Black Sheep Flight Officer, was leading a division consisting of Bob McClurg, Paul Mullen, and Tom Emrich. These four Black Sheep attacked 16 Zeros in a diving turn to the right. Ewing crowded over so much toward the other three planes in his division, which were on his right, that McClurg had to cross under him to give him room. In doing so, he was left on the outside of the turn and could not stay with his three division mates.

Ewing kept crowding over on Mullen, trying to get into a position to fire. Mullen continued to slide over until he saw a Zero in a steep dive on a Corsair to the left below them. Mullen and his wingman, Emrich, cut under Ewing and got in a burst at the attacking Zero. The Zero spun, smoked, and then went off to the side in a controlled dive.

When McClurg leveled off at 21,000 feet he looked around for his division, but couldn't spot them. Then he looked for any friendly plane to join up with. Off to his left he spotted a rust-colored Zero on its back, firing at a friendly plane. McClurg immediately headed in that direction. The friendly plane began to burn and went down vertically.

The Zero rolled out at the same altitude as McClurg and came at him in a head-on run from about 400 yards out.

"I could see puffs of smoke coming from his wings so I knew he was firing at me," said McClurg, "but I couldn't tell whether or not he was hitting me. I just held the trigger down as we came at each other. My tracers seemed to be crossing right in front of his engine, apparently having no effect at first.

"At the last possible instant before we would have collided, the

Zero rolled over and dropped into a diving turn to the right with black smoke pouring out of its engine.

"I circled to the left above him and watched as flame burst from the engine and shot back to the cockpit. Then he spun down burning."

Boyington, leading the Black Sheep's first division, heard the "Tally Ho" call, but saw no enemy planes near him. He pushed over and went down through a layer of clouds looking for them. He was in a sharp circle to the left with Don Fisher, his wingman, about 200 yards behind him when a Zero came in from the left, crossed between the two Black Sheep, and circled in a quarter pass on Boyington. Fisher fired a burst at the Zero, which went into a slow roll to the left.

"I closed in on him," related Fisher, "and gave him another burst at the top of his roll. Flames shot out of his wing roots, and then the whole plane exploded.

"I looked around for Pappy, but before I could spot him, a Corsair passed in front of me with a Zero on its tail. I fired a short burst and missed, but caused the Zero to pull up into a slow roll to the left. I gave him a continuous burst as he was on his back. He scooped his slow roll and then began to smoke heavily. He fell off on his left wing and spun down. I followed him down, firing, to 4,000 feet. He spun in, burning."

Shortly after he lost Fisher, Boyington saw a Zero pull alongside, waggle his wings, and pull ahead, passing within 100 feet of him. The Zero had somehow mistaken Boyington for a friendly plane as this is the signal to join up. Boyington accommodated him by giving him a burst from 50 yards. The Zero flamed from the cockpit and spun down burning.

Looking for his flight, Boyington could see no planes at all, so he started for home. Ten thousand feet below him, he spotted several Zeros making passes at the rear of our bomber formation. Pappy pushed over and dived on one of them, opening fire at 300 yards and closing fast.

"The Zero exploded completely when I was about 50 feet from him," said Boyington. "I threw up my arms to protect my face and flew through the debris."

Boyington's plane had dents in the cowling and leading edges of his wings from this debris.

"I climbed back in the sun to 18,000 feet and looked around. A Zero was diving on the right flank of the bombers.

"I started to dive, and as I did so, the Zero overran his target and pulled up to about 11,000 feet. I leveled out a little and caught him on the rise as he climbed. I opened fire at about 300 yards and held the trigger down as he went into a loop. I stayed with him in the loop for a moment; then he pulled inside of me, and as I was on my back, I looked below and saw him flame and spin down.

"I climbed back in the sun and took another look. Zeros that had been heckling the bombers were now leaving them and heading for home in pairs at about 6,000 feet. I spotted what I thought was a single, and knowing I'd have too much speed in a power dive, I slid down on him in a throttle-back glide.

"The Zero began to make a gentle turn to the left and was just a sitting duck. I knew this was entirely too easy so I looked around for the catch. Sure enough, there it was—the bait's wingman was off to the right waiting for me to make a pass and sucker in.

"I continued my pass, watching the hovering Zero out of the corner of my eye until he dove in on me. Then I suddenly jerked on the stick and kicked my rudder. My Corsair cartwheeled to the right and I was in a head-on run at the second Zero.

"I could see pieces flying off his cowling as I held the trigger down during the run. The Zero pulled up and I passed directly under him and then pulled up in a chandelle to the left and saw that he was smoking badly.

"I followed him, climbing, intending to finish him off, but he went down in a flat glide and crashed into the water.

"I didn't want to crowd my luck too far, so I headed for home again. However, I spotted a pair of Zeros about 3,000 feet below me. They turned on me, evidently thinking I was a cripple.

"Since a strong offense is the best defense, I made a head-on run at the leader. When he pulled out to the right, I swung toward the second one. He began to smoke, but I was low on gas, ammunition, and altitude, so I continued on for home, climbing to about 10,000 feet.

"I then spotted a single plane, only about 3,000 feet off the water, which I thought at first was a Zero, although it was headed toward Vella Lavella. Then I saw two planes attack the single and knew that they were the Zeros. I pushed over and opened fire at extremely long range, hoping to drive them off the friendly plane.

"One Zero pulled straight up in the air, and I followed him, firing a succession of short bursts. Then he slow-rolled, going practically straight up, and I held the trigger down and stayed with him. Suddenly, four of my guns quit firing, but I didn't need to fire anymore—the Zero burst into flames and spun down, leaving me on my back in a spin at 10,000 feet.

"After getting straightened out, I looked around but couldn't see either the friendly plane or the other Zero, so I headed south again and pancaked at Munda."

At Munda, it was evident why four of his guns quit firing: they were out of ammunition. He had only 30 rounds left in two guns and barely enough fuel to taxi to a revetment!

I added up our Black Sheep score for the day: 11 Zeros shot down for sure and 9 probables—a fine score for a group of replacement pilots whipped into a squadron practically overnight. In those few minutes, they had become a combat team of fighting men. Referring to this mission in his book *Strong Men Armed*, Robert Leckie says: "Soon the baaing of the Black Sheep would be heard all over the South Pacific."

It was a fine score—but "Rootsnoot" Ewing didn't come back. The last seen of our 23-year-old Flight Officer was when he crowded over to make that initial run. He wasn't in trouble at that time.

But he didn't come back.

What had happened to him? No one could say. He might have been shot down and died at the controls of his plane. He might have bailed out and been killed in his chute. He might have landed safely in the water and been picked up and made a prisoner. The possibilities were many. It was too late to search for him that night.

Sadly, I wrote "MIA" for "missing in action" beside his name in my War Diary. We all hoped he'd turn up soon, and I could erase those letters.

But he never did.

8 | Munda

In the evening, Boyington and his pilots went over the lessons learned from the Ballale action.

Later, an operations officer came in and told us that we were to move to Munda the next day. At 7:30 A.M., five of us left in a transport plane, while the rest of the Black Sheep took off to search for Ewing. They were to land at Munda on their return.

Munda, on New Georgia, was an example of the costs of war. One entire end of the island had been leveled by bombs, artillery, and naval gunfire. A few splintered stumps were all that remained of a huge coconut grove. Wrecked airplanes lay all around, pushed to one side if they interfered with the work on the strip, otherwise left where they were. Some were upside down; some had tails high in the air; others were broken into several pieces. The shallow water at the end and one side of the strip was studded with them. Roundels identifying some as Japanese stared at us like big red eyes. Here and there, crashed American planes showed that the vital strip had not been won without cost.

Everywhere there was activity. Bulldozers worked in the glare at one end of the runway, lengthening and widening it. Trucks buzzed around. Aircraft landed and took off regularly.

A truck hauled us along the strip, around its end, and up a winding hill to our camp area—a cleared space, bulldozed out of the jungle. Back under the trees were the tents and the mess hall.

Doc Reames and I moved into one of the 16-foot-square tents along with Boyington and Bailey. Our new home had a wooden deck and two six-foot foxholes. The sides of the tent were rolled up to take advantage of any breeze that might come along.

It was hot, steamy. A foul odor pervaded the air. Flies were having a field day: there'd been no time yet to bury the dead Japanese.

We walked back to our truck and went down to the airstrip and our "office." The fighter intelligence office was another 16-foot-square tent with a long table constructed from rough-hewn teak boards. A couple of homemade bulletin boards lined one side. We looked forward to the return of our men from the search mission, but when we saw their long, sweat-streaked faces, we knew that they'd seen nothing of Ewing.

They flew patrols, photo escorts, and search missions all day. At seven o'clock, the last flight in, darkness covered the island. The strip was secured and we climbed into the trucks to go to our camp area for chow.

A sign over the mess hall door read: "MAUDIE'S MANSIONS—A HOME FOR WAYWARD PILOTS."

We crunched along the rolled coral floor, sat on splintery mahogany benches at long, rough mahogany tables, ate fly-covered Spam and beans with dehydrated potatoes, and drank warm chicory. (To this day, I can't stand Spam!)

After our evening meal, we found our way to our tents and took off our sweat-crusted clothes. Then, dressed only in field shoes, we slung towels over our shoulders. With a bar of soap in one hand and a flashlight in the other, we picked our way around the stumps and mud puddles to the showers in a corner of the camp area. A raised frame had been built some three feet off the ground. Over this had been laid a few strips of the steel Marsden matting that was used to provide a firm surface on coral airstrips. On racks above were a dozen 50-gallon oil drums, and hanging on the nozzles were tin cans with holes punched. These were our showers. The cool water felt good as we soaped and chattered contentedly. Life here was reduced to its lowest common denominator: if you were alive and comfortable and not hungry, all was well. The showers were a luxury. So was our only woman within hundreds of miles: the well-endowed nude (being chased by three pilots) painted on the corner of the mess hall sign.

Back at our tent, we lighted a candle and sat on our bunks and talked for a few moments. Then we adjusted our mosquito nets and stretched out nude, sweating again from the mild exertion of having walked from the showers.

The dark, heavy, green foliage pressed in on us almost visibly, working its way back over the area that had been cleared. Jungle birds, tree lizards, and frogs called to each other with eerie, screeching cries. Rain began to pound on our tent and run off its sides in solid sheets. It was like a scene from the movie *Rain*. Now I really understood what the phrases "coming down in buckets," "raining in sheets," and "frog strangler" meant. It was as though a giant had suddenly dumped an entire swimming pool onto our tent.

I raised my netting and put my hand out under the solid stream; the water was as warm as a YMCA pool.

It was only nine o'clock, but we had to be up at 4:00 A.M., and that would give us seven hours of sleep, we thought.

We thought wrong.

It started with a dull humming inside my head. It grew louder and louder. I shook my head and turned over, but the hum—now a wail—persisted, beating and beating at my brain. Then I heard a scuffle of feet, thuds, the crash of bodies moving through the jungle. I suddenly sat up, bumping my head on my mosquito net support pole.

An air raid! It was 1:00 A.M.

Nothing happened for a few minutes, so we stepped outside the tent. It was clear and bright. The rain had stopped. A full moon illuminated everything, and I knew what "Bomber's Moon" meant.

Boyington, Bailey, Reames, and I—we were a strange sight, naked except for steel helmets and field shoes; shirts and trousers wouldn't have been any help.

Suddenly, a searchlight flung its long finger upward, probing the sky like a surgeon probing a wound for a bullet. Another one flicked on, and another and another, fingers interlocking and opening and moving about relentlessly.

We could hear the uneven drone of unsynchronized engines.

"Yes, that's Charlie," said Bailey.

The searchlights continued their restless movement until one passed across the enemy formation; it jerked back and clung there. The others quickly swung and there, like tiny moths caught in the glare of our lights, were six Japanese bombers, making no effort to evade. Our antiaircraft opened up. Ka-bloom, boom; ka-bloom, boom; one after the other the shells burst, at first low and to one side, then closer and closer as the directors began to get the range.

A shell burst alongside one of the flanking planes; it faltered a moment and then began to go down in a long flat glide, trailing smoke.

Like the roar at a baseball game when a batter hits a home run, a cheer went up all over our camp.

"Time to get in our foxholes," said Boyington.

"Nobody has to tell me that!" Doc Reames said, who was already in his.

The rest of us started toward our foxholes and ended up diving in when we heard the whistle of bombs. Down on our hands and knees, we heard them come closer, and then the earth shook with the concussion as they detonated. Bits of rock and coral bounced down the sides of the hole. We crouched there for ages, our shoulders hunched against another blast.

When we crawled out, everything looked the same. Twenty minutes later, the all-clear sounded; we went back to bed.

I woke immediately the next time I heard the siren. It was 2:35 A.M., and Washing Machine Charlie was back. This time it was a lone plane. He flew a straight course in spite of the lights, made no effort to dodge either them or the AA bursts, which came close but never touched him. Once again we ended in a scramble for our foxholes, and the bombs crashed somewhere toward the strip.

We were hardly back on our bunks when the siren wailed again. By the time the all-clear sounded, it was four o'clock and time to get up.

Breakfast consisted of grapefruit juice, chicory coffee, and creamed hamburger on toast—which Marines had awarded the expressive and alliterative title of "shit on a shingle," or SOS.

The air raid sirens wailed again as we climbed into the trucks to go to the strip. Since no planes could be seen, however, and the Black Sheep were scheduled to take off at five o'clock for a rendezvous with a convoy coming up from the south, we started out. The moon had gone down. All lights were out. Everything was soft, warm, clinging blackness.

Our driver, who would rather have been in a foxhole, wound up the truck in second gear and raced at 45 miles an hour down the slippery coral road to the airfield. We rounded the curve at the bottom without mishap and straightened out on the road that crossed a long open area.

Suddenly, the antiaircraft batteries sprang to life and the searchlights came on again. Our driver jerked on the emergency brake and jumped out of the skidding truck, leaving us in a heap on its floor. We scrambled out and lay down in the muddy ditch along the road, feeling more than a little exposed.

The flight of bombers passed over us and unloaded some of their eggs before the lights lost them. We lay there awhile till the lights had all flicked off, leaving the island blacker than it had been before. Then we piled into our truck, and our jittery driver raced once more toward the strip.

We hadn't gone half a mile when the AA opened up again, and once more we scrambled out and flopped into the ditch. But this time we climbed back into the truck as soon as the planes passed over us, realizing that even if they had released their bombs directly overhead, they would fall some distance away.

We reached the field at ten minutes to five, and the Black Sheep were gathering their gear when the AA started again. We sprinted for a huge foxhole, covered with coconut logs and sandbags, beside our ready tent. Not all of us made it. A stick of antipersonnel bombs walked right down the taxiway, past our tent and past our foxhole, one bomb detonating within 30 feet of us.

I still have the tail fin off that bomb, and the scar it made.

One of the mechs dived under a truck that had been parked only a short time. Bomb fragments were flying all around, and in the midst of it, we heard an agonized groan from under the truck. We tried to help the man out.

"Don't touch me. I'm hit bad. Blood all over."

In the beam of the flashlight, we could see him huddled face down, his head on his folded arms. The "blood" was warm oil dripping from a hole in the crankcase of the truck's engine.

Later that morning, Harper had a new name: "The Mole." During the air raid, he'd hit the ground on his hands and knees and hadn't wasted time to get up; instead, he had scuttled along the ground on all fours, dived into the huge open foxhole, and then tried to burrow into the side of it.

Repeated bombings or not, we still had our Task Force cover to get off. The pilots were only five minutes late despite the confusion.

The Task Force was bringing men and supplies for our beachhead at Barakoma, Vella Lavella, north of us. Black Sheep pilots, in four- and eight-plane divisions, covered the convoy two hours at a stretch all day long, relieving each other on station.

At 1:30, Bill Case came in, reporting downing a Zero. I had hardly finished recording his success when a plane called our control tower requesting clearance for an emergency landing. It was "Wild Man" Magee.

He nursed his crippled Corsair into the groves, eased down carefully as though he were handling a crate of eggs, and then rolled free. As he flashed by us, we could see that one tire was flat, and jagged tears showed in his tail, fuselage, and wings. The actual count was 30 bullet holes.

"I got off late because I had to change planes at the last minute," Magee told me. "Then I couldn't locate my flight, so I joined with three other Corsairs over Vella Lavella.

"We spotted 30 dive bombers heading toward Bougainville. We nosed over, gained speed, and came up under them in a low stern pass. One of them pulled off to the side and I followed him, giving him three medium bursts. He caught fire in the middle and went down burning.

"At this time, I spotted 15 dive bombers heading for our shipping off Barakoma. I'd lost the other Corsairs by then, and our batteries were throwing plenty of stuff up at the dive bombers, but I knew they couldn't get them all. I pushed over and went down at them."

"All by yourself?"

"Well, yes, there were no other friendlies around. I caught them about 100 feet off the water and made a high side pass at the formation. One broke loose, and I chopped his tail off. He nosed over and crashed in the water.

"The dive bombers jettisoned their bombs and headed for home, so I picked out a straggler and started a high side pass at him. I passed over him before I could get in an effective burst, so I circled and made another high side at him. He turned in to me, and we came head-on. I gave him a long burst and saw pieces of his cowling and fuselage flying off. Then he nosed under me.

"I was going to circle and finish him off when I heard that old typewriter sound and saw holes begin to appear in my right wing. I kicked hard left rudder and then hard right alternately and dived toward our AA. Looking back, I could see four Zeros on my tail. They pulled off as I went down, so I circled and climbed back on station."

"You climbed back on station?" I asked him. "When you knew your plane had been shot up? Why didn't you come home?"

"I hadn't been relieved yet. There were no other friendly planes in sight, so I thought I'd better stay. In about 15 minutes a flight of New Zealand planes showed up, and I came on in."

"You ought to get the Navy Cross for that performance, Maggie. I'm going to write up the recommendation."

"Hell, I don't want any medals," he said. "Just killing the yellow bastards is enough fun for me!"

But I wrote up the recommendation anyway, and Maggie did receive the Navy Cross.

On the ground, Magee was quiet, reserved; in the air he was a junior edition of Boyington, a wild man, man-handling his plane like a cowboy bulldogging a steer. But he could fly with a delicate touch, too. Three days later, his engine was hit while he was strafing Japanese barges and quit as he flew parallel to our field. Instead of bailing out and letting the plane go into the water, he brought it in.

Life at Munda was grim. The pilots were flying all day, everyday. One or two divisions were up at 4:00 A.M.; others were never in until after dark. Doc Reames and I were up with the first and waited at the field for the last.

It wouldn't have been so bad if we could have slept at night, but enemy air raids were nightly occurrences, usually spaced so as to prevent our getting more than an hour or two of sleep at a time.

The food had a nauseating sameness about it—Spam, beans, dehydrated potatoes, and SOS. Flies ranged regularly from the bodies of the dead Japanese, still unburied, to the "heads" (toilets) and onto our food. Dysentery ("GI runs") was common. We all had a dull laugh one day when Doc brought in a piece of literature he'd received in the mail. Prepared by a board of doctors and surgeons in Washington, it was a detailed report on the importance of proper nutrition for pilots. Never, it said, should pilots be fed greasy foods or beans. Fruits and green vegetables should be regularly on their diets.

"Does it say anything in there about fried flies, stewed flies, boiled flies, or just plain flies, Doc?" asked Bragdon.

At night, tree toads chirruped in the jungle. Sometimes they crawled into our tent, along with lizards three or four feet long that looked like something out of a lost world.

Huge coconut crabs scraped across our floor at night, often dragging our shoes about. Rats as big as cats pilfered our belongings. One night, one of them chewed on Burney Tucker's thumb as he slept, after he inadvertently flung his hand outside his mosquito net.

It rained regularly. Everything was mildewed. You washed out your shirt in a bucket of water and hung it up in your tent to dry, and it stayed damp for a week. Our foxholes, although covered by the tent, seeped full of water.

One night during an air raid, I stood nude above my foxhole and shone my flashlight down into it. It was four feet deep in muddy water. Two rats had fallen in and were swimming about, unable to climb its straight slippery sides.

"I'm not jumping into that, bombs or no bombs," I vowed. But when the bombs began to fall, I jumped in, all right, and thrashed about in the dark, beating off the rats as they tried to climb up my chest and back.

We had no night fighters at Munda then, so all we could do during raids was sit and hope our antiaircraft fire would knock the bombers down or scare them away.

Tired of these sleepless nights, Boyington requested permission to fly one night to try to knock off one of our nocturnal visitors. He took off at one o'clock one morning and stayed up for four hours. Enemy planes were all around us all night long. They'd close in when Boyington dropped down to get off of oxygen, and then circle away as he climbed to meet them. That night we had only one alert; no planes came close, no shots were fired, and no bombs were dropped.

A good many thousand men blessed Pappy for giving them the first uninterrupted night's sleep they'd had in a long time.

Boyington landed at 5:00 A.M.; at 5:40 the sirens sounded. Four Black Sheep were among those scrambled to intercept the enemy; John Begert was knocked down by a bomb blast as he ran to get into his plane, but sustained only a few cuts, scratches, and bruises.

The other three Black Sheep and two pilots from another Marine squadron got off and were directed out on two separate courses. The other squadron's pilots sighted the enemy bomber, chased it for 75 miles, and shot it down.

We hoped that would slow up the air raids, but the next night we had an alert in the middle of evening Spam. We stumbled across the muddy clearing and sat down on our cots in our tent. No planes appeared; no searchlights went on.

"Let's go down and get our showers," suggested Bailey.

The two of us undressed, and shielding our flashlights so that only a tiny streak showed between our fingers, we picked our way back across the clearing.

We had the showers all to ourselves and were covered with soap when the searchlights came on and immediately picked out a bomber only 15,000 feet up and coming directly over us. We looked around frantically for a moment. We had no place to go—there were no foxholes by the showers and no time to get back to our tent. There was nothing we could do, so we took our razors and began to shave as the AA shells burst around the Nip plane.

It was like having a front seat at a mammoth Fourth of July celebration. The searchlights played brilliantly across the sky; the batteries flashed around us; their shells exploded brightly high above us. Then the enemy plane unloaded its bombs. We could hear them whistling down, then detonating over toward the strip. Bailey and I finished shaving, showered again, and dried off. The all-clear sounded as we fumbled for our field shoes.

Life on those islands was feelingly expressed by a young Marine who scribbled off this poem one night:

Tropical Serenade

Down where there are no Ten Commandments
    And a man can raise a thirst,
Lies the outcast of civilization
    Where life's at its very worst.

There in those fever-soaked islands
    Are the men that God forgot,
Fighting the Japs (for the rest of the world)
    And the itch and tropical rot.

Nobody knows how they're living,
    The few that would don't give a damn.
Back home they are soon forgotten,
    Those Marines of Uncle Sam.

Covered with sweat in the evening,
    They lie in their foxholes and dream
And wish to Hell there were liquor
    To help dam up memory's stream.

Where even no natives are living,
    There in that sultry zone,
They fight alone in a man-made Hell
    Thousands of miles from home,

> Where there's no such thing as liberty
>   And no one draws any pay,
> And there's nothing to do in the evening,
>   Unless bombers are coming your way.
>
> Vermin in your bed when you use it,
>   Ills that no doctor can cure.
> Hell no, we are not convicts,
>   Just Marines on a foreign tour.

The constant roar of planes taking off and landing made sleeping difficult; the fine coral dust blew over everything, interfering with our work, our card games. Some of the boys went souvenir hunting and found Japanese flags, guns, aircraft instruments. The Seabees who were working on the strip could make anything: beautiful brass ashtrays out of artillery shells, necklaces from a kind of seashell called "cat's eyes." The prize souvenir salesman, however, was the Army corporal who tried to sell us a U.S. .45 pistol he'd swiped as it hung in our parachute tent!

We had some laughs. The story got around that one of the Japanese bomber pilots called our control tower on our frequency and said in good English: "Here's a present from Tojo."

The tower operator said, "To hell with Tojo."

The pilot dropped his bombs and, after the explosion asked: "What do you think of Tojo now?"

"Tojo is a son of a bitch," said the tower Marine.

The Japanese pilot sputtered for a moment, thinking of the foulest thing he could say, and then blurted out:

"Babe Ruth is a son of a bitch."

Another story involved an officer looking for transportation to the forward area from Espiritu Santo who managed to arrange passage in a torpedo bomber. He stowed his footlocker, seabag, and bedroll in the bomb bay of the aircraft in the afternoon, figuring on leaving early the next morning. However, one of the pilots took the plane up for a practice flight that same day and made a mock attack on an abandoned hulk out in the ocean.

He scored a direct hit with the major's footlocker, and near misses with the seabag and bedroll.

Between their strikes and patrols, the Black Sheep ranged over enemy territory, strafing barges, troop concentrations, antiaircraft and coastal gun positions, and transport vessels. No place was safe from their whistling Corsairs and hails of 50-caliber machine gun slugs.

On 21 September, four of them headed by Boyington caught a Japanese steam launch in the channel off southern Bougainville and blew it up.

Another day, they asked permission to make a strafing run over Kahili Airdrome itself, home of hundreds of Japanese aircraft. Dr. Boo Bourgeois took his division off for this dangerous mission at 3:30 P.M. Junior Heier, Sandy Sims, and Don Moore were with him. The four circled to the northwest and roared across the south end of the heavily defended airfield at 300 miles an hour only 50 feet off the ground. Holding their triggers down, the Marines in echelon formation burned a deadly swath across this vital area. In the face of late, scattered AA fire, they strafed a bivouac area near the strip, burned up eight Zeros parked along the runway, battered an AA position just west of the strip, and sieved some boats and troops at the mouth of the river immediately west of the AA position.

Heier was the farthest inland of the four-plane division. On the swing, he was outside and having trouble catching up. At this point, a ground explosion threw debris in front of his plane, and he swung to get out of the way, plowing through a palm tree as he did so. The sturdy Corsair staggered out into the clear with the prop vibrating badly.

Heier nursed the plane along, losing oil all the way, and just as he rounded the corner of Vella Lavella, the oil pressure gauge went right to the top, indicating that the engine was about to seize up. He kicked the plane over onto its back and fell out head down. When the parachute opened, he told me, his head and feet traded positions as though he were on the end of a bullwhip.

He hit the water so weighted down with his survival gear that he just dropped toward the bottom of Kula Gulf like a bomb. At a depth of about 25 feet, he popped his life jacket CO_2 cartridge and shot back to the surface, inflated his rubber boat, and paddled to shore, having lost one of his beautiful Australian flying boots—highly prized by the pilots—in the process.

Then he saw a Japanese scow coming after him.

"I got out my .45 and said to myself, 'I'm going to get as many of them as I can.' I had no intention of being captured—I'd been reading all those atrocity stories—so I figured I'd shoot as many of them as I could and then shoot myself."

Emotionally drained by the strain of nursing his crippled plane 100 miles over unfriendly territory, shaken by the parachute drop, wet and cold, he was a forlorn figure as he resolutely stood his ground, his .45 in his hand, as the craft moved along the shoreline.

"Then I heard one of them say, 'The son of a bitch is around here somewhere; there's his parachute,' and it was our Seabees! They were using the Japanese scow as a garbage boat.

"I hollered, 'Over here, fellas'. As they came toward me, I saw I only had the one flying boot. Realizing one boot was worthless, I threw it out into the water and walked along the beach to be picked up."

As he waded out to board the boat, he saw his other boot in the shallow water. But he couldn't find the one he'd flung away.

---

9 | I Got That Old Feelin'

"I got that old feelin'," Quill Skull Groover told me on the morning of 23 September, as we were discussing the day's scheduled strike on southern Bougainville.

Groover's "old feelin'" was as sure a forecaster as your grandpa's rheumatism. This Georgia boy's "feelin'" forecast aerial combat action, and we had already come to respect it.

This morning, he must have had the feelin' pretty strong. Only two and a half hours later, with a broken right arm and leg, he fought his bullet-riddled Corsair 150 miles back to our base and landed it raggedly on the coral strip. He was helped out of his bloody cockpit, stained from the flow of a dozen wounds along his right side.

Groover was one of nine Black Sheep flying high cover on a joint Army, Navy, Marine, and New Zealand strike that day. The Black Sheep attacked 40 Zeros that were snapping at the heels of Army Liberators returning from the strike.

As the fight began, Big Bob Alexander, who was on Stan Bailey's wing, reported his engine was missing. Bailey directed him to return to base, but just at this point, three Zeros attacked Bailey.

Instead of returning to base, Alex guided his limping plane about the sky to protect his division leader. He soon had the three Zeros on his own tail and enemy tracers whistling past his ears. He went into a dive, and his engine quit. The Zeros, fortunately, turned away.

Bob managed to get his engine going spasmodically and headed for home, losing altitude all the way. He radioed in to the uncompleted Vella Lavella strip, instructing them to prepare for an emergency landing. As he came over the ridge north of the field, clearing the trees by only five feet, he saw the runway covered by trucks and bulldozers and men working. He had no choice now, so he put his plane down to one side of the strip, kicking right and left rudder, dodging trucks and bulldozers as he rolled along at nearly 100 miles an hour.

His plane hit a huge ditch, bounced, struck something solid, and turned over on its back, crushing his Plexiglass canopy.

Alex was lifted out, unhurt, by a naval officer, who looked at his face and said, "Jeez, aren't you from Davenport, Iowa?"

He was a Seebee ensign and a hometown friend.

Bailey, in the meantime, was playing sieve again: the three Zeros got in several hits before he could shake them. He tried to join up with other Corsairs, but kept running into Zeros, which made passes at him from all angles.

He finally headed back and climbed over the tail end of the returning bombers. Two-thirds of the way home Bailey saw six Zeros strafing a parachute in the water. He pushed his bullet-damaged plane over and attacked, driving them away from the helpless pilot.

He brought his Corsair safely into Munda with four 20-millimeter shell holes and 30 machine gun holes in it.

Black Sheep John Bolt, separated from his division in a cloud, came out in the clear and climbed into the sun to 20,000 feet. He attacked the last of a flight of six Zeros, opening fire at 200 yards. The enemy plane flamed and spun down.

Another Zero cut across in front of him, evidently attempting to join the remaining five. Bolt circled in behind him in a diving turn, bore-sighted him, and flamed him with a short burst.

Quill Skull Groover was on Moon Mullen's wing when the action began. They opened fire from 300 yards on a Zero to the right of them and then noticed a flight of Zeros waiting for them to lose altitude.

Moon and Groover pulled up in a climbing turn, looking for friendly planes to join, but none were in sight, only the 10 to 20 enemy planes.

As the two Black Sheep attacked, Groover saw one Zero pull in a tight loop and swing in toward Mullen's tail. He turned in to it as Mullen straightened out.

Three more Zeros came in on Groover's tail.

Mullen saw tracers eating into Groover's plane and then saw the Georgia boy's wing catch fire. Mullen circled and fought off the swarm attempting to finish Groover.

As he battled them, one of the Zeros made an overhead pass on him, hailing him with machine gun bullets. One shattered as it entered the Plexiglass canopy and wounded Mullen in the left shoulder.

Mullen turned toward the Zero and it dived out. Another came in from the left; Mullen swung on him, raking him from stem to stern. The Zero flamed and went down burning.

Mullen pushed over and dived after Groover.

Groover was badly hit. A 20-mm shell had exploded in his wing, setting it on fire; at the same time, another shell had entered the right side of his cockpit, breaking his right arm and ankle, wounding him all along the right side, and setting fire to the cockpit. Quill pushed over in a dive and beat out the cockpit fire with his hands; during the dive, the fire in his wing went out.

Shaking off the attacking Zeros, Groover leveled at 10,000 feet, put his nose down, and headed for home. On course, he began to take stock of his damage. Half his instruments and his radio were shot out; his right aileron was gone; he had two huge holes in his left wing. His right arm was useless, his right leg numb, and blood had soaked through his clothing from wounds in his arm, side, and leg.

As he got out his first aid kit to treat himself, the engine quit! Dropping the kit, he worked over the remaining controls till he got the engine running, holding the stick with his knee as he did so.

We saw Groover as he brought his plane onto our field. From a long way out we could see the huge hole in his wing. We kept our fingers crossed as he limped cautiously in, and with one aileron control and one elevator not functioning, put his Corsair safely down on the strip.

Quill was through for this tour; Doc bandaged him up and loaded him on a plane for Guadalcanal and the naval hospital there.

Mullen's wounds were slight; after being patched up, he insisted on flying another mission that day.

Our box score for the day was four Zeros destroyed and two probably destroyed, while all our pilots got back to base. The squadron totals were now 18 and 12.

And we had gained even more respect for Groover's "old feelin'."

10 | Zeros Snapped at Their Heels

On Sunday, 26 September, we sent 11 Black Sheep to Bougainville as high cover for a Marine torpedo bomber strike on the Japanese anti-aircraft positions near Kahili Airdrome. The Marine bombers thoroughly plastered the target, then joined up and headed for home. As they did so, the fight began. Seven Black Sheep attacked and scattered a dozen Zeros that were harassing the bombers, sending one down smoking.

The other four Black Sheep, with Moon Mullen leading, ran into real trouble—some 20 Zeros. Rollie Rinabarger, in Mullen's second section, found his engine heating up and could not stay in position.

Lagging slightly on a turn, Rinabarger received a long burst from a Zero that dived on him. One 20-mm shell exploded in his right stabilizer, another in his left wing gas tank. Machine gun bullets beat a steady tattoo on his tail and worked up his fuselage; one entered at an angle just back of his cockpit, nicked his knife, and hit him in the left hip. The slug traveled on down through his thigh, stopping just under the skin about eight inches down on his left leg.

Rollie attempted to stay in formation but couldn't do so. Then the shells really began to hit him as the enemy planes all piled onto the cripple. A second 20-mm shell exploded in his left wing; a third struck the right side of his cowl, breaking his oil line and putting one cylinder out of commission; another entered his fuselage and exploded back of his cockpit, starting a fire; still another hit his left wing, bursting his tire and destroying his flap control on that side, while machine gun bullets raked him fore and aft.

Mullen brought the remainder of his division around as sharply as he could and engaged the swarm of Zeros as Rollie dived out, smoking badly. For 140 miles these three Black Sheep fought off the pack of Zeros attempting to finish off their squadron mate. They worked gradually toward Munda, keeping the Zeros several thousand feet above Rinabarger, whose engine was smoking badly.

The fire in the fuselage behind Rollie burned out, but oil obscured his windshield; blood ran out the leg of his trousers, filled his shoe, and covered the floor of his cockpit. He limped into Munda, coming in too fast—about 140 miles an hour—because his air speed indicator had been shot out and his left flap was damaged; he was unable to see through the oil on the windshield, and one tire was flat.

He drifted too far without his flaps but sat down well in spite of the flat tire, rolled down the runway, and might have made it except for a grader parked to the right. His right wing struck the grader; the Corsair spun, rolled over, and was washed out.

Doc Reames rode with Rollie up to the hospital, and Boyington and I went up to see him as soon as the flight was in. He lay on a canvas cot in the hospital, a long tent with open sides and a bare, muddy coral floor. His face was pale, and we could see that his wound was painful.

"Gee, Skipper, I'm sorry I wrecked the airplane," he said. Rollie was evacuated to New Zealand to recover.

The next day, our Black Sheep knocked down four more Zeros to run our score up to 23, plus 13 probables. Ten Black Sheep tangled with 50 Zeros in that action, which took place off southern Bougainville.

Boyington had Mo Fisher on his wing, with Bill Case leading his second section and Red Harris on Case's wing.

These four attacked 20 Zeros and shot down three, Boyington, Fisher, and Case each getting one. The remaining six Black Sheep jumped 30 Zeros, and Don Moore sent one spinning down.

In the scramble, the Black Sheep became separated and then had to battle a storm for 15 minutes before coming out into the clear.

Case and Harris were apparently alone in the sky as they came out in the vicinity of Treasury Island, so the two of them headed for Vella Lavella. Almost there, Case looked back and saw a swarm of Zeros attacking the rear of the bomber formation that had just broken clear of the storm. One bomber was smoking.

"Red, we've got to go back," he radioed to Harris, and the two turned to try to fight the Zeros off the flight of Army Liberators. As they drew closer, they could see about 40 enemy planes.

Climbing as they went back, the two Black Sheep gained altitude and then came down on the Zeros, scattering them. They pulled back above the bombers and scissored over them as the Zeros reformed still farther above. One after the other and in pairs, the Zeros began to dive on the two Corsairs and then pull out.

The bombers were going very, very slowly, and the Black Sheep were buying their passage, foot by foot.

Suddenly, Japanese planes were coming in from all directions; one was directly on Red's tail. Case turned and fought him off, but a 20-mm shell exploded in his left wing and a flight of bullets went past him. He slid under Harris and came back at the Zeros. They were hitting him from all sides. He went into a diving turn, looking for Harris, but couldn't see him. Then he pushed straight over and went down, shaking his attackers.

Behind him, as he leveled off, he saw a plane splash into the water. It might have been Harris's, because Red didn't come back.

As Case climbed back into position over the bombers, one of them radioed him: "Corsair, you're smoking. Get the hell home."

Landing at Vella Lavella, he found his plane riddled with 20-mm and 7.7 bullet holes.

And at Munda, I wrote "MIA" beside Red Harris's name in my diary. It had been three months to the day since Red had kissed his new wife, Maurine, goodbye at San Diego.

The next morning McCartney and Matheson, returning from a patrol mission, spotted a barge filled with 15 enemy troops in Kape Harbor by the enemy-infested island of Kolombangara, just across the channel from us. They went down and made several passes at them, chopping them to pieces with their 50-caliber slugs.

"That's for Red," called Mat as they headed for home.

That day and the next the Black Sheep shot up anything that moved in enemy territory.

11 | The Squadron Comes of Age

On 29 September our men were out hunting again, although the weather was not good. I noticed a civilian sitting near our ready tent and learned that he was George Weller, a war correspondent for the Chicago *Daily News*. He was en route to MacArthur's command in Australia but had been weathered in at Munda.

Seeing an opportunity to get the Black Sheep some of the recognition they deserved, I invited him into our ready tent and opened the diary of biographical information I'd collected on each of our pilots.

Three of our Black Sheep were Chicago boys, I told him, and supplied details: their home address, their schooling, their performance. I pointed out that the Black Sheep had already scored 23 planes and 13 probables, although they'd been in combat only three weeks. I explained how the squadron had been formed and how we'd selected our name. He scribbled furiously and asked me to repeat some of the statistics. As the boys checked in, I introduced him, and he talked to them himself.

As a result of that stop, he wrote a series about the Black Sheep, stories that were syndicated all over the United States and among our Allies. The Black Sheep were on their way to becoming a household name.

The night of the 29th, we received orders to return to the Russell Islands the following afternoon.

The next morning, on their way back from dawn patrol, Bailey, Alexander, and Tucker spotted four boats at Ropa Point off Sosoruana Island near Kolombangara. Bailey radioed instructions:

"Don't fire until I give the word." He flew low, recognized them, and radioed: "Don't fire, they're our own PT boats."

Apparently not receiving the message, or perhaps accidentally tripping his trigger, Alexander opened fire. The PT boats responded, and the next thing Bailey and Tucker knew, Alex's plane had crashed on the Kolombangara beach in flames, sliding into the jungle. Bailey and Tucker circled the spot but could see nothing but a column of smoke.

When Bailey came in to report, I could tell that something had gone wrong.

"What is it, Stan?"

"Alex is dead." Unshed tears balanced on his lower lids as he told me what had happened.

"I sure loved that kid," he said.

I wrote "MIA" beside Alexander's name in my diary, but I knew he didn't have a chance of getting out alive. The all-American boy was gone . . . one of the tragic errors of war.

At 1:00 P.M., 30 September, 14 Black Sheep took off for the Russells via transport plane. At 4:30, eight more followed in Corsairs. Boyington, Reames, and I went down the next morning.

The Russell Islands really looked good. Although actually only 130 miles from Munda, it was a million miles away in comfort. We had good food, swimming beaches, clean clothing, and practically no bombing raids. For three days, we had no missions except scramble alerts.

And we had *mail*—six huge bags of it for us alone. It was the first we'd received since we left Espiritu Santo 19 years—no, days—before. Some of the boys got as many as 75 letters.

After a shower and a change into clean clothing, I went to dinner with Doc Reames, and afterward we walked to the outdoor movie and sat through one of the horse operas that seemed to have been made exclusively for showing overseas. By the end, half the audience had left.

Following the rootin', tootin', hootin', and shootin', Doc and I went back to our hut.

"Sit down a minute," said Doc.

"Let's go over to the big hut where most of the gang is staying."

"You sit down a minute. I need your help."

"Sure," I said, "what is it?"

Doc was fumbling in his bag.

He came up with a pint bottle of champagne.

"I want you to help me drink this," he said. "We're going to celebrate."

"Celebrate what?"

"I've been carrying this bottle around with me for eight months. Ever since I left to come overseas. I knew I wouldn't be able to get it over here."

He split the bottle in our two canteen cups.

"What is it, Doc?"

"My wife's having a baby tonight."

"What! How do you know?"

"Tonight's the night, boy."

"O.K.," I said. "Here's to Junior."

"And here's to Rosalita."

We clicked our canteen cups.

Outside, a tropical rain had begun to beat down. The wind rustled the palm trees about us; an occasional coconut fell to the soft earth with a thud.

And inside, a candle flickering between us, Doc Reames and I drank warm champagne out of canteen cups in an 8,000-mile toast to his wife, whom I'd never seen, and to his son, whom he'd never seen. It was two more months before he learned that he had, indeed, become the father of a son at about that time.

For a few nights, our choral society really flourished. We gathered in the long hut where most of the boys were quartered and shook the coconuts with our singing. With Ashmun, Mo, Moon, Mat, Oli, and Sandy leading, we sang such songs as "Wreck of the Corsair," "Blood

on the Runway," "Bless 'em All," "I'm Gonna Lay Down My F-4-U,"
"After Rabaul Is Over," "In a Rowboat at Rabaul," and, of course, our
own "Black Sheep Song." We had parodied the Yale drinking song
which, in turn, had been taken from Rudyard Kipling's "Gentlemen
Rankers":

> To the one-armed joint at Munda,
> To the foxholes where we dwell,
> To the predawn takeoffs which we love so well.
> Sing the Black Sheep all assembled
> With their canteen cups on high,
> And the magic of their drinking casts a spell.
> Yes, the magic of their singing
> Of the songs we love so well,
> "Mrs. Murphy," "One Ball Riley," and the rest,
> We will serenade our "Pappy"
> While life and breath shall last,
> Then we'll pass and be forgotten
> Like the rest.
>
> We are poor little lambs who have lost our way.
> Baa, baa, baa.
> We are little Black Sheep who have gone astray.
> Baa, baa, baa.
> Gentlemen Black Sheep off on a spree,
> Damned from here to Kahili,
> God have mercy on such as we.
> Baa, baa, baa.

We also sang old favorites—"When You Wore A Tulip," "I Want A
Girl Just Like the Girl That Married Dear Old Dad," "For Me and My
Gal"—and many that were considered risqué at that time: "The Bastard
King of England," "One Ball Riley," "The Man in the Moon," and
dozens of verses of "In China They Never Eat Chili."

Some energetic individual once gathered many of our songs, had
them mimeographed, and circulated a few copies under the title:
"South Pacific Serenade, a collection of bawdy morale-builders chiefly
contributed by Marine Pilots, dedicated to Marine Aviation, whither-
soever dispersed."

My musty-smelling copy is one of my favorite souvenirs.

On 4 October, Pappy led five other Black Sheep off the Russell
Islands coral strip in Corsairs that had been sent down from Munda for
major overhauls but had not yet had them. The six Black Sheep were to
act as medium cover for a Marine bomber strike on Malebeta Hill, an
enemy AA position next to Kahili Airdrome.

They were still 50 miles south of Kahili when they saw dust rising from the airdrome as 30 Zeros rose to meet them.

There was plenty of time to count them.

Pappy took his flight down in a high stern run from 3,000 feet above, coming too fast, and almost overran his quarry. He chopped back on his throttle, skidded sideways, settled back into position, opened fire, and chopped a Zero's tail to pieces.

The Zero spun in.

Still in a tight turn, Boyington came in on his second Zero in a high port quarter pass.

After a very short burst, the Zero pilot popped out of the cockpit, parachuting to safety.

Continuing in his sharp circle, Boyington swung in on the tail of a third Zero, opened fire, and closed in on him, firing. The Zero flamed from the wing root and went down.

Three Zeros in 30 seconds! Pappy had run his score to 15 (including his Flying Tiger kills) and the squadron total to 26.

The Black Sheep reassembled and looked about, but the remaining 27 Zeros had left the field of battle.

For the next six days, our pilots saw no combat action. They flew task force covers, local patrols, escort and search missions.

On 10 October, however, "recess" was over, and we all flew back to Munda.

It was a different squadron from the one that had arrived there just 23 days before. This time, our pilots were an integrated fighting team, battle tested and battle wise.

We had hardly unloaded our gear when 20 Black Sheep were assigned to cover a twin Army and Marine strike on Kahili and Malebeta Hill. Army B-24s were to attack the airstrip while Marine dive and torpedo bombers were to go after the AA positions.

Only two Black Sheep made contact with the enemy, attacking ten Zeros that were harassing the rear of the B-24 formation. Ed Olander made his first sure kill in a high six o'clock run on a Zero as it made a pass at one of the B-24s. The Japanese plane literally flew to pieces in the air, and its debris sailed downward, burning.

Ed had already scored three probables in previous aerial engagements, so we were especially glad to see him get his first "certain."

On 11 October, Bill Case nailed a Nip plane in an impossible shot from 800 yards out.

The 13th of October was the last day we had to live—the Emperor of Japan had so decreed in an Imperial Rescript, and Tokyo Rose talked about it on her excellent program (the only decent music we could get down there): every white man on Munda was to be killed before 14 October. She didn't say exactly how—just that we were all going to be wiped out.

We did nothing different; no special precautions were taken, and we were all alive the next morning.

All, that is, except Virgil Ray.

Ray had left at 10:00 A.M. of the 13th on an errand to Guadalcanal and the Russell Islands. He left the Russells at 4:30 P.M. for the 45-minute return flight to Munda. A storm developed between the two bases after he took off.

Had he become lost in the storm, and crashed into a mountain on one of the islands? Had he run out of gas? Had a flight of enemy planes picked him off? "MIA" was the catchall for those possibilities.

At first light the next morning, and all that day, every available plane in the area combed both water and land for signs of him. He never showed up.

During the 14 October searches, Bill Case and Long Tom Emrich were scrambled to intercept approaching enemy planes. They caught up with two Zeros at 20,000 feet, 20 miles north of Vella Lavella. Case destroyed one, and Emrich probably destroyed the other. It was Case's fifth Zero, making him the second ace in the Black Sheep Squadron.

12 | A Change in Tactics

Around Munda, some of the pilots were developing a feeling of futility in our missions to Bougainville. Flying regular bomber escort, our fighter pilots would beat off the Zeros that attacked the bombers. Next day, the enemy fighters would be out again in full force.

Trying to protect the bombers while tangling with enemy fighters was like trying to box with one hand tied. Our planes were confined to the small escort area, while the enemy had the whole sky in which to maneuver. We were pecking at them and knocking them down, but not nearly fast enough.

Before Bougainville could be invaded, Kahili had to be eliminated as a fighter base. Taking a page from World War I tactics, Boyington suggested the answer: the fighter sweep.

Why not send up fighters to *seek out* the enemy fighters and shoot them down? Taunt the enemy into fighting, keep after him, knock his planes down until his reserves ran dry—then, when his fighter strength was exhausted, let our bombers go in and plaster the place and soften it up for the Marine landing!

This would be something new in the Solomons—aerial combat in its purest sense. The two formations would battle it out in the skies, our advance agents clearing the way for the big, slow heavyweights to get in. It was a way to even up the odds.

Could our Corsairs and the Marines who flew them do it? Boyington was sure they could and laid his plan before the powers that directed our aerial campaign.

They were skeptical, but Boyington had an unplanned opportunity to show what he meant on 15 October. Scheduled to act as cover for a B-24 strike on Kahili, Boyington was held up at the takeoff. Thinking the B-24s would proceed directly to the target, he led three other Black Sheep in a high-speed, direct run to the Japanese airstrip, arriving well ahead of the bombers. With Kahili all to themselves, the four Black Sheep attacked 16 Zeros, destroying six and probably three more, without damage to themselves.

It was Boyington's tenth Zero for the Black Sheep Squadron. Case brought down two to bring his score to seven; Emrich got two (his first sure ones); and Burney Tucker made his first kill. The Black Sheep total was now 35, plus 17 probables.

No Japanese planes got within miles of our bombers that day. When the reports were in, there was no longer any opposition to Boyington's plan. A fighter sweep was scheduled for 17 October, and Marines were assigned the job; fittingly enough, Boyington and his Black Sheep were to lead.

On the 16th, Bolt, returning in extremely bad weather from an escort mission to Kahili, spotted Tonolei Harbor, on the southeastern corner of Bougainville, loaded with Jap ships and barges.

Although Bolt recognized the strafing opportunities, he was low on fuel. He turned his plane away and bent to his instruments to navigate back to Munda through the storm. On the way in idea struck him, and he changed course to land at Vella Lavella instead.

There, he ordered mechs to service his plane quickly. When they had done so, he took off and headed toward Bougainville, alone and on instruments.

Bolt broke into the clear at 15,000 feet, just short of the busy harbor, and roared down on the enemy shipping with his six guns blazing. Flashing up the entire length of the harbor, he left a swath of death and debris behind him.

His slugs chopped to bits a barge loaded with troops, leaving them dead and dying in their sinking craft. His shells walked up the water and sieved another barge, a tug, and a transport vessel, leaving them burning.

Reaching the end of the harbor, Bolt chandelled up and around, and came back down on a new path, braving the ground batteries that were opening up on him. His bullets beat down on a dock, two boats anchored there, and another barge before he headed for home, pursued only by a few shells that splashed in the sea behind him.

That was the Black Sheep spirit at it best—attack, attack, attack; hit 'em everywhere, anywhere, but hit 'em.

Bolt got the Distinguished Flying Cross and a personal "well done" message from Admiral Halsey for his action that day.

On Sunday, 17 October, we were up before daylight and down to the strip and into our ready tent, where we gathered around the hissing Coleman lantern to hear Boyington's final instructions for this new sort of mission. There was an unusual tenseness in the air.

"We'll go up at about 20,000 feet. One division will fly ahead at 6,000 to act as bait and get the Nips to come up and fight."

This was not just defense; they were going out *looking* for trouble. The Marines loved it. The night before, Boyington had had trouble selecting the 13 Black Sheep who were to accompany him. All of them wanted to go. He finally chose Moore, Case, McClurg, Olander, Matheson, Bolt, Harper, Hill, Ashmun, Magee, Heier, Mullen, and Tucker.

With the Black Sheep were to be seven Marine fighter pilots from Squadron 221.

"There's going to be action," Boyington went on. That's what we're going for. If they won't come up and fight, we'll make them. Just keep your altitude; if you lose your division, join with someone else.

"Let's stay in there. The sooner we shoot down all their planes, the sooner they'll have to give up."

We didn't know they were to do their job so effectively that Marines would land on Bougainville just 16 days later with virtually no aerial opposition.

With four Corsairs out in front at 6,000 feet as bait, and the remain-

ing 17 planes climbing, the formation headed north past Kolombangara and Vella Lavella. Through scattered clouds in a now bright
blue sky, the Marines reached Kahili without incident and made a lazy
circle over the field. Black puffs of AA bursts appeared beneath them.
Streaks of dust showed on the airstrip as Japanese fighters began to
take off in twos and threes.

"Here they come, boys," called Boyington into his throat mike.
"Don't get too eager. Pick your targets."

Boyington did a perfect job of tactical organization with his flight.
He took two divisions down in big, sweeping S-turns, instructing the
remainder to stay on top till the fight began. This the remainder of the
formation did, making a slow figure eight turn over the strip.

Boyington led his eight-plane formation in an attack on 20 Zeros
that were climbing to meet them. Above him the remainder of his flight
contacted 35 Zeros, and the battle was joined: 21 Marines against 55
Zeros!

For the next 40 minutes, the sky was filled with heaving, roaring,
whining, and straining planes, the chatter of machine guns, flashes of
flame—and falling Zeros. The radios went wild: "Look out!" "I got the
bastard." "Coming in at eleven o'clock." "Watch behind you." "Watch
him burn!" The fight ranged all over the sky from Kahili to Ballale and
Fauro Island to the Shortland Islands. The Marines fought the Nips
right down to the water. Then the fight was suddenly over as the
Marines ran too low on fuel to pursue the fleeing enemy.

Back at Munda, we tallied up the mounting score as our pilots
straggled in.

The 21 Marines had, without a single loss, shot down 20 Zeros for
sure and God only knew how many probables—the battle was too
violent to worry about probables. Black Sheep pilots had scored 12 of
the kills, to bring our squadron total to 47. Bolt had downed one to
make his third. Junior Heier had knocked down his first two. Olander
had got his second one, and Burney Tucker had scored a double to
bring his total to three.

Wild Man Magee got two to bring his score to four, and Mat
Matheson had downed his first Zero. Boyington had blasted three Nip
planes out of the sky. He now had 19 (counting his six in China) and
was within sighting distance of the record of 26 held jointly by Eddie
Rickenbacker and Marine Joe Foss.

The Black Sheep had not escaped completely, however. Moore,
Matheson, and Harper had their planes shot up extensively; the three
aircraft came home with total of 123 bullet holes and six 20-mm shell
holes. Both Matheson and Harper had been wounded by 7.7-mm

bullets that shattered as they entered their cockpits. Matheson was hit in the legs and Harper in the neck.

In the midst of a sudden tropical storm, Matheson made a perfect landing despite serious damage to his left wing and elevator. Harper, his hydraulic system destroyed, had to make a belly landing when his wheels refused to come down.

Nevertheless, our ready tent was a scene of wild hilarity as the victory-high Black Sheep crowded around my table, all talking at once, while Doc bandaged up Harper's and Matheson's wounds and dispensed small bottles of anti-jitters brandy. Rain beat down on the roof, blew in under the side of the tent, and muddied the coral floor, but the Black Sheep continued to talk, laugh, and shout like a football team that has just won the big game.

I leaned my chin on my hand, watching them. To have told them that they were heroes would only have invited a jeer.

After the excitement had calmed somewhat, Harper came over and stood beside my table. "You know," his face serious, "I learned something up there today."

It was the third time he'd told me this. Twice before he had flown back from Kahili with his plane full of holes, and the men in the squadron were calling him "the Sleeve," after the tow targets on which they practiced gunnery runs.

Today, I said, "Did you, Harpo?"

"Yes, Red, I really learned something up there today. They can't touch me now!"

I looked out at his perforated plane, which was being hauled away, and then back to the bandage that Happy Jack Reames had put on his neck. "They can't touch you, huh?"

"No, they can't touch me now."

And though he was in several actions after that, in which he shot down a Zero and two probables, no enemy aircraft ever did put another hole in his plane.

Navy Corpsman "Weavo" Weaver was a big help, not only to the Black Sheep, but to all pilots based at Munda. He set up a tent behind our quarters in the camp area, installed a couple of homemade rubbing tables, and worked most of the night, every night, massaging the tension out of tired pilots' bodies. We never knew where he came from or how he got started. One night we came in from the strip and there he was, all set up for business. He never had to drum up trade; there was always a string of pilots waiting their turn.

It was amazing to watch a highstrung, jittery pilot calm down under Weavo's ministrations. Fighter pilots are sort of like racehorses.

They're an entirely different breed from bomber pilots. Accustomed to hurtling through the air at hundreds of miles an hour, they think fast, move fast; their minds and bodies are alert, quick. The mere taking off or landing of a red-hot fighter plane requires the fullest concentration and coordination of mind and body. Add to this the constant threat of death in the air all about them, and it is no wonder the pilots were tense and jittery after a day of combat.

Weavo would stretch them out and probe into taut nerves and muscles with his capable fingers, and the pilot would loosen up, relax, and often fall asleep on the table. All that Weavo expected for his timely treatments was a signature in his logbook. During the time he was operating, he got signatures and notes of gratitude from all the pilots who flew out of Munda; his logbook was a fine souvenir. Weavo had the last signatures of some Marines who never came back, some of the high-scoring aces, and some who were given up for lost and then incredibly returned.

At 9:00A.M. on 18 October, Boyington led 12 Black Sheep to cover a bombing strike on Ballale. The bombing was highly successful and enemy fighters were observed in the vicinity; but none came in to challenge. Bob McClurg's engine cut out on him at 26,000 feet and he nosed over in an attempt to get it started. He got it running—but running rough—at 15,000 and headed for home. Spotting two Zeros at 2,500 and aware that attack was his best move, he slid down and knocked both out in one continuous run. It was his first positive score.

At 3:30 the same afternoon, Pappy zoomed off the Munda strip to seek out the enemy once more, leading 11 Black Sheep and eight Marines from Squadron 221. Matheson and Harper insisted on going in spite of their wounds.

Boyington led them up the slot to Kahili, and the blue Corsairs circled the airdrome at 15,000 feet. The antiaircraft batteries opened up, but no Zeros came out to meet them.

"Come on up and fight, you yellow bastards," screamed Boyington over his radio. He knew that the Japanese listened in on our frequencies; when he had been up over Kahili only a few days before, a clipped Oriental voice had spoken into his earphones:

"Major Boyington, what is your position, please?"

He knew that it was a Nip, not only from the accent but also because one of his Black Sheep would have said: "Hey, Pappy, where the hell are you?"

Boyington had replied: "Right over your lousy airfield, you yellow bellies. Come on up and fight."

This day, he expected a reply to his challenge. He got it. "Why don't you come down, Major Boyington?" queried the Japanese monitor.

Instructing the remaining Corsairs to stay aloft, Boyington pushed over and went down in a screaming dive, spraying the field with his six 50-caliber guns. AA fire burst all around him, but the Corsair zoomed up and away, untouched.

Rejoining his flight, Boyington taunted the Japanese once more: "Now, come up and fight, you dirty yellow bastards!"

There was no answer. But there is the "oriental face," and the morale of thousands of Nip troops on the ground must have been rapidly ebbing. The flight of Marines audaciously circling and mocking them was too much for the Nip commander. Japanese pilots raced out to their planes, and one after the other they took off until there were 40 Sons of Heaven.

Boyington and his flight circled slowly, waiting for them. It was like the moment before the kickoff: mouths were dry, hearts beating fast, palms sweaty even at that altitude.

Giving the enemy a chance to get well bunched, Boyington waggled his wings and then took his formation down in huge S-turns to meet them. The enemy was brought to action at only 6,000 feet.

Like the spring on a broken clock, everything fell apart, and the sky was a wild, seething mass of hurtling planes. Results began to show immediately, with Zeros falling into the water "like AA shells," as one of the Black Sheep put it. In 15 minutes the beaten Japanese scattered, leaving the field of battle to the Leathernecks.

Once again the Black Sheep stormed hilariously into our ready tent, shouting and waving their arms in the familiar fighter pilots' gestures, showing with their hands the planes' positions and going through the gyrations and maneuvers as they talked.

The final score showed 18 Zeros knocked down with one Squadron 221 pilot missing, the only loss of the day. Boyington's plan was working: in the two missions on two successive days, Marines had shot down 38 Zeros, with only one pilot missing in action.

The Black Sheep score jumped eight more to bring our total to 57 planes destroyed since the 16th of September, only 32 days before—55 of them over enemy territory, an important factor. Fighting over enemy territory meant that if you had to go down, there was little chance of being picked up by friendly forces. The fact that all but two were fighter planes was also important; the slow-moving bombers were easier to shoot down. Our score was run up the hard way. Only those planes actually seen to burn, explode, or crash were counted, according to the

Navy and Marine system. "Probables" and those destroyed on the ground were frosting on the cake.

Boyington had welded a conglomeration of casuals and replacements into one of the deadliest aerial combat squadrons in history. He was not only a savage past master of individual aerial combat; he was also an inspiring leader.

Reames, a broad grin on his face, was circulating and slapping backs, looking the Black Sheep over and passing out his two-ounce bottles of "nerve medicine" as I gathered notes for my official action report.

Boyington had downed another plane; it made him an even 20. Tall Jimmy Hill of Chicago had made his first kill. Wild Man Magee had become the third Black Sheep ace: he'd shot down three Zeros to bring his score to seven. Moon Mullen got one to become a near-ace with a total of four and one-half planes to his credit. Ed Olander had scored again.

Burney Tucker, separated from his flight on the way back, made his return count by coming, alone, across a Japanese troop bivouac area in Faisi Island and gun emplacements on Poporang Island in a high-speed strafing run, expending 1,400 rounds of ammunition as he chopped down tents and troops. On his way out, he dodged shells from the AA and coastal gun positions; one of them splashed in the water under his wing.

It was perhaps this day that Bill Case got religion. Because he was short, he usually raised his seat several inches in order to give him better all-around vision out of the cockpit. On this flight, for some reason, he'd raised his seat only slightly, perhaps two or three inches less than normal. In the melee, Case got his eighth plane but did not escape unscathed. A 7.7 bullet had pierced his Plexiglass canopy, split his scalp as it skidded across the top of his head, and then lodged in his gunsight. Had he had the seat in its usual position, the bullet would have hit him squarely in the back of the head and killed him instantly. He was never able to figure out why he'd flown with his seat lower that day.

During the afternoon, our relief squadron had come in. We were to go back to the Russells the next day.

The Japanese aerial defense of Bougainville was in shambles.

13 | "Your Steeplechase Is Over"

Waiting for a lull in the celebration, I told the pilots that our relief was in and that we were scheduled to leave the next morning. With a whoop, they pounced on Doc Reames.

"How about unlocking that medicine cabinet of yours, Doc? It's time for a party," they shouted.

And Doc didn't have to be urged. We moved out of our tents and gathered in a big Quonset hut (a recent innovation at Munda) that night. We drowned out the lizards and tree toads as we sat, naked, on our canvas cots, babbling about the day's action, singing, and talking about Sydney, where all squadrons were sent for seven days of R-and-R leave after each six-week combat tour.

It was about two o'clock when the last of us stretched out and dozed off.

The beam of a flashlight across my face awakened me.

"Strafe Kahili!" I heard Doc exclaim.

Boyington stood beside me, feet wide apart, sweat glistening on his hairy, stocky body. His square jaw was thrust forward; his blood-shot eyes peered out between half-closed lids.

It was 3:45 in the morning. I rolled over; what the hell *was* this? Our squadron had been relieved, but here was an operations officer nervously rattling some papers and bringing us news that Operations wanted four planes to strafe Kahili and Kara, the latter another airdrome adjacent to Kahili.

"What the hell's the matter with the squadron that just relieved us?" I asked.

"They're not yet familiar with the area," the officer replied. "Fighter Command said to give the Black Sheep the mission."

"All right, they want Kahili strafed, we'll strafe it," said Boyington. "This is no time to take a regular division. Who wants to go with me?"

It never entered Pappy's mind that he could send someone else in his place.

Pappy selected George Ashmun, Wild Man Magee, and Bob Mc-Clurg. The four of them and Doc and I got up, drank a cup of coffee, and went down to the strip. It was 4:25 A.M. when we got there.

Everything was black night. Strain as it would, even the Coleman lantern gave up after pushing the darkness only a few feet from the table.

"You fly my wing," Boyington told McClurg. "We'll strafe Kahili. George, you and Maggie take care of Kara.

"We'll take off, stay together, go up along the west coast of Choiseul, split up into our two sections there, and make our runs at about the same time."

The Black Sheep had started out when Doc saw that Boyington was barefooted! "Pappy, where the hell are your shoes?"

"I don't need any shoes." Pappy stamped his feet on the sharp coral to prove it.

"You'll sure need them if you go down."

"Don't worry, Doc. I'm not going down."

"I don't want you going up there without any shoes, Skipper. Here, take mine." Doc pulled off his shoes.

"O.K., Doc, if it'll make you feel any better."

They took off at 4:50, headed north, and almost immediately ran into a violent thunderstorm that would have justified their returning to base. They switched on their wing lights in order to stay together, however, and flew grimly on, buffeted about like matchsticks by the squall.

Suddenly, Ashmun was separated from the others. Afraid of colliding with them in the turmoil, he dropped a thousand feet and continued northward.

In the meantime, McClurg had joined Magee, thinking he was Boyington.

Ashmun, believing he was far enough north, began to let down through the storm. He broke into the clear over Fauro Island, too far offshore to get to Kara, so he made a strafing run on the Ballale airdrome. He roared the length of the strip, a little to one side, 40 feet off the ground, and sprayed the revetment areas and the control tower. He had to lift one wing to keep from hitting the tower.

The other three continued north, managing to stay together in spite of the heavy weather until Boyington nosed over, flicked off his lights, and disappeared.

Magee and McClurg flew on up the east coast of Bougainville, went down to 2,000 feet and then to 800 feet, and circled inland about a mile north of Kara airfield. When they were sure they had located it, they went down to 40 feet and sprayed the length of the runway. Eight bombers lined up on one end were left burning from their incendiary shells.

Boyington had made his run from the water, inland over Kahili, but didn't see anything, so he pulled around in a tight circle and came back down the runway, firing, while enemy antiaircraft shells and tracers lit up the sky.

"I wasn't fully awake till then," Boyington told me, "but I sure as hell woke up fast."

Holding into his run, the Black Sheep skipper poured a long burst into three bombers parked on the end of the strip. They exploded as he passed over them. Coming out into the clear over the water, he circled to the left and hurtled into the mouth of Tonolei Harbor, strafing the small boats anchored there.

The antiaircraft batteries opened up, and in their flashes he made out the outline of a huge destroyer at anchor. He kicked slight right rudder, bore-sighted the destroyer, and held his trigger down. The ground fire intensified as Boyington poured hundreds of rounds into the warship, skimmed over it, and out over the ridge back of the harbor.

Circling out to the right, he stayed low and searched the coves along the coast of northern Choiseul until he found an enemy barge. He destroyed it with the remainder of his ammunition. Then he returned to Munda and gave Doc back his shoes.

Later that day, 12 Black Sheep went out again to Bougainville as cover, but not a single enemy plane rose to challenge them. The next day, eight more Black Sheep covered a Marine dive bomber strike on the Kakasa area of Choiseul, and again no enemy planes were sighted.

Finally, our squadron received a characteristic dispatch from Admiral Halsey: "Your steeplechase over; you are retired to stud."

The following morning we all flew to the Russell Islands and got ready to go out of the combat area. While the rest read mail, ate and slept, or went swimming, I worked over my books, bringing squadron records up to date and preparing official reports. The last few days at Munda had been so hectic, I was way behind.

Busily writing, I heard the door open and a voice say, "Hello, Red."

It was Quill Skull Groover, his hair standing straight up as usual. I let out a whoop. "How are you? Are the leg and arm O.K.? Can you fly?"

"Sure, I can fly. I appreciated your letters and I read about what the Black Sheep were doing, and I sure wished I was along."

"Hell, you did your share, boy. But we've missed you."

About that time some of the gang came in, and an impromptu celebration began.

A couple of days later, we all loaded into transport planes at 7:30

one morning, flew to Guadalcanal, changed planes, and then flew on down to Espiritu Santo.

By the time we got loaded into trucks and hauled over to the camp at Espiritu Santo, it was about 4:00 P.M. After the combat area, the place looked like a country club to us. Set in a coconut grove, the camp was quiet and well kept. Cool green grass covered the ground between the Dallas huts. The coral roads were smooth and white. A clean, sandy beach ran down to the warm water of the channel. A dock jutted out some 150 feet, and a bathing platform was anchored 50 yards away.

There was even a mascot—a lady goat smuggled in from Sydney when she was very young. Under loving attention from so many pilots, however, she had grown difficult to handle. One day, after a squadron consultation, it was decided that Nanny needed a boyfriend. She was taken back to Sydney; a groom was found; and she was married off with 40 pilots attending the ceremony.

The hut that Boyington, Bailey, Doc, and I shared had just been vacated by a squadron going north. It was dirty; the previous occupants had moved out in a hurry. Papers littered the ground about it, but we were too tired to care.

"We'll clean up in the morning," Boyington said.

It was well after midnight when a flashlight beam swept over our little hut.

"Boyington."

"Yeah. What is it?" And then, recognizing the colonel commanding the Group, Boyington swung his feet to the floor, stood at attention, dressed only in a pair of shorts and said, "Yes, sir?"

"You know the rules around here. Why haven't you and your men got your mosquito nets up? I've been around to the huts of all your squadron, and not one of them has his net up.

"Furthermore, your area is dirty. Why isn't it cleaned up? You know the rules. You're the commanding officer of your squadron. You will take immediate steps the first thing in the morning to remedy this situation, understand?"

"Yes, sir."

"And report to me as soon as you do. We don't live like a bunch of pigs down here."

"Yes, sir."

The door slammed.

The colonel had developed an intense dislike of Boyington, stemming from earlier conflicts. When he made out the next fitness reports (which become part of each officer's individual file jacket in Washington), he marked Pappy as low as he possibly could without Boyington's having to write a reply and thus see it. He added a notation: "This officer is a good combat pilot, but can't command men because of his drinking."

When we got the boys together first thing in the morning I told them what had happened and then Boyington took over.

"We want to make it a point to conduct ourselves so that there won't be the slightest cause for complaint. The first thing we'll do is clean up our huts and our camp area. Do a thorough job; don't even leave a cigarette butt. After everything is cleaned up, get your mosquito nets set up—and use them. I know it's silly, here where there are no mosquitos and where our huts are screened in, but the regulations say that we must sleep under mosquito nets—so we'll sleep under mosquito nets. Now, let's get to work."

We cleaned our camp area and our huts as they had never been cleaned before. Even Bragdon, Sims, Mullen, and Fisher—who had never been known to hang up a shirt or touch a broom—polished up their quarters. Then we all went swimming in the lukewarm water off the channel that ran in front of the club.

We spent the next few days turning in final reports on the tour, getting physical exams, writing letters, lying in the sun, swimming, and getting ready to go to Sydney.

Rollie Rinabarger, wounded on the 27th of September, joined us. The boys crowded around him and brought him up to date. We'd missed his lanky figure and his dry wit.

However, he didn't look at all well. He was pale, gaunt, and his eyes were deeply sunken. We suspected he had talked the doctors into letting him out of the hospital in time to go to Sydney with us.

14 | Sydney

Daily, the tales grew wilder of that wonderland to the south, Australia, where the food was fresh and varied; the liquor excellent and plentiful; the girls beautiful and plentiful, too.

Ah, Australia, where everything was upside down—where it was summer when it was supposed to be winter and vice versa; where it was spring in the fall and fall in the spring. Land of peculiar animals: the duckbilled platypus, the kangaroo, the koala bear.

Australia, where you had to pay $6.00 not to vote. Where the men are pretty tough customers but don't let their "cobbers" (pals) down. Where the highest compliment you can pay a man is to tell him he's "game as Ned Kelly" (a "bushranger," or backwoods highwayman, about whom the Aussies talk as we talk of Jesse James).

The Aussies are rough and tough, we were told; the best thing they can say about you is that you're a "bloody fine barstud." They are confused by all the "pleases" and "thank you's" tossed about by the Yanks. They think all that is sissified. Yet their Sunday "Blue Laws" fixed it so you couldn't get a drink, go to a dance, or even to a movie on Sunday. But the girls had learned how to make Sundays pleasant for the visiting Yanks in spite of the Blue Laws.

The stories flew thick and fast as we completed our physical exams and cleaned up our squadron paperwork.

Everyone took his atabrine faithfully because he didn't want a little thing like malaria holding up his trip to Sydney.

We stood in a long line outside the laboratory tent to have our malaria smears taken. Spears of sunlight through the coconut palms shattered on the hard-packed coral pathway and bounced to tanned, sweating faces and bodies.

Physical exams over, it was back to our quarters, bathing trunks on, and out to the beach to swim and lie in the sun, to get those "clear blue eyes, rippling muscles, and bronzed body that looks good on white sheets."

Tom Emrich combed his black hair, doublechecked his technique. He hadn't tried it on Aussie girls yet. Would he enjoy the same success he always had in the States?

A period of anxious waiting for our blood tests to come back. A positive malaria would mean you couldn't go. Doc was the man of the hour, and the men pestered him regularly.

Then one day, he brought in a sheet of paper.

"Well, I got the report, fellas. It's all O.K., except one man got a positive malaria smear."

Everyone was apprehensive, waiting for the bad news. Doc raised his head. "I'm sorry, Tom," he said to Emrich.

Emrich's face paled. "Oh, well, I might have got in trouble anyway," he said, but his tone was not as jaunty as his words.

Then we looked at Doc. He had his head down again, but we could see he was having trouble hiding a grin.

"I was just kidding, Tom. Everyone goes."

After our formal report and request for transportation had been turned in, we were in a turmoil of preparation—26 eager young men planning to cram over 10,000 minutes of fun into their seven-day leave, living each minute as though there would never be another opportunity for them to see civilization, streets, buildings, civilians, real food, women, again. "What should I take?" was the standard question.

Since we were to fly, we were limited on weight: 300 pounds total, including yourself, was the rule. Mo Fisher heard this with a long face. With his huge bulk, he would barely be able to get aboard himself, let alone take any trade goods.

Yes, we took trade goods. American cigarettes, we'd heard, were extremely hard to come by in Australia, and the Aussies liked them better than their own brands. You could get anything for cigarettes, from a bottle of whiskey to a taxi ride, a car, an apartment, food, or a girl.

Of course, there were regulations, there were customs inspectors, and dire repercussions threatened anyone caught trying to smuggle cigarettes into Sydney. You were supposed to take only what you would normally need for your own use. Each man's interpretation of that, of course, was different. Most of us figured that we could squeeze through the seven days on 20 cartons, but Mo managed to get 50 into an oversized parachute bag. We took only Camels, Lucky Strikes, and Chesterfields; the Aussies looked askance at some of the "Joe Magee" brands that had been shipped out for free distribution to the troops on the fighting fronts.

Be sure to take your own soap and toilet paper, too, we were told—they're very scarce in Sydney.

We were divided into two groups of 13 each, to go on successive days. The last night came for the first group. We were to be picked up by trucks at midnight and driven out to the transport field across the island. The evening was long and loud as we celebrated our departure;

the singing put particular emphasis on "I'm Gonna Lay Down My F-4-U." Some of the boys folded up early in order to catch a little sleep; others stayed with it till time to catch our trucks.

The men were quiet as we waited beside our mess hall. The moon was down. The sky was clear. The broad whiteness of the coral road narrowed away from us. We could hear the crunch of the sentry's feet as he walked his post. There was a damp chill in the air.

Then the trucks rolled up and we piled aboard. With the usual stop and starts—where's Fisher?—we finally were on our way, screaming a raucous goodbye to the old MAG 11 camp as we rolled out. Our choral society—Ashmun, Fisher, Olander, Mullen, Sims, Matheson—took over and roused the owls in the jungles.

At transport headquarters, our first job was to weigh in—and straighten out small arguments over the weight of our gear.

Looking about, I saw a sign on the wall. How different from stateside airline offices. It read:

SOUTH PACIFIC COMBAT AIR TRANSPORT COMMAND

• We give you the privilege of carrying your own baggage.
• We carry combat supplies; sorry that you have to sit on them.
• When you get there, watch your own gear—SCAT valets will be noticeably absent.
• It may seem silly to get you up at 2:00 A.M. to take off, but this is war and schedules come before personal comfort.
• Stay put when we take you to the plane. Wanderers get lost in the jungle while the plane takes off without them.
• Men to keep planes clean are scarce. Stuff that half-eaten sandwich in your pocket.
• We do not run hotels. If you happen to find any bed bugs, they do not belong to us.

I'd barely had time to read this message when an open truck backed up, and we were told to throw our gear aboard. We did, piled aboard ourselves, and jostled out to our plane.

It was similar in shape to a civilian airliner, but there the resemblance ended. An unsightly coat of dirty dull brown paint covered its normally gleaming silver sides. Comfortable seats were nowhere in evidence, just a bare, empty fuselage. A stack of parachutes was secured in one corner. I counted them: eight. Thirteen passengers climbed aboard. I mentally reviewed the scramble that would ensue if 13 men should try to divide 8 chutes in an emergency.

The extra gear began to come aboard. Boxes, bags, packages, and crates were thrown in, stacked high and tied down. When the pilot climbed aboard, he barely had room to crawl over the top of the pile.

We squirmed about on the boxes and crates and made ourselves as comfortable as possible. The pilot started the engines; the big plane jerked around and lumbered down the taxiway, engines coughing. Everything was matter of fact. As we stared out the little windows into the darkness, we could see an occasional mechanic working on a plane, but they didn't even turn to watch us rumble by. And we were going to *Sydney*.

The plane paused at the end of the runway, reared its head and roared, coughing and spitting blue flame from its exhaust stacks. Then it began to move, gathering speed slowly as the pilot pushed the throttle forward. The Black Sheep halted their babble of conversation to help "sweat" the ship off.

The big ship wasn't gaining speed fast enough.

"She'll never make it."

"Jesus, get the tail up."

"Here we go, boys."

"Everybody forward." And with the last shout, we all scrambled to take some of the weight off the tail and put it on the wing. We lay there like groaning sardines, each mentally saying a quick prayer!

"Don't let us crash—not when we're on our way to *Sydney*!"

The plane staggered off the ground and strained upward, protesting to its very last rivet the load it was required to lift.

Some three and a half hours and 460 miles later, we jarred down onto the runway at Tontouta, New Caledonia. It was barely daylight. We halted only long enough for a sleepy driver to bring up a gas truck and service the plane.

Then we sweated out another takeoff for the 1,200-mile hop across the southern edge of the Coral Sea. There was no place to go but forward or back once you took off, not even a coral reef on the way. In an emergency landing, we'd have had about four minutes to scramble out the emergency exits. We screamed ineffectually at each other for a while, and then gave up any attempt at conversation, since it was practically impossible over the racket of the engines. The choral society gathered as usual, however, and our combined voices joined the engines' roar. We sang "Silver Dollar" several times, and there was a strong leaning toward the old western favorite, "Back in the Saddle Again."

We droned along some 8,000 feet above the surface of the water; outside, just the water and a few clouds. No land was in sight in any direction. It was a matter of sweating out the eight-hour flight.

We all crowded eagerly to the windows when land finally came into sight. We floated slowly across Sydney's red buildings and slanted into the airport. Everything was bustling efficiency. Trucks stood by to haul us into town. An officer handed each of us a slip of paper that told us when we were due to return and where to call to check on our return trip. We were hauled into town past huge factories engaged in what is apparently one of Australia's major industries, the tanning of sheep hides.

Sydney was a city of about a million and a half people, and to say that it looked wonderful to us after months of life in the jungles, where the tallest building was a ten foot tent, is to put it mildly.

And the girls—real girls. It had been months since we'd seen a white woman; nurses and Red Cross workers hadn't gotten to Munda yet. The wolf whistles were loud and long and frequent.

We found that we could stay in dormitories, hotels, or apartments. Doc Reames and I rented an apartment, paying $100 for the week we were to be there, though it was worth probably $35 a month. But it had a "wireless" and a "lift"—in most of the apartment houses, you had to walk up, no matter how many floors the place had.

Doc and I threw our gear on the floor and looked over our vacation home. It had a bedroom, living room, kitchen, bath, and a simple color scheme: red plush sofa and chairs, red curtains, red rug, red rose wallpaper, red bedspread, red draperies, and a floor lamp with a red shade.

Doc and I cleaned up, changed from our crumpled khakis, and went out to see the sights. Most of us wanted food, liquor, and women—not necessarily in that order. Next, there were the secondary things: steam bath, massage, shave, manicure, movies, golf, and shopping.

Everyone naturally gravitated to the lobby of the Australia Hotel (and the sidewalk in front of it) and its bar, which was called the "Snake Pit" or "Passion Pit,". It was known throughout the South Pacific. The "Passion Pit" was filled nightly with females of all sizes, shapes, and ages, usually with but one inclination: to have a good time and to help the Yanks have a good time.

We soon learned that the two local clip joints were Princes and Romanos. Both had their eyes open for suckers—Yanks a bit under the weather. In one of these, we paid our bill three times; in the other, twice.

And suckers we were; we had seven days leave, and we might

never have another. We figured on spending a month's pay each; some of the boys spent as much as a year's salary.

For my first breakfast, I ate 13 eggs, just to break a dozen. After a long diet of doctored-up powdered eggs, they were hard to get used to. One of the boys commented, "No taste to them."

Walking along the street after breakfast, I saw a sign: "American Milk Shakes."

"What are 'American Milk Shakes'?" I asked.

"They have ice cream in them," the trim little girl, dressed in blue and white, told me.

"What flavors have you?"

"Vanilla, strawberry, chocolate, and pineapple."

"I'll have one of each," I said, and tossed off all four. During the day I drank eight more, but did not let them interfere with my sirloin steak and fried oyster lunch, or my filet mignon dinner.

Butter, tea, and sugar were rationed, and everything had ceiling prices, but we found the usual black market operations. The grocery stores hid out nice big, ripe tomatoes for the customers who would pay double. You could buy *anything* for money or cigarettes.

Drugstores were "chemists," and street cars were "trams." Restrooms usually had coin-operated doors that required depositing a penny; hence the common expression: "I want to go spend a penny." Desserts were "sweets," and if you wanted a pitcher of milk, you asked for a "jug" of milk.

Since civilians got three gallons of gas ("petrol") a month, many cars had been equipped with coke-burners: large, unwieldy devices that looked like washing machines. Others had huge gas bags on top, about 12 to 15 feet long, 6 feet wide, and 5 feet deep. These could be filled with natural gas at a filling station. One filling would run the car just 15 miles.

It was easy to see why the Aussie girls went for the Yanks. I watched a Digger (Aussie) and his girl one day. He was dressed as though he'd come from the trenches. His hat was dirty, he was unshaven, his trousers were baggy, and his shoes were unshined. He pushed out the door of a restaurant, and as the door slammed behind him, his girlfriend got caught in it. He stood on the sidewalk picking his teeth with a toothpick while she struggled out. When she finally caught up to him, the Aussie started off in long strides, swinging his arms, eyes ahead, intent on where he was going.

Nearing the corner, he shouted something to his girl, who was trotting along beside him; he took off in a lope and caught a streetcar on the fly. The girl ran doggedly after it, and the Aussie leaned against the post on the step, twiddling his toothpick and watching as she barely made it—without benefit of a hand from him.

Contrast this with the young Marine sergeant who came out the same door but held it open for his Australian companion, talking to her as he did so. His eyes and his mind were on her; the rest of the town didn't exist. He matched his step to suit hers, and when he hailed a taxicab, he helped her in, then climbed in and sat beside her, hardly ever taking his eyes off her.

No wonder it is said of the Sydney girls: "Never have so many given so much to so many for so little." All they wanted was a kind word and a little attention.

It was not until we got to Sydney that we found where the name ANZAC came from: it was made from the initials of the Australian and New Zealand Army Corps, which fought in World War I. ANZAC troops were now fighting in New Guinea.

We learned that when an Aussie described someone as a "fair cow," it was quite uncomplimentary, equivalent in meaning to our term "jerk." And when a taxi driver told me about his "trouble and strife," he was discussing his wife.

The bar in the Australia Hotel seemed to be the gathering place for all service personnel. It was presided over by Frieda, a buxom, pink-cheeked, friendly gal who reached down and came up with a "U.S. Marines" flag when we walked in.

Naturally we all hit the barber shop as soon as we could, stretched out, and asked for "the works." Next stop was the turkish bath on the seventh floor of the Australia Hotel. Here, Charlie held forth. When he got through with you, you felt like a different person from the jittery, headachy individual who had stumbled in a couple of hours earlier.

We made the rounds of the department stores, buying and shipping home souvenirs; the sheepskin rugs were especially nice.

There was the zoo, the horse races, golfing, the beach, movies, the clip joints, *and* the Passion Pit. The seven days flicked by like the riffle of a deck of cards.

Too soon we sat again in the waiting room at the airport. Some of the boys were chattering away; some were quiet. Some looked rested, some tired. Some looked as though they'd just stepped from a warm bath; others, with traces of lipstick, as though they'd just slipped from a pair of warm arms.

One of the weighing officers spotted the case of Australian beer we had brought along to drink on the return trip. "You can't take that. Too heavy."

He may have wanted it for himself; not bloody likely:

"Gather round, men. We can't take this beer," shouted Fisher. The 12 quarts were gone in a flash. We put the case with its 12 empty bottles before the officer's blinking eyes and clambered aboard for the long trip back to work.

The huge plane had hardly lumbered off the ground before most of us were sound asleep—sleeping the sleep of men who have played hard and long and said: "To hell with tomorrow!"

---

15 | New Black Sheep

We got back to camp at Espiritu Santo about ten in the morning. Most of the boys promptly hit the sack and spent the rest of the day there. Having a good time had been tiring.

The next morning we were surrounded by a group of dewy-eyed second lieutenants, fresh from the States.

"What was Sydney like?" they asked.

"Oh, it was O.K.," Bragdon told them, then deadpanned, "Coming back was rough, though. We ran into bad weather and began to lose altitude. We pitched over everything loose on the plane, but she was still losing altitude, so we had to pitch over three second lieutenants. Too bad. They were nice guys."

Our 30-man flight echelon had dwindled to 21. Regulations in effect at that time allowed pilots to return to the States after three combat tours. Five (Bailey, Begert, Bourgeois, Case, and McCartney) had had two tours before joining us and were therefore transferred to a squadron due to return to the United States. These five along with our four losses (Ewing, Harris, Alexander, and Ray) brought our pilot strength from 28 to 19; the flight surgeon and I made it 21.

As we resumed training, we learned that a new plan had gone into effect that called for fighter squadrons to be manned by 40 instead of 28 pilots. So on 19 November we got 21 new pilots to add to the 19 we still had.

Twenty-seven-year-old Major Pierre Carnagey, a blond, husky, soft-spoken South Dakotan and a career man in the Marine Corps, had joined in February 1940 after graduating from the University of Southern California. He now called Corpus Christi, Texas, his home. His wife, Mary Jeanette, was a nurse's aide there. He had had one tour of combat duty and was assigned as squadron executive officer to replace Major Bailey.

Major Henry Miller, a thirty-year-old legal eagle from Jenkintown, Pennsylvania, was a serious, sober-minded, straight-faced stickler for detail. We immediately nicknamed him "Notebook Henry" because, if you asked him to meet you for lunch in 15 minutes, he'd make a note of it; and if you asked him the time, he'd make a note of that, too. He knew the insides of an airplane the way a jeweler knows a watch; with a few moments to adjust his notes, he could no doubt tell you what the plane was thinking!

Henry had had two tours with Marine Squadron 214 before it was broken up and the number assigned to us, and he had won the Navy and Marine Corps Medal for attempting to rescue a pilot from a flaming aircraft. He was assigned as Flight Officer, a perfect choice.

J. Cameron Dustin was a 22-year-old Bellevue, Nebraska, boy who'd had two and a half years at Omaha University before joining the Marines in April 1941. He was tall, husky, quiet, tanned, good-looking. This was his third tour; the first two had been Guadalcanal, Russell Islands, and Munda.

Gelon H. Doswell was 23 years old; he had a wife, Elizabeth, waiting for him in New Orleans, and a seven-month-old baby daughter he'd never seen. He had had two and a half years at Tulane before joining up in April 1941. He was immediately dubbed "Corpuscle" because his pasty face indicated that he needed some; he continually asked where he could get a pint of plasma. Corpuscle had been with Dustin on his two previous tours.

Twenty-eight-year-old Marion J. "Rusty" March, though he was born in Preston, Idaho, called Seattle his home, and he had graduated from Stanford, where he had been a track man. Rusty was a book hound, and not at all averse to getting in a little sack time when the opportunity arose. This was his first tour of combat duty.

Fred Avey, at 31, was old for a fighter pilot (some weeks older than Boyington). Like several in the first group, he had come into the Marine Corps early in 1942 after a year in the RCAF. We called him "Lighthorse" because he was small, and it was said that Fred devoted at least one hour a day to a vain search for the muscles God forgot to give him.

He had left the States in December 1942 but had not been able to get in his first combat tour until October 1943, when he scored one and a half kills.

Twenty-one-year-old Jimmy Brubaker had been with Fred on his first tour. His home was in Clearwater, Florida; he had joined the Corps after two years of junior college and a start at the University of Florida. He had left San Diego for ovrseas duty on 22 June 1943, the same day his brother (a B-17 bombardier) was shot down over Germany.

To direct attention from his thinning hair, Jimmy could usually be seen sporting a Pepsodent smile. He generally carried off the honors at bridge.

Bruce Ffoulkes came from San Mateo, California, but his heart was in Portland where Harriet, the girl he was engaged to, lived. After three and a half years at Stanford (gymnastics and golf), he had joined the Marines in August 1941.

"It's rough ass," was Bruce's favorite expression, whether he was discussing flying or any of his other multifarious activities. A photo addict, he spent a lot of his flying time taking pictures of everything in view, including volcanos and Nip AA positions. He had done one tour with Avey and Brubaker.

Henry "Red" Bartl, 22 years old, lived in Sacramento, California, where he'd graduated from Sacramento Junior College. He was the squadron's jive hound. When he had that faraway stare on his freckled face, you could be sure he was dreaming his way back to the Palladium for a night with Benny Goodman. It was said that more than one California chick was brokenhearted because Red, choosing between her and the Palladium, chose the latter. Red had been out of the States barely a month.

Glenn L. Bowers, 22, had had three years at Penn State as a zoology major. He had left a wife, Betty, in York, Pennsylvania, when he'd shoved off for overseas duty a month before. He had one child and was sweating out another.

John S. Brown, 25, of Indianapolis, was the typical football player. Big, loose, quiet, easy, Brownie had trampled Purdue's gridiron for three years.

Rufus "Mack" Chatham, 21, was the new Texas boy in our squadron. Beaumont was his hometown, and he'd had three years at Texas A&M before joining the Marines. When you heard "Come Nina Ross, the Winnin' Hoss," rise above the clink of glasses at the Officers' Club, it'd be a fair bet that sackhound Mack was at those galloping dominoes.

J. Ned Corman, 22, from Bellefonte, Pennsylvania, had graduated from Penn State in 1942, where he'd lettered in soccer; he joined the Corps shortly afterward. Like "Open Sesame" to Ali Baba, Sydney was the magic word that put a gleam in his eyes; he couldn't wait to get down there and see if it was all true.

William L. Crocker, Jr., age 23, hailed from Worcester, Massachusetts. During his two years at Springfield College, he'd lettered in swimming. Whatever you wanted, Crock could get it for you—and at wholesale. He was immediately made a junior member of the Quartermaster Kids' club and soon was teaching them a new angle or two. Crock was a jungle scout of parts, too, taking off on long jaunts and coming back with tall tales of the strange sights he'd seen.

William H. Hobbs, Jr., 22, was a Missouri lad. Another book man, he plowed through everything readable and spent a good deal of time writing to his wife, Ann, in Webster Groves. Hobbsy had spent four years at the University of Missouri.

Herb Holden, Jr., 23, called Elizabeth, New Jersey, home, and had graduated from Williams College in 1942. Herb put all the squadron in his debt when he joined the Black Sheep choral society, and whipped up an arrangement of "Why Do They Call Me Snowball, When Snowball Ain't My Name."

Alfred L. Johnson, 23, of Utica, New York, had spent two years at New York University. "Shorty" ranked with Junior Heier in the realm of quick comebacks, and the whole squadron was waiting to pit him against Frieda, the famous Sydney barmaid.

Harry S. "Skinny" Johnson, 22, had left his wife, Dorothy, back home in Birmingham, Alabama, and if her accent was anything like his, it must have been mighty pretty to hear. We elected him Second Vice-President of the Yamheads. Skinny was at his best trying to speak English in his southern lingo thick enough to cut with a dull knife; his explanation of why he had to fire 3,000 rounds of ammunition to test his guns was a masterpiece of Yamhead oratory.

Perry T. Lane, 22, came from Rutland, Vermont. "When I left home," Perry confided, "my mother warned me to avoid drinking and gambling, but I can't see where her advice has done me much good."

A nine o'clock glance at Perry's eyeballs, which looked as though he had used a mercurochrome eyewash, verified this observation. We could never figure how he was always able to work up that infectious smile. Perry was always lost: he was never sure which was Kahili, which were the Treasury Islands and which the Shortlands; he even had trouble identifying Choiseul.

Fred S. Losch, 22, of Larryville, Pennsylvania, was one of the preflight "muscle men"; he was always stretching out his stringy arms and inviting one of the boys twice his size to take him on. We understood that he had a string of squealing gals awaiting his return to the States. Mat gave him the nickname "Rope Trick" one night as Fred was squatting cross-legged on the floor, his brown body nude except for a pair of shorts.

"You look like a God-damned Indian fakir. When the hell are you gonna do your rope trick?"

Alan D. Marker, 21, Park Ridge, Illinois, had spent two years at Maine Township Junior College, where he'd played baseball and basketball. A bad landing and a broken arm put him out of action shortly after he joined us, and he was evacuated to a rear area hospital in spite of his protests.

These were the 21 additions to our squadron. Bolt immediately got things rolling by coming up with a fish fry. He took a sack of hand grenades, went out somewhere, and came back with a couple of gunnysacks full of fish. Mo Fisher, Bragdon, Mullen, and Sims rounded up 15 cases of beer. By the time the beer and fish were gone, the new men had become full-fledged Black Sheep.

16 | Trouble at Home Base

Hearing that we were to go north in six days for our second combat tour, Boyington worked the pilots hard, breaking the new men in on Black Sheep tactics and formations, organizing the divisions, and indoctrinating them with the Black Sheep approach to aerial combat: aggression.

No one had been in any trouble since our cleanup episode, so it was an unworried Boyington who went to the Group Commander's office in response to a summons. He came back to our hut with a long face.

"I'm not going back with you," he said.

"WHAT!"

"The Colonel asked me how the squadron was coming along, and I told him, 'Fine'; that we were ready and eager, and that I understood we were to leave in a few days.

"He said, 'Yes,' but that I was not going. He said they need a major for operations officer at Vella Lavella and he was sending me. All I could say was, 'Yes, sir,' and about face. I knew it was useless to argue with him."

Boyington shook his head. "Looks like he finally caught up with me."

"You're not gonna stand for that, are you?" I asked.

"What can I do?"

"I know what you can do. You can go over and see General Moore. I'll bet he doesn't know it."

Major General James T. Moore, Assistant Commanding General of the First Marine Air Wing, had been in command at Munda most of the time we were there. He had developed a solid respect for Boyington's leadership and fighting ability, while we had come to admire and respect the general for his quiet, friendly manner and his calm, efficient handling of his command.

"Yes, that might help. I'll go over there tonight after chow."

"You'll go right now," I said. "You change your clothes; I'll get a jeep for you."

I hustled Boyington into the jeep and off he went, while I sat with fingers crossed and waited. To take him out now would destroy the morale of the whole squadron. When I heard four Black Sheep go into the hut next to ours, I went over and told them the bad news, and the five of us worried together. Other members of the squadron dropped in, and by three o'clock a sizable representation of the squadron was crowded into the 16-foot-square hut.

Around four o'clock, the Group Commander stopped by, and I stuck my head out.

"Is Boyington around?" he asked.

"No, sir."

"When he comes in, I want to see him."

"Yes, sir."

At five o'clock, the Colonel was back.

Still no Boyington.

At six o'clock, the Colonel came by once more.

No Boyington.

The Colonel sent a runner at seven, eight, nine, ten, and finally eleven—still no Boyington.

"Be sure you tell Boyington that the Colonel wants to see him when he comes in," the runner said.

We debated what had happened to Pappy. We knew General Moore well enough to know that he'd give Pappy a straight answer, without sitting on the fence, so we agreed that only two things could have happened: Pappy was either drowning his sorrows in one of the island Officers' Clubs if he was out, or celebrating in one of the same if he was still in the squadron.

It was after midnight when he finally rolled home, happy, mellow. "I'm back in," he said, with a wide grin.

"Tell us about it, Pappy. What happened? What did the General say?"

"Give me a drink, and I'll tell you the whole story."

Fisher quickly found him a bottle of beer.

"Well, I went over to call on General Moore. Naturally, I couldn't call for the purpose of complaining about my new assignment because that would not be going through official channels, so I just dropped in to pay him a visit. We chatted awhile about the days up at Munda.

"Then he asked me how our squadron was shaping up. I told him it was fine; the new boys had fitted in O.K. He looked at his schedule, and said we were due to go north in a few days, and he expected I was eager to get into combat again.

"I told him the boys were eager to go, and so was I, but since I had been assigned this operations job, naturally I wouldn't be with them.

" 'What!' he shouted.

" 'Yes, sir,' I said, 'the Colonel told me this morning he had assigned me as operations officer at Vella Lavella, so I wouldn't be going up with my squadron.'

"The General hit the ceiling. He called his Chief of Staff. 'What's this about Boyington being taken out of his squadron?' he asked.

" 'I don't know, sir.'

" 'Get me MAG 11.'

"When he got the Colonel on the field telephone, he said, 'What's this about taking Boyington out of his squadron? . . . What? . . . Well, put him back, do you hear? Put him back immediately. . . . I don't care how senior he is; he's the best combat pilot we've got, and he's to be left in command of his squadron where he belongs, understand?'

"The General banged down the receiver and looked up at his Chief of Staff who was standing before him. 'There's too goddamned much of this business of transferring squadron commanders around without my hearing about it. You get a good man in command of a squadron, and then somebody wants to take him out. In the future, I want to know about it before any squadron commander is transferred. Is that clear?'

"The Chief of Staff mumbled 'Yes, sir,' and went out. The General was still sore, banging the desk and swearing, when I thanked him. He shook hands and wished us luck on our tour when I left.

"The guard at the gate stopped me when I came in and told me the Colonel wanted to see me."

"Yes," we said, "he's been looking for you all day. What the hell, there's not much he can do. You're back in the squadron, and we're due to shove off in a few days."

But next morning, after Boyington reported to the Colonel, he came back with a serious face. "I slipped up, and he's got me. Group Regulations say that when you leave the camp, you must notify the Adjutant. I didn't do that when I left yesterday, and he's put me under official arrest."

A few minutes later, a runner brought over a sheet of paper. "The Colonel wants you to sign this, sir."

The typewritten page read: "I hereby acknowledge that I violated rule number so and so of the Group Regulations"; there was a space for Boyington's signature over his typewritten name. Boyington reached for a pen.

"Don't you sign that," I said.

"Why not?"

"That's going into your official file in Washington. For all anyone knows who reads that, that rule you violated might be murder or stealing." I turned to the runner. "Take this back and have it retyped to read, 'I hereby acknowledge that I have violated rule number so and so of the Group Regulations, which reads, quote,' and then quote the rule."

The runner took the sheet and left. He returned in half an hour with the revised sheet which read:

I violated Group General Order Number One, dated 17 January 1943, quoted herewith:

GROUP GENERAL ORDER NUMBER 1, 1943
Official trips to the First Marine Aircraft Wing or other higher offices.

1. All officers of this Group will not make trips to the subject offices for personal or departmental benefit without specific permission of the Group Commander.

2. The exceptions to this order will be the Group Quartermaster and his staff, who may deal with higher offices as in the past.

Boyington signed it. A little later, the runner brought a memorandum over the Colonel's signature. It read:

1. You are hereby placed under arrest for a period of 10 days for disobedience of orders.
2. The limit of your arrest is that you re restricted to the Turtle Bay Airfield Area exclusive of the Officers' "Wine Mess."
3. You are informed that this report, together with your statement, will be forwarded to the Commandant, Marine Corps, for file with your official record.

The same afternoon, however, the following letter was forwarded to Boyington:

FIGHTER COMMAND
AIRCRAFT SOLOMONS
APO 717

15 November 1943
FROM: The Commanding General, Fighter Command Aircraft Solomons.
TO: The Commanding General, First Marine Aircraft Wing.
SUBJECT: Combat efficiency report, case of Major Gregory Boyington.

1. Major Gregory Boyington, while Squadron Commander of VMF 214, came under the operational control of this Command from 15 September 1943 to 20 October 1943. His activity during this period was marked by a brilliant combat record, readiness to undertake the most hazardous types of missions, and a superior type of flight leadership. The superb caliber of his work is indicated by the fact that he destroyed 14 enemy aircraft during this period.
2. Major Boyington enjoyed the complete confidence and respect of his superiors and his squadron mates as a combat leader. I consider him one of the five outstanding combat fighter pilots that have operated in this theater since the beginning of operations.

D.C. Strother
Brigadier General, USA
Commanding

The payoff came the following day when the Colonel himself was ordered to take over the operations job!

Three days later our entire squadron took off via SCAT transport planes for our second combat tour.

At Guadalcanal, while our planes were being serviced, we were standing near them talking when Rinabarger suddenly slumped to the ground, unconscious. He hadn't looked well at all since he'd rejoined us, and Doc Reames had told him he should be back in the hospital. But Rollie had begged so earnestly to stay with the squadron that Doc had reluctantly let him do so. Now, Doc examined him and ordered him to the hospital.

"I'm O.K., Doc. I'll be all right."

"No, you need a long rest, Rollie. I'm sending you to the hospital and recommending that you be transferred to a cooler climate to recuperate."

Rollie was evacuated to New Zealand and then home. He was ready to go overseas again with a Marine carrier squadron when the war ended.

17 | Vella Lavella

Vella Lavella was a lovely little island, solidly covered by jungle and coconut groves except where the airstrip, roads, and camp areas had been cleared. The runway had been built by the simple expedient of blasting out the coconut trees and then grading down the surface dirt to the firm coral underneath. It lay along the southeastern coast of the island, bounded on one side by coconut trees and on the other by the clear, warm waters of Vella Gulf. From there, we could look directly out to Kolombangara, some 35 miles away, rearing its 6,000-foot peak into the clouds. It was there that Alex had crashed on our previous tour.

Our new temporary home was typical of all the Solomon Islands. Only about as far from the equator as San Diego is from San Francisco, it was hot and steamy. Rainfall averaged some 140 inches a year with most of the rain falling during the period from November to March, which meant that we were getting as much rain every month as San Francisco averages every year. We learned to appreciate the phrase, "It isn't the heat, it's the humidity," because although the temperature was rarely over 90 degrees, we were sweltering.

Kahili Airdrome lay only 75 miles to our northwest; the enemy fortress at Rabaul, with its fine harbor and five loaded airdromes, was 300 miles farther.

Marines had landed at Empress Augusta Bay, on the west coast of Bougainville, 26 days before. They were engaged in heavy fighting to secure the tiny perimeter, about half a mile deep and four miles long, that they'd carved with their blood out of the side of the 3,900-square-mile island. This new landing had taken place about 15 months after the Marines had swarmed ashore at Guadalcanal; in that time, the Marines had come 500 miles closer to Tokyo. At that rate, it would take them another six years to cover the remaining 2,500 miles to the heart of Japan.

But our pace was accelerating all the time. The distance, though small, represented a tremendous gain in tactical position. And it represented an even greater gain in attrition of enemy men and materiel. A note in the diary of a Japanese officer killed in the Munda campaign made this clear. He had written: "Oh the cursed South Seas—that have swallowed countless noble souls and closed over weapons sweated from the blood of citizens—cursed be the Sea of the Solomons!"

As our farthest-advanced air base, Vella Lavella was of enormous tactical importance, particularly if the Japanese decided to contest the air over Bougainville. However, for nearly three weeks, the Black Sheep saw no enemy aircraft. They flew dawn patrols, local patrols, dusk patrols, task force covers, and strafing missions without air opposition.

Then one morning, on patrol over the precarious Marine beach-head on Bougainville, they got a call from the ground. Marines were pinned down and getting cut to pieces by enemy mortar fire. Could our planes help?

The ground Marines laid out a huge arrow in white panels and asked that the airmen strafe enemy mortar positions 500 yards off the tip of the arrow. The Black Sheep made eight strafing runs over the area, putting 25,000 rounds of armor-piercing, incendiary, and tracer slugs into it, cutting down trees, chopping away the underbrush, and leaving the enemy crews sprawled about their broken weapons.

The smashing success of that operation helped the Black Sheep to realize the importance of strafing missions. After that, when they were relieved from a patrol or cover mission, they went hunting over enemy territory. They chopped to pieces and burned bivouac areas, huts, wharfs, small boats, barges, ships, buildings, AA positions, trucks, airfields, villages, troop concentrations, supply dumps, and bridges. Nothing in Japanese territory that moved or was usable was safe from their guns.

The dispatches began to speak of "the irrepressible Black Sheep," the first time a squadron had been mentioned by name in these official reports.

In the air the Black Sheep were relentless killers, but on the ground they passed the time much the same as anyone in the States. We played volleyball; we went swimming—took off our clothing and walked across the coral taxiway to the water. Leaving our shoes on a convenient log, we'd dive in and splash about, but care had to be used in putting our feet down because the bottom was littered with wrecked aircraft— silent testimonials to the violent battles for the skies waged over this tiny coral atoll that doesn't even appear on most maps of the world. Nor did anyone venture far; lurid stories of the quantity, size, and ferocity of sharks and barracuda roaming the waters prevented that.

After swimming, we'd pull on our field shoes and walk back to our office tent, keeping our eyes half-closed against the brilliant glare of the sun.

The camp area was pleasant in spite of the usual lizards and coconut bugs. The island abounded in tropical fruit. We had limeade for every meal; an ice-flaking machine was kept going 24 hours a day. And in spite of what we'd read about headhunters in the Solomons, the natives were friendly. We bought some of the trinkets they made out of shells, bits of coral, carved ebony, and mahogany.

The natives watched with open mouths as the planes taxied to the end of the runway, gunned their engines to test the magnetos, and sped off. They loved to ride in our jeeps, and watched carefully the manipulations required to operate them. One night a couple of them got a little high on their native beverage (fermented coconut milk) and stole a jeep. They got it going, drove along the strip to the head of the runway, roared the motor once, flicked the lights off and on, and then—just as they'd seen the airplanes do—took off wide open down the runway.

They were doing about 50 when they went over the cliff at the end.

We took advantage of the comparative lull in activities to make a trip over to Kolombangara to see if we could locate the spot where Alexander had crashed. I telephoned the PT boat base that had been established at Vella Lavella and made arrangements for one of their boats to take us. Seven Black Sheep (Boyington, Mullen, McClurg, Reames, Moore, and I, along with Burney Tucker, who'd seen him crash) boarded the powerful 65-foot craft shortly after dawn on Sunday, 5 December.

The Navy lieutenant commanding the twin-engined boat ordered the lines cast off, and we moved out into the rough, choppy channel in the midst of a tropical downpour. Dressed only in trousers, shoes, oilskins, and sou'westers, we bowed our heads into the driving sheets of steamy rain and clutched onto handholds as the boat rolled and lurched and pounded like a bucking bronco.

The weather cleared as we neared the coast, and the skipper headed in close to shore. We purred along slowly, with a sailor on the bow to watch for underwater obstructions in these uncharted waters. We scanned the coastline for some indication of the spot where Alex had gone in. Because of the rapidity with which the tangled jungle closes in on everything unless a major effort is made to keep it back, we were afraid we might not find the place.

"There it is," said Tucker quietly. He'd spotted it well. Under his direction, the PT boat moved in near a small promontory and stopped about 100 yards off shore.

"Right there," Tucker said, pointing to a spot where the solid jungle was scarred as though a giant scythe had made a sweep through the tree tops.

Rubber boats were lowered; we climbed into them, pushed off, and paddled in. Although our forces had, by now, bypassed and sealed off the island, Japanese troops were still scattered through this portion of it. For this reason, in addition to machetes for cutting through the brush, we also carried our service pistols.

Wading ashore, we hacked out the mass of twining vines and cut our way inland. A few birds rose, screaming. Flying foxes, hanging upside down from limbs high above us, awakened, let go their holds, and swooped about crazily. Brilliant flowers such as I'd never seen grew in wild confusion all about us. Delicately tinted orchids festooned the vine-wrapped trunks of trees. A huge lizard nearly eight feet long, with horns running down its back, blinked at us from one of the tree trunks.

Time had stood still in this strange, far-off world.

We chopped, following the path of Alex's plane by the splintered tops of the trees, until we came to a burned-out section. Here were parts of the plane.

Above, Corsairs of the Black Sheep Squadron over the Solomon Islands, September 1943. *Below,* Pappy Boyington reviews tactics with Black Sheep pilots at Espiritu Santo. Kneeling, from left: Boyington, Stanley Bailey, Virgil Ray, Bob Alexander. Standing: Bill Case, Rollie Rinabarger, Don Fisher, Henry Bourgeois, John Begert, Bob Ewing, Denmark Groover, Burney Tucker.

Runway at Munda. *Below,* Black Sheep home life at Munda.

The Black Sheep at Vella Lavella. The baseball caps were gifts from the St. Louis Cardinals: one cap for each enemy plane shot down. From left, on the ground: Chris Magee, Bob McClurg, Paul Mullen, Greg Boyington, John Bolt, Don Fisher. On wings: Sanders Sims, George Ashmun, Bruce Matheson, Jim Hill, Ed Olander, Bob Bragdon, Frank Walton, Ed Harper, Warren Emrich, Bill Heier, Burney Tucker, Don Moore, Jim Reames, Denmark Groover.

South Pacific barbershop.

Walter R. Harris (*left*) was one of four Black Sheep pilots lost during the squadron's first combat tour. (Others were Robert T. Ewing, Robert A. Alexander, and Virgil G. Ray.) Pierre Carnagey and Harry R. Bartl (*below, left and right*) were lost in the air battle for Rabaul on the second combat tour. (Others missing in action over Rabaul were James E. Brubaker, Bruce Ffoulkes, J.C. Dustin, Donald Moore, and George M. Ashmun.) Two Black Sheep pilots— William L. Crocker and William H. Hobbs (*bottom, left and right*)—were lost on combat missions over the Northern Solomons after the squadron was disbanded.

Pilots on scramble alert at Vella Lavella.

Left, John S. Brown

Don Moore explains to intelligence officer Frank Walton how he shot down a Zero, while Bob Bragdon and Herb Holden watch. *Below*, Walton with Corsair named for his wife.

New Year's Eve at Vella Lavella. Pappy Boyington is holding the jug, flight surgeon Jim Reames wearing the derby.

Seattle welcomes Pappy Boyington home after his release from
Japanese prison camp, September 1945.

Boyington after receiving the Medal of Honor from President
Truman, October 1945. Walton is on the right.

Spreading out, we searched the surrounding area. We found a wheel here, a bit of stabilizer there, parts of the wings, the fuselage. We found the plate that definitely identified the plane.

And then we found Alex.

The violence of the crash had torn the seat loose from the rest of the plane, and we found Alex's bones beside it. There was a rusty knife one of the boys had given him a few days before his last flight . . . his crushed canteen with his initials scratched on it . . . a few metal buttons.

With our machetes we scooped a shallow grave, laid his bones in it, and covered them up. Then we carried some clean white rocks up from the beach and put them around the grave. Searching about, we found a blade from his propeller, painted his name on it, and erected it at the head of his grave. We were undecided which end to make the head until Boyington said: "Let's have him looking toward Japan so he can follow our advance all the way to Tokyo."

No formal prayers were said, but Boyington lined us up on either side of the grave and called us to attention. Then he whipped his hand up in a salute, and we all followed.

"So long, Alex," he said.

We felt that Alex would rest more easily now that friendly hands had put him to bed. And there Alex sleeps today, I hope, his grave grown over now. Blanketed by the vines and creepers, orchids and other tropical flowers, he sleeps quietly through the warm Solomons days and nights in a spot where no white man had ever been before him.

And where no other might ever go again.

18 | A Change in Boundaries

The boys were more anxious than ever to get into some aerial combat. We all wondered why we weren't hitting Rabaul, which was now within fighter range. Rabaul's five airdromes were loaded with enemy planes, but they were staying in their own back yard. We asked why our planes couldn't go, but no one seemed to know the answer, and almost everyone was content to wait for orders. Not Boyington.

In typical fashion, he climbed into a plane one morning and flew down to Air Command Headquarters at Munda to find out. It was 12 December, eight days after his birthday. He was 31 years old, and knew he wouldn't be allowed to stay in fighter planes much longer. Very few fighter pilots live that long—if they keep on fighting.

The boys in the squadron averaged some seven years younger than Boyington; because of this and the wide difference in combat experience, they had begun to call him Pappy shortly after the beginning of our first tour. Now Bragdon began to call him "Gramps."

Knowing that he would never be permitted to make another combat tour, Boyington realized that it was now or never if he hoped to break the 26-plane record held jointly by Eddie Rickenbacker and Joe Foss.

At Munda, he found out why the Black Sheep couldn't get a crack at Rabaul. Some months before, Admiral Halsey and General MacArthur had agreed on a geographical line to separate their areas of responsibility. The line ran west of Bougainville and then curved as it went north so that Rabaul was in MacArthur's territory.

Boyington suggested that the line be revised, or that a dispatch be sent to MacArthur requesting permission for our forces to attack Rabaul. Four days later, all squadron commanders were ordered to Munda for a meeting. Late in the afternoon, Boyington jumped off the truck and strode into my office tent with a spring to his step and a grin on his face.

"Here we go, boys," he said, as he put a sheaf of papers on my desk.

"What's up, Gramps?" asked Bragdon, who had been playing bridge with Brubaker, Olander, and Doc Reames.

"We're going to Rabaul tomorrow," Boyington answered.

Everyone shouted and then began to throw questions at him.

"Wait a minute," he said, and turned to me. "You've got a big job.

Eighty planes are going up in the first fighter sweep over Rabaul tomorrow, and you're to brief all the pilots tonight in the mess hall after chow. I brought you the latest photos of the area. You don't have much time to get your material together, but I told them you could do it."

"I'll get right at it now, if all you guys will go in the ready room and give me a chance to think."

They went out chattering, and I went to work. I got out my maps, the photos of the area, the latest intelligence reports, studies of the Bismarck Archipelago, survival information, weather and current data, the operations plan that Boyington had brought, and the landing instructions for our airstrip on Bougainville. It was nearly eight o'clock before I bundled up everything, climbed into a small truck that was standing by, and went up the hill to the mess hall.

The room was full. The long tables had been cleared, and the pilots were sprawled about them, not doing a great deal of talking. This was another night before the big game.

I passed out strip maps to all—small maps showing the compass headings the pilots were to take to the target and back. All pilots also got maps of Rabaul Harbor and the surrounding area, while all division leaders were given eight-inch-square target maps that showed the location of the airdromes in the Rabaul area.

"Your mission is a fighter sweep over Rabaul," I told them (see Appendix E for complete briefing notes). "Eighty planes will participate in the sweep: 24 New Zealand P-40s, 24 Navy Hellcats, and 32 Marine Corsairs.

"Major Boyington will be Tactical Commander.

"The 32 Marine planes will fly top cover, with VMF-222 at 26,000 feet; 223 at 23,000; 214 at 20,000, and 216 at 20 to 25,000. The 24 Hellcats will fly at 15,000 to 20,000 feet; the 24 New Zealand planes will spread between 10,000 and 15,000.

"Takeoff from here begins at 0445 tomorrow.

"All planes will pancake at Bougainville for topping off gas tanks. All turns are to be made over the water and not inland.

"At 0830, the first plane will take off from Bougainville for the strike. The last plane will be off by 0900.

"You are scheduled to be over Rabaul at 1020. At this time, an Army photo plane will be over the area at 35,000, making a photo run.

"You will leave the Rabaul area at 1045; planes low on gas will refuel at Bougainville; others return here or to Ondonga.

"Your rally point is Cape St. George, the southernmost tip of New Ireland.

"Latest intelligence shows 160 aircraft on the five fields around Rabaul; 91 of them are fighters—Zekes, Hamps, Tonys, and Tojos. Zekes and Hamps are, of course, the round- and square-wing-tipped Zeros with which you're familiar. Tony is an in-line fighter that resembles a P-40. It's faster, and more heavily armed and armored than the Zeros but not as maneuverable. Tojo is a new fighter plane about which little is known except that it's very fast, very maneuverable. It's a short, stubby, easily recognized aircraft.

"Lakunai Airdrome, on the outskirts of Rabaul, is loaded with about 100 of the 160 planes in the area; 65 of them are fighters.

"Strong antiaircraft positions ring the coastline, and all the airdromes. There also is a strong series of AA positions on Hospital Ridge, back of the town.

"As for rescue procedure, two Venturas will patrol the line between Bougainville and Rabaul from 1000 until 1200. Two Catalinas will be on alert at Bougainville between 0730 and 1500. For rescue planes, call DANE base.

"If you have to go down and have any choice, hit the water west of Bougainville. The currents will bring you south along the west coast. The wind in this area is generally southeast this time of year.

"Your best bet is to go down on the water, get in your rubber boat, and wait for a rescue plane. However, if you do have to go down on the land, you still have a good chance of getting out O.K. We have Coast Watchers on both New Britain and New Ireland, as well as on Bougainville. They move about, sometimes within a stone's throw of the Japanese airfields.

"On New Britain, head for Open Bay; on New Ireland between Cape Siar and Cape Bun Bun. You'll find help and supplies in both places.

"You have every chance of getting out if you keep your head; hide your chute; move quietly; make use of the information you've been given regarding native fruits and vegetables.

"In the event of bad weather, the code word 'Dagwood' means that the flight is called off.

"Are there any questions?"

There were none. All the pilots were studying their maps.

"Are there any questions any of you would like to ask Major Boyington?" I further asked.

"Yes, I have one," said a stocky Navy squadron commander. "I'd like to ask what tactics he plans on using if we contact the enemy."

Boyington rose. "Tactics? Hell, you don't need any tactics. When you see the Zeros, you just shoot 'em down, that's all."

There were no more questions.

The field was busy long before daylight the next morning, 17 December.

The darkness and the moisture in the air combined to muffle all sounds. The whine of trucks descending the hill to the taxiway; the cough, the sputter, and then the roar of engines being started; and the voices of the pilots and mechanics as they stood in small groups discussing the day's mission or looked over their planes—it was all a single, subdued jumble. Conversation was on the brief side. Tempers were short. The ready tents were dark, and I could hear the pilots swearing as they fumbled for their gear on the racks.

A long line of planes lumbered awkwardly along the taxiways, roared, gathered momentum, then were airborne, blue flames licking their bellies. The trees shuddered with the reverberation of their engines; the sky was dotted with twinkling lights. Then suddenly the sky was empty; everything was quiet, and I sat with Doc Reames, as usual, on the knoll overlooking the end of the runway.

Very little was done around Vella Lavella that day. I called Operations every half-hour to see what news had come in on the radio.

In exasperatingly slow succession, I learned that all planes had topped off their gas tanks at Bougainville on schedule; that they had taken off again on time; that the weather was clear. Ffoulkes had nosed over on landing but had borrowed a plane to complete the mission.

Shortly after noon, Operations reported that the first planes back from Rabaul had landed at Bougainville and more were coming in fast. It wasn't until 4:30 P.M., however, that the first planes swooped into the traffic pattern, circled, and landed at our field.

Boyington threw down his helmet as he walked in. "They wouldn't come up. Just a few strays. We were over Lakunai at 1045. About 40 fighters were lined up on the strip, but they wouldn't take off.

"I dived to 10,000 feet and fired a few rounds at them to try to stir something up, but they just wouldn't stir."

Our Black Sheep did manage to find and shoot down three Zeros, McClurg getting one and Moore, two. That ended the scoring for us for the day, and it brought the squadron score up to an even 60.

"We scared them," Boyington said. "We ought to send up only about 24 planes, so they'd be sure to come up and fight."

General MacArthur had announced several weeks previously that

Rabaul had been neutralized, but the tens of thousands of Nip troops, the seamen manning the aircraft carriers, cruisers, destroyers, and submarines, and the hundreds of Nip pilots had not been consulted on MacArthur's communiqué.

If Rabaul had been neutralized before, it had to be neutralized again, so on 23 December 24 Army B-24s were ordered to bomb both Rabaul and its harbor. The bombers were to be covered by 48 Navy and Marine fighter planes, while 48 Army Air Force and Marine fighters were to take off later and act as a rear guard for the bombers on their return trip.

Pierre Carnagey led five other Black Sheep as low cover for the bombers, while Boyington led nine others in the rear guard sweep.

Rendezvous with the bombers was late, and the entire formation was 30 minutes behind schedule as it crossed over New Britain. As the bombers went into their runs at 21,000 feet, some 15 or 20 Zeros piled down on them from above. Possibly because of the bad timing, only four Hellcats were in position, and the Zeros whined through them and on top of the Black Sheep positioned immediately above the bombers. One bomber was hit in one of its engines but feathered the prop and stayed in formation.

The fight increased in intensity. Japanese planes began releasing aerial bombs, which exploded into huge white phosphorus balls like silver creampuffs with 15-foot silver streamers.

More Zeros joined the original group, and the six Black Sheep were battling for their own lives as well as those of the B-24 crews. Two lost: Pierre Carnagey and Jimmy Brubaker.

Meanwhile, Boyington's group, scheduled to arrive in the area 45 minutes behind the bombers, was actually only 15 minutes behind them. It was well that they were early.

In the action that followed, Boyington got four Zeros to bring his total to 24. Bolt and McClurg scored two each to become our squadron's fourth and fifth aces. Magee got one to make eight, Heier got two, and Miller bagged his first. But we lost Bruce Ffoulkes.

At Vella Lavella, I added up the score. The Black Sheep had downed 12 planes to bring the Squadron total to 72. But the cost was high. I wrote "MIA" beside the names of Carnagey, Brubaker, and Ffoulkes.

19 | Crescendo

Things were getting rough over Rabaul now. The Nips were throwing everything they could round up into the air battle, in a desperate effort to stave off our advance.

Rabaul was the keystone to the entire Southwest Pacific. If we were able to neutralize it, any threat to Australia, New Guinea, and the Solomons would be permanently eliminated. The enemy would have to pull in their horns all the way back to the Philippines and the Marianas. They weren't going to give up easily.

In spite of the furious deadly battle that he was so brilliantly spearheading, Boyington was happy. He wrote his mother: "I've got the swellest bunch of kids in the world with me; I'm flying! I'm killing Japs."

Another day, he wrote: "The Japs are getting pretty tough out here. I don't know whether I'll be able to beat Joe Foss's record before I go home, or not. As you have always taught me, there is nothing worthwhile unless you earn it. You taught me that the faith I held could beat anything in the world. Maybe I can appreciate it now after working for it. I was sidetracked for a while.

"You will never have to worry about me again, because this experience has taught me how to live and how to forgive. Some men, it makes better. Now I'm as calm and happy as I've ever been in my life.

"I've learned that many things have to be done to achieve a good purpose. I've had to send men to their deaths. I've had to write to their mothers and fathers; to young wives with children. The only consolation is that I've led my boys into everything they went into.

"I've thanked God a good many times in the last few months for the training I had at home.

"Gosh, how I'd love to be back and have some of those old friendly arguments at the family dinner table. After all is said and done, there isn't a family that had as much fun as we had. It must be the Irish in us!

"Give my darlings my love and have a nice Christmas for them."

Christmas Eve on Vella Lavella was a far cry from Christmas Eve in Okanogan, Washington.

The Black Sheep had roamed the skies over New Britain that day without sighting any Nip planes and had disgustedly bounced their Corsairs back onto our strip without having fired a round of ammunition. That night we gathered in the tent now occupied only by Boyington, Doc, and me, since Pierre was missing.

In a big aluminum kettle, Doc and I had made up a concoction that had some faint resemblance to eggnog. It consisted of powdered eggs, powdered milk, sugar, nutmeg, water, AND five quarts of whiskey. The kettle was in the middle of the tent, and we sprawled about it, dipping in and filling and refilling our canteen cups. There had never been, for any of us, a Christmas like this.

Instead of the traditional snow and cold and rosy cheeks and frost and exchange of presents and glittering store windows, we had the jungles and steaming tropics as we lay about with only a pair of shorts on, sweating, batting at mosquitoes, and brushing an occasional centipede out into the hovering darkness.

Had anyone sung "White Christmas," we'd probably all have bawled.

We stayed carefully away from any such sentiment, however; the talk was of flying and of Sydney; the songs were our own Black Sheep songs. Loud and crude, they served, with the help of the "eggnog," to release pent-up emotions that have no place in the hearts and minds of those who are going out tomorrow to fight. Late in the evening, Bragdon, in his terse, impersonal manner, spoke what was in all our minds.

"Listen, Gramps, we all want to see you break the record, but we don't want you to go up there and get killed doing it."

"Don't worry about me. They *can't* kill me. If you guys ever see me going down with 30 Zeros on my tail, don't give me up. Hell, I'll meet you in a San Diego bar six months after the war, and we'll all have a drink for old times' sake."

"Here's to that San Diego bar," said Moon Mullen, and we all drained our cups.

"How about 'That Little Ball of Yarn,' K.O.?" shouted one of the boys to K.O. Toomey, who had been named after the comic strip character because he wore a derby hat everywhere except when he was actually flying. A pilot with another squadron, he should have been a Black Sheep, and did the next best thing by spending all his spare time with us.

K.O. had a stock of songs that he performed with a fine Irish brogue in a hoarse whiskey tenor, perfect for the time and place. He had made many dull evenings pass pleasantly because of his singing and his ability to turn a neat phrase, and he came through again this night by jamming his derby onto Boyington's head and singing "Ball of Yarn" for us.

I have a treasured photograph of this Christmas Eve party, showing Boyington, dressed only in shorts and K.O.'s derby, surrounded by the rest of the Black Sheep.

As the hour grew late, the canteen cups were scraping on the bottom of the kettle, and the light from our Coleman lantern began to wane. The boys gradually slipped off to their tents until only Boyington, the Doc, and I were left. Each of us sat on the edge of his cot, chin in hand, a little reluctant to go to bed, trying to retain the sense of pleasure the party had brought but feeling it slipping away. We sat there, silently, for a long time, and then Boyington repeated what he'd said the night before: "It's sure lonesome in here without old Pierre."

"It sure is, Pappy," said Doc.

The next day was Christmas, but it was just Saturday on Vella Lavella.

While the strikers back home were holding up production for more money, and those defense workers who weren't striking were getting double time, the Black Sheep were at 21,000 feet over Rabaul—just happy to be alive.

Eight of them tangled with 40 Zeros in a mad melee, and when I tallied up the score, they'd knocked down four more Zeros to push our squadron total to 76 sure kills and 27 probables. Avey, Corman, Fisher, and Tucker had made the kills—Corman's first, Avey's first with us (he had 1½ from a previous tour with another squadron), and the fourth for both Fisher and Tucker.

Sunday, the 26th, the boys ranged over New Ireland without opposition.

On the 27th a fighter sweep was scheduled, the type of flight Boyington had originated in the Solomons. Fittingly, Pappy was assigned as tactical commander of the formation of 44 Marine Corsairs and 20 Navy Hellcats.

Although it was customary for our pilots to take any plane on the line, in order, as they were dropped off, Pappy chose the "Lady Carol W.," a plane I'd named after my wife.

In a masterful job of tactical leadership, Boyington took his formation up over Rabaul and circled Lakunai, putting his flight in a long column behind him, and then let down on the climbing Japanese in a huge tilted Lufbery circle. Sixty Zeros gave battle; in spite of the odds, the Black Sheep completely broke up the Nip formation and shot down six without a loss. The Black Sheep score was now 82. Boyington, Avey, Harper, and Mullen made one kill each; Fisher downed two.

It was Fisher's fifth and sixth, to make him the squadron's sixth ace. Mullen's single brought his score to five and a half, and he became the

Black Sheep's seventh ace. Boyington's score was now 25—just one short of the record, but he wasn't satisfied.

"I was pressing up there," he said. "God, I should have had four or five—there were plenty of them."

That night, Fred Hampson, an Associated Press correspondent, dropped in at our island base. He wanted to interview Boyington.

"All right," I said, "I'll bring him over and you can interview him just once. But you've got to remember he's under a hell of a strain, so after this interview, you've got to leave him alone until after he breaks the record."

The three of us and Bus Holt, Marine Public Information Officer at Vella Lavella, talked until late.

"Sure, I'd like to break the record," said Boyington, in response to Hampson's question. "Who wouldn't? I'd like to get 40 if I could. The more we can shoot down here, the fewer there'll be up the line to stop us."

But the questioning didn't end with Hampson's interview. In the mess hall, in the ready room, in the revetments, even in our tent, a steady stream of well-wishers kept Boyington's mind continually on the specter of that 26th plane: Could he do it? Would he do it? Did he want to do it? When would he do it? How did it feel to be so close? Was it tough? What did he think?

The rest of the Black Sheep realized the strain he was under and never mentioned that *other plane*, but hundreds of others did.

"Christ, I don't care if I break the record or not, if they'd just leave me alone," Boyington told me.

"You've got to stay with it, Greg," I said. "The whole squadron is pulling for you and you can do it—you'll never have another chance. It's now or never."

"Yes, I guess you're right."

On the 28th of December, Boyington led 12 Black Sheep over Rabaul again as part of a 46-plane fighter sweep. Boyington was not in tactical command of the formation, and the inexperienced leader let the Japanese planes get altitude advantage on his flight.

Suddenly, the 12 Black Sheep were engaged in a desperate battle, with 60 Zeros swarming all over them like flies on a dead carcass. The boys shot down four (one each for Magee, Matheson, McClurg, and Olander) to bring our score to 86, but at great cost: the lives of three more Black Sheep. It was the same story: no one saw the three in trouble; they just were not among those who winged their way back to Vella Lavella and taxied into the revetments.

I wrote "MIA" beside the names of Dustin, Bartl, and Moore, and their tentmates gathered up their belongings for the sad duty of sending it home.

We had a standard routine, both written and unwritten for this. Two officers segregated the belongings into three piles. One contained the man's valuable belongings, such as his money and jewelry. In another were his nonvaluable personal belongings: his uniforms, his photographs, etc. These two piles were packaged and sent back to the States, where they eventually found their way to the family.

The third pile consisted of his GI equipment—khaki shirts and trousers, pistol, flight gear, etc.—which was returned to the quartermaster for reissue.

Any gear of use to the remaining boys in the squadron might be retained: rubber air mattresses, extra goggles and the like, writing pads, slippers. If the items had any value, the boys bought them and included the money with what was sent home.

Usually all of the man's letters were burned.

I had often read, in the pulp magazines, about the carryings-on of pilots in the First World War. In most of those stories, their names were listed on a blackboard, and when one was shot down or turned up missing, an officer would draw a line through the name. Then someone standing in front of the board would break down, and a sympathetic squadron commander would lead him off as he screamed, "When is it gonna be my turn?"

Actually, it doesn't work out that way. When you live, eat, sleep, and fight with someone 24 hours a day, you develop a deep respect and love for him. When he's gone, you're left with a feeling of emptiness, of loneliness. But you don't scream about it. You just seal over that empty spot in your heart, and there it always remains.

On the 30th on a bombing escort mission that was partially aborted because of bad weather, Olander scored one Zero to become our squadron's eighth ace and bring our total to 87.

Boyington was getting wound up tighter. He went off by himself and stared at the rain. He was jittery.

When we went to chow, the newspaper correspondent sat down at the long table, across from us. "Well, Pappy, what do you think? Are you going to get another chance at the record?"

"I don't know."

"Well, if you do, are you going to break it? Are you going to be satisfied with just one or two, or are you going after more?"

Boyington blew up. "Goddamn it, why don't you guys leave me alone? I don't know if I'm going to break it or not. Just leave me alone till I do or go down trying." He slammed his fist down on the table, catching the edge of his plate and splattering food into the face of the correspondent, and left the mess hall.

"I told you to leave him alone," I said. "You guys never learn."

That night, Doc and I talked it over and decided it would be better if Boyington didn't fly on New Year's Day. He was still asleep when the boys took off for Rabaul, and he was fit to be tied when he found they'd gone without him.

However, he didn't mind so much when they returned without having made contact with the enemy.

In order to give him some exercise and get his mind off flying for a while, I got Doug White, a Marine combat correspondent, and Crocker, our jungle expert, to take him out in the jungle on a wild goose chase looking for a mythical Zero that was supposed to have crashed there. Doug and Crocker tramped what Boyington termed "a thousand miles" and brought him in about five o'clock, ready to go to bed.

He took a shower, stretched out for a nap before dinner, and slept soundly until time to get up for the 2 January sweep over Rabaul.

---

20 | Finale

On 2 January 1944 the weather was good. Boyington led 36 Marines and 20 Navy fighters to Rabaul. Only three of our Black Sheep accompanied him.

After they'd gone, Doc and I rubbed our hands. This, we thought, was *the day* when Pappy would break the record.

It was not the day.

When they got back, I found that the four Black Sheep had attacked 15 Zeros but shot down only one, and that score was made by Rope Trick Losch, bringing our squadron total to 88. Boyington never got a shot. His engine was throwing oil so badly that he was unable to see through his canopy.

Everything appeared to be stacking up against Pappy: the weather, the people, and for the first time in 100 combat hours, his engine. When Pappy came in at five o'clock, all conversation ceased.

"Had a little tough luck up there," he said, quietly.

"There's another big hop tomorrow, Greg," I told him. "If you're not too tired, you ought to go."

"No, I'm O.K."

"I've got some sandwiches on the way down. You'll have to take off in 40 minutes to go back up tonight. The schedule calls for a 6:30 A.M. takeoff from Bougainville."

"O.K."

The last we saw of him, he was standing in the bed of the truck, munching a sandwich, as the truck pulled out to take him, Ashmun (who was to fly his wing the next day), Matheson, and Chatham down to their planes.

We expected the flight back to Vella before noon, and long before that the ready tent was full of people wanting to know if he'd broken the record.

At 7:00 A.M., Operations told me the flight got off on schedule, and that the weather was good.

At 10:00 the first planes were back at Bougainville.

At 11:30, Matheson landed and brought the first word. He'd seen Pappy and Ashmun attack 15 Zeros, and Pappy had shot one down!

We all talked excitedly—that one tied the record. Were there any more?

Matheson didn't know. He and Chatham had had their hands full with another 15 Zeros; he'd shot one down, and then Chatham's electrical system had gone bad, and Matheson had to return with him to Bougainville. Our squadron total was now 90.

As the time dragged by, other pilots came in. I talked to all of them. No, they hadn't seen either Boyington or Ashmun. I asked Operations to check Munda, Ondonga, Treasury, to see if they'd landed. They *had* to be down somewhere; their gas would be gone by now.

And then, gradually, it began to dawn on us. Fred Hampson's report described it:

The Skipper didn't get back!

The news spread like a chill wind from revetment, to the ready room, to the tent camp on the hill. The war stood still for a hundred pilots and 500 ground crewmen.

It COULDN'T be true. The Japs didn't have a man who could stay on the Skipper's tail.

But as the minutes rolled into hours and negative answers to our queries came in from all fields, we began to comprehend that Pappy and Ashmun were both missing.

"Let's go up and look for them. They may be down in their rubber boats," suggested Mullen. Miller and I went to the Operations office and requested permission to send a flight up to scout for them.

"No, the weather's closed in. There's no use looking," the Operations officer told us. By this time, the Operations office was crowded with pilots. An angry murmur surged through them.

"I think from the standpoint of morale, it would be a good idea to let us at least look," said Miller. "These pilots all want to feel that every effort will be made to locate them if they go down."

"Oh, all right, go ahead."

In five minutes, eight Black Sheep took off in the only planes we had in commission. They gassed up at Bougainville and then were on instruments nearly all the way to Rabaul, finally climbing into the clear over a fleecy mattress that totally obscured the water below. Getting their bearings, they went down through the thick, soupy fog to the very surface of the water but had to give up because they couldn't see a thing.

That night, Doc and I sat alone in our tent. Pappy's bunk was rumpled, just as he'd left it. A pair of trousers lay in a heap beside it. A shirt hung over the frame supporting the twisted mosquito net. We both remembered what Pappy had said about Pierre.

"It's sure lonesome in here now," Doc said.

I just nodded my head, and swallowed.

For the remaining three days of our tour, every mission included a search for the Skipper and George.

The Black Sheep raged like wild men, up and down the coasts of New Ireland and New Britain, shooting up barges, gun positions, buildings, bivouac areas; strafing airfields; killing Nip troops; cutting up supply dumps, trucks, small boats.

They did wild things; dangerous things; foolish things—heroic things.

Every rumor of a sighting of any kind—flares, smoke, markers, chutes, rubber boats—brought a horde of Black Sheep whistling down so close to the sea that their prop wash left white wakes in the water.

Aerial combat was incidental; they wanted to get down to look for their Skipper and George. Nevertheless, they shot down four more Zeros to bring the squadron's grand total to 94 planes destroyed, 35 probably destroyed, 50 damaged in aerial combat, and 21 destroyed on the ground.

Mullen got his seventh plane, Bolt his sixth, and Groover and Harry Johnson each got his first.

Those last few days of our tour pointed up an important factor of the Black Sheep performance that had been missed by many observers. The Black Sheep was a *team*; their record was a *team effort*. Although Boyington was the acknowledged combat leader and had shot down the most planes, he had had the benefit of fine protection by his teammates. On more than one occasion, they had shot Zeros off his tail.

As for the record itself, the other Black Sheep had shot down 74 planes while Boyington was shooting down 20 (actually 75 and 22, as we learned later: see Appendix A). Everyone had made his contribution to the squadron performance, some by shooting down planes, others by providing protection for those who did the shooting. Some had given their lives in attempting to provide that protection.

The squadron's last score was made on 6 January 1944 by Skinny Johnson. He was all alone over Cape Gazelle because he'd taken off from Bougainville late after arguing the Air Officer into letting him join the flight. Suddenly, he was attacked by a swarm of Zeros. Twenty of them buzzed around him.

One came gliding down on him in a high head-on run. Johnson lifted his nose, opened fire, and raked the Zero from prop to tail. The Zero spiraled down and crashed into the water.

"Hey, fellows," called Johnson into his radio, "come over here, there's lots of them over here."

"Where the hell are you?" asked one of the other Black Sheep.

"Over here, over here; hurry before they get away," shouted Skinny, figuring he had 20 Zeros cornered.

He spotted one in a gentle turn slightly below and ahead of him, and immediately nosed over to attack. As he did, he remembered Boyington's voice of experience: "When you have an easy shot, and they're in a gentle turn, look for the catch."

Johnson looked around and saw two Zeros coming down on him in high stern runs. Without further fiddling, he pushed the throttle all the way forward, nosed down, and dived out and into a cloud, safely.

That was the last activity of the Black Sheep.

On 8 January we returned to Espiritu Santo, but it was more of a wake than a joyous homecoming. We'd lost eight pilots—and one of them was the Skipper.

After we got squared away in huts at our group headquarters camp, Miller and I went over to see General Moore. When we told him about

Pappy, tears ran down his cheeks. "He was the greatest combat pilot we ever had," he said.

"They're talking about breaking up our squadron, sir," said Miller. "We thought you'd understand why we want to stay together. We feel we've got a spirit built up in our squadron that will stay there if we're together but will be destroyed if we are scattered as replacements in other squadrons. We only need 13 new pilots to bring us up to full strength."

"The kind of spirit the Black Sheep have is the kind of spirit that wins battles," General Moore told us. "Certainly, you ought to stay together. Write me a letter outlining your request."

Miller and I went back to our camp to prepare the letter (its full text is in Appendix F). The letter received two very different endorsements. Lieutenant Colonel W.B. Steiner, Personnel Officer of Marine Air South Pacific, wrote: "Put these pilots in the pool . . . the VMF 214 number has already gone back to the States." But General Moore insisted, in his own handwriting: "Keep this combat team intact. Do not split this group."

Waiting for action on the letter, we spent our time swimming and catching up on our mail; we were so sure of success that we discussed possibilities for our next combat tour.

We knew the Black Sheep had done their share in turning the war around and putting the Japanese on the defensive. Although much hard fighting remained, the result was clearly in sight. The Japanese had used up their skilled pilots and most of their aircraft. What was left were desperation efforts such as the ill-fated Kamikaze attacks.

As Robert Sherrod reports in his *History of Marine Corps Aviation in WW II*, "The attrition of the Solomons was telling fatally on the Emperor's stock of Wild Eagles."

By February 1944, only token Japenese aerial resistance was put up. Like a broken log jam, the drive toward Tokyo accelerated.

Unfortunately, General Moore was transferred to another command, and we learned our fate from a news broadcast by the Associated Press in a story datelined "20 March 1944, An Advanced South Pacific Base":

The Black Sheep are no more.

The famed Marine Corsair Squadron led by the missing 26 plane super ace, Major Gregory Boyington . . . has been broken up after shooting down 94 Japanese planes in 12 weeks of combat in the South Pacific.

Its members are being scattered among other Marine Fighting Squadrons, the Solomons Air Headquarters announced.

The Black Sheep long had been recognized as one of the hardest hitting and most eager teams of air fighters and a squadron which was nourished by the fighting competitive spirit of its lost skipper. . . .

The Black Sheep started as a squadron of nobodies, being formed from a collection of flyers and replacements on the spur of the moment. . . . Within a matter of weeks it became the best Japanese-killing outfit in the Solomons and, in some respects, the most unusual squadron ever to fly the South Pacific skies.

Our squadron number went back to the States, and the new pilots assigned to it proudly adopted the famous Black Sheep name. But for us in the original Black Sheep Squadron, there were only 51 Black Sheep, the ones who lived and fought together—and died—during those 84 hectic days in the Solomons.

The Black Sheep scattered. Some, having completed the required three combat tours, returned to the United States for new assignments; others were sent to Bougainville or Green Island.

Quick to recognize good public relations when they had it, the Marine Corps made "Black Sheep" the permanent designation of VMF 214, a name already become almost as much a legend in Marine Corps history as "The Halls of Montezuma."

Boyington's name remained prominent as well. On 29 January 1944, in an impressive ceremony, the officers and men of Marine Air Group 14 dedicated an amusement park on Ondonga (an island near Munda, in the New Georgia group) to Boyington. The plaque they erected read: "To the outstanding heroism; to the excellent record-surpassing accomplishment achieved in aerial combat against the Japanese by Major Gregory Boyington, a member of this Group, this amusement area is respectfully dedicated by the officers and men of MAG 14 and is hereafter to be known as BOYINGTON PARK."

And throughout the length and breadth of the Solomons, on carriers, back in the States—everywhere combat fliers gathered—the questions were always raised:

"What do you suppose happened to Pappy?"

"Do you think he had a chance of getting out alive?"

"Did he get shot down?"

"Did he and Ashmun collide?"

"Did he get hit by an AA burst?"

"Did he get captured?"

"If so, is he still a prisoner? or did they kill him?"

"Could he be hiding out in the New Britain jungles?"

"Will he keep that date in San Diego?"

"They can't kill that guy. He'll turn up, sure as God made green apples."

"Not a chance. After all, the man was human—even he could only take so much."

Then the rumors began. Boyington had been picked up by a submarine and was already back in the States. He was hiding in the jungle waiting for a chance to get out. He was one of several pilots hiding along the coast of New Ireland, and a PT boat was going to pick them all up. His Mae West life jacket had been found, full of holes. He was working his way along the New Britain coast, trying to make it to our forces at Cape Gloucester.

In my capacity as Intelligence Officer, I saw top secret messages, and I knew that none of these rumors was true.

It *was* true, however, that Boyington had been awarded the nation's highest military decoration. The press release came in the mail, dated 12 April 1944:

Major Gregory Boyington, U.S.M.C., of Okanogan, Washington, who shot down 26 Japanese fighter planes and is now missing in action, has been awarded the Congressional Medal of Honor by the President of the United States for "extraordinary heroism."

The citation accompanying the medal says the Marine ace, "a superb airman and determined fighter against overwhelming odds," led his Black Sheep fighter squadron against the Japanese in the Central Solomon Islands from September 12, 1943, to January 3, 1944, when he failed to return from a mission over Rabaul.

The citation was signed by President Franklin D. Roosevelt.

But one day, I felt a wave of excitement as I thumbed through the Top Secret file. I read the message again: Marines who'd captured Saipan had picked up a document which said that Boyington had passed through Saipan on his way to Tokyo. Thrilled, I read it again. And again.

And then soberer thoughts came. If the Japanese knew who he was, they'd probably have killed him. They'd killed a lot of captured allied troops. All that could be done was watch the message traffic and hope.

I completed a 16-month tour overseas, returned to the States, and was assigned as assistant chief of staff for intelligence at the Marine Fleet Air West Coast Headquarters in San Diego. Nearly a year went by.

Then one morning, it was there! "Pappy Boyington rescued from Japanese prison camp."

Checking by telephone and dispatch, our public information officer found that Pappy was being flown to San Francisco.

We spread the word to the 21 Black Sheep on the west coast. All were there to greet him when the big Navy transport plane slid down through the fog over Oakland before dawn on 12 September 1945.

We picked him off the plane; carried him on our shoulders into the waiting room; watched as he told his story to a battery of half a hundred newspaper reporters, to the accompaniment of flashing photographers' bulbs. Then we took him to our hotel in San Francisco.

That night at the St. Francis Hotel we had the Black Sheep party Pappy had always said he'd attend "even if I go down with 30 Zeros on my tail."

The Marine Corps assigned me to accompany Boyington on a several weeks' tour of the country selling war bonds. Included were a homecoming to a stupendous welcome for him in Seattle and a stop in Washington, D.C., where we met the rest of the Black Sheep. We all watched as Boyington received his Medal of Honor from President Truman.

It was a fitting conclusion to the Black Sheep story.

TWO

The Black Sheep Forty Years Later

War talk by men who have been in a war is always interesting; whereas moon talk by a poet who has not been in the moon is likely to be dull.

Mark Twain

Frank Walton

Following the Black Sheep reunion in Washington in 1980 on the occasion of the Corsair induction ceremony at the Smithsonian's National Air and Space Museum, it took me another two years to meet and talk with each of the Black Sheep (I criss-crossed the country twice from Maine to California and from Washington to Florida); to have some 60 hours of tapes transcribed; to do additional research; to get the material assembled.

They were nostalgic years, journeying back 40 years to those stirring, eventful days and filling the gaps in the participants' lives between then and now. I'll start with myself.

After the Black Sheep broke up, I went to Guadalcanal to become Air Command Intelligence Officer for what was planned as an assault on Kavieng—a Japanese stronghold some 180 miles northwest of Rabaul—but turned out to be a less bloody landing at Emirau, a tiny island some 70 miles farther north. The Japanese had been driven out of Guadalcanal, bottled up on Bougainville, and bypassed in the Bismarck Archipelago; at Emirau we were effectively interdicting their efforts to supply their bases.

Nevertheless, one of the highlights of my tour of duty on Emirau was a chance to be a temporary commando. Among the bravest and least recognized of those who fought the war in the South Pacific were the Coast Watchers, a number of Australians and New Zealanders who lived among the natives in those jungle islands and radioed Allied forces when Japanese air raids were headed their way.

One of these, an Australian who had been operating on Tabar Island, had been betrayed by a German national, captured by the Japanese, and beheaded. His brother suggested that we mount a small raid to Tabar, try to capture the German, and see what intelligence material we might pick up.

We made the 150-mile trip by PT boat at night, and pink streaks of dawn stretched across the sky as we approached Tabar. By the time we'd paddled a rubber boat to shore, about a hundred fuzzy-haired natives—tall, muscular, blue-black, and armed with spears—had assembled on the beach. Some of them had bones in their noses. Many had boars' tusk bracelets and necklaces. They wore nothing but basic

Left and below, Frank Walton

Below, left and right John Bolt

G-strings. None was smiling. Not even Lloyd's of London would have quoted odds on our lives.

The Australian questioned the chief in pidgin English—"Massa Manheim, he come along here?"—but got no response until he brought up the butt of his submachine gun and knocked the chief to the sand—while the PT captain and I crouched with our weapons at the ready, envisioning ourselves in iron pots as "fresh meat."

The Australian said: "You talk-talk, plenty fast, savvy?" The chief scrambled to his feet and motioned us to follow.

We found the German's place, all right, but he had gone. We destroyed a warehouse containing several tons of rice, burned his house, stove in and burned a small power-boat that he had hidden in the mouth of a stream. Then, aware that the rising smoke would cause enemy reaction, we hurried back to the PT boat. In my den, I still have the sign I took from the rice warehouse: in Japanese it reads: "Do not touch, Japanese Civil Government in charge."

From Emirau, I was sent to Bougainville to act as Assistant Chief of Staff, G-2, for Air Command, Northern Solomons. The tiny beachhead that the Marines had carved at Empress Augusta Bay was barely large enough to contain the runways and the supporting buildings.

The Japanese dragged artillery pieces into the mountains surrounding our base and lobbed shells into our camp.

Among my duties was the presentation of a daily intelligence situation briefing to the senior staffs of the various commands present, and once a week our section provided an intelligence briefing for all the troops at the movie theater.

With the war in our area winding down, however, we had time for recreation: volleyball and swimming in the ocean. For the rest of my life, I'll remember swimming off the black sand beach of Bougainville while our planes blasted Japanese positions surrounding us on three sides.

After the war, released from active duty, I returned to the Los Angeles Police Department, and an appointment as lieutenant (I had taken the examination in the South Pacific, a towel wrapped around my arm to keep the sweat from staining the papers). I also resumed my college education and earned a master's degree in government, and was a member of the 1948 U.S. Olympic water polo team.

I retired in 1959 to accept an appointment as a Foreign Service Officer in the Department of State and spent the next 12 years in Vietnam, the Philippines, Thailand, Libya, Laos, and Washington, D.C.

I remained a member of the Marine Corps Reserve, was called up for a year's service during the Korean War, and finally retired as a colonel after 27 years' total service.

I live in Hawaii now, swimming, playing golf, and doing some writing—this book, for instance.

Barrister and Fisherman

John Bolt

New Smyrna Beach, Florida, population 14,000, is about a dozen miles south of Daytona. Here, in an office not far from the remains of a sixteenth-century Spanish fort, John Bolt carries on a busy law practice. Behind the desk in his office, silver-haired, dressed in a business suit, the slender, soft-spoken Bolt bears no resemblance to the intrepid, aggressive combat pilot he once was. Yet he is a jet/prop ace, the only one the Marine Corps has had. He shot down six Zeros with the Black Sheep, and followed that up by scoring six MiG kills during the Korean War. He is one of only seven Americans who were aces in both World War II and Korea.

Mementos of the Black Sheep, as well as of his Korean service, dotted the wall. I noted the date on his Law Degree: 1969. He'd earned it at age 48.

"Bring me up to date on your career," I asked.

"Well, it's kind of checkered. I retired from the Marine Corps in 1962 after 20 years' service. I'd been able to get my bachelor's degree in military science. But I felt that the military life was hard on teenage children, and I had one in high school and another coming up. Also, I always had a strong feeling for my hometown of Sanford. I had an opportunity to go into a business with what looked like a good stock option, and I worked there for about seven years. It wasn't turning out as it had been presented to me, though, so I dropped it and went to law school, going straight through in 27 months. Then I stayed on the faculty for two years.

"After leaving Gainesville, we came to New Smyrna Beach and I opened up my own law office."

"Looking back on your Black Sheep experience, did our squadron differ from others you served in?"

"Yes, in several ways. The most significant thing about that tour was the introduction of the Corsair with a capability that just overwhelmed the Zero, which had only about half its horsepower. We were just learning to use the Corsair. It's a great experience to introduce a fighter plane that has twice the horsepower of your opponent's. In my opinion, the Corsair was the real hero of the Pacific war. The squadron got the credit because Americans like people to be heros, not weapons or weapon systems.

"However, the spirit of the Black Sheep was different, too. The pressure and the accomplishments, along with Boyington's leadership, made it a great team. Unfortunately, Boyington has tended to minimize the contribution of others; people like Emrich, Harper, and Tucker haven't received the credit they're due."

"Do you think the day of the man-to-man aerial dogfight is over?"

"Yes, it's not the intimate experience we had when we got pieces of the enemy plane stuck up against our planes. I remember Ed Harper shot a Zero, then flew into its fireball. His plane was covered with soot when he landed. In Korea I got a piece of MiG, molten aluminum, stuck in my armor glass."

"If you had it to do over again, would you stay in the Marine Corps?"

"I've told my wife several times that I should have gone to law school after the war. Dottie protests this. She loved the Corps and thinks I'd have gotten tired of practicing law if I'd started so soon. We enjoyed the Marine Corps and the friends we made there, and we certainly have no regrets."

"Why did some shoot down planes, and others not?"

"Well, Waldo, I couldn't have answered that at the end of World War II, even after a second tour aboard carriers. I learned the answer in the Korean War. The answer is that you simply want to shoot down airplanes more than anything else in the world.

"When I was flying F-86s with the Air Force, I failed to capitalize on a couple of opportunities because I was too conservative. I determined at that point that the next one I saw was a dead man, and I didn't care where he was or how many protectors he had—he was a dead man.

"That particular time is on film: in the middle of a gaggle of MiGs about 43,000 feet, I'm pounding away at this one guy.

"I see this in animals: lions, other predators, when they attack the grass eaters. The grass eaters may be scattering in all directions, cutting back and forth between the predator and his target, but he never changes target. He selects his target and that's it; the others can run off. They don't distract him.

"It's true in quail shooting, too. The guy who doesn't shoot any quail is the guy who tries to kill the whole covey. The guy that gets the birds, gazelles, lions—whatever—and the fighter pilot who makes his kill is the one who selects his target and stays with it ignoring everything else."

"Singleness of purpose?" I asked.

"Absolutely, and a dedication to it that gets you up early in the morning, and puts you to bed late at night. It's a commitment like anything else, but there, of course, you're playing with your life."

"That's a long time ago. What's your attitude now?"

"I'm a workaholic—I like my law practice. But I go skin-diving frequently, too. My son likes to dive. You don't have good diving until you're down to about 95 feet. There are strong currents out 23 miles. I damn near got killed out there about three years ago and haven't gone back. We can get lots of lobsters in the Keys.

"But my big sport these days is cast-netting for mullet. I sell them commercially. It's hard work, slogging through the mud and eel grass. The mullet eat algae on the bottom of the eel grass. This past Sunday I caught 150 pounds. I gave away one full box, and sold 104 pounds.

"I also do a little hunting. I keep in close touch with a few Black Sheep and will see them at the New Orleans Marine Corps Aviation Association Convention."

John Begert

Accounting for 20 percent of the nation's wheat output, Kansas ranks as one of our chief agricultural states. Topeka, the state capital, is a city of some 120,000 near its eastern boundary. It lies on Interstate Highway 70, a few miles south of the Potawatomie Indian Reservation.

I drove out to John Begert's old family home on the western outskirts of Topeka, part of a farm that has been in the family for years. One wall of his den is covered with Black Sheep memorabilia; shelves on another wall are filled with gold trophies—John is a four-handicap golfer.

Begert had sent me a letter in 1944 about what to expect when we got home: "Be prepared for a wonderful welcome. . . . The attitude of the people toward anyone who was in combat is more than gratifying. It made me feel sheepish not to be able to say I'd done more. Merely the fact that you've been 'out there' makes you a hero to your old friends."

Now, John was lean, tanned, healthy. It was easy to see how he would have a four handicap.

He pulled out reams of files of orders, photos, news stories, and we spread them out on a huge table to refresh his memory.

"Seven or eight of us went out together from the States. We had two combat tours before the Black Sheep were formed. Boyington was with us on one of them, but he broke his leg in a barroom brawl and missed the second. He'd been sent to New Zealand to recuperate, and when he got back, he was placed in command of the newly formed 214.

"Before that, we sat around doing nothing. There was some idiot colonel in charge of the base; I think in the TV show he was Colonel Lard. He made us go out and pick up cigarette butts, and he was hot on using mosquito nets, poking his flashlight into every tent. He was lucky he didn't get shot.

"While we waited, 20 or so more people came in, including Fisher, Bragdon, Harper, and Olander."

"So that's how there happened to be enough for a squadron," I said. "Compare the way Boyington ran things to the other COs."

"I thought Stan Bailey ran the squadron as far as administration was concerned." Begert replied.

"Boyington was very strict on air discipline, but he didn't worry too much about what went on on the ground," I agreed.

"Right, but I'd say the main reason we made the records was

John Begert

Ed Harper

because of training—we did more training with that squadron than we did with both the others—and the bull sessions we had at night about tactics."

"When you first went out in combat, were you scared?"

"I was scared all the time." Begert said.

"What kind of scared? Like your anticipation before a football game? Or like going into a dark alley with some muggers?"

"I would say more like an athletic contest, the big game. I think our psychology was completely different. We went in there after Joe Foss and Marion Carl, and I think all of us secretly wanted to make a record for ourselves. It was a combination of fright and opportunity. I think your analogy to a football game is good. When you go into a game like that, you're scared you're going to get hurt, and you want to be a hero."

"Were the guys you went out with your closest friends?"

"Yes, Bourgeois in particular, but only in the rear areas. I think we were each afraid something would happen to the other in combat, and we didn't want to be that close.

"I'll never forget one night after a mission. I got into my cot, and there was an empty cot on my left and on my right, and an empty cot across the way from me.

"Case was missing, once, and they gave away all his clothes. When he showed up again, they were quite embarrassed and had to start getting it all back."

"Let's jump ahead. Where'd you go after you had your home leave?" I asked.

"I was sent to the First Marine Division in China, after the war, as Air Officer to General Peck."

Begert has a couple of citations: one, dated 15 April 1946 expressed the appreciation of the Tientsin Chief of Police for his excellent service and cooperation in apprehending two people engaged in smuggling $100,000 in Japanese currency out of China.

The other is from General K.E. Rockey, Commanding, Third Amphibious Corps, for "excellent service in connection with operations to effect the formal surrender of the enemy in the Tientsin area." Begert assisted the Provost Marshal in the investigation of an international narcotics smuggling ring by volunteering to join the criminal organization, "fully aware of the desperate character of the individuals, and the personal danger involved." He successfully accomplished his mission.

"I resigned my regular commission after I left China; Case and Bourgeois stayed in. My dad wasn't well and needed me at home. At that time, we had three farms, this one; one 400 acres about a mile and a half from here; and another, 160 acres, about 15 miles away. We also had the major interest in an overall factory in Atchison.

"I came home and built a duplex. Dad died about ten years before my mother, and Betty and I have taken care of things ever since. We've sold off all our property except one acre around the house.

"I'm a stockbroker with Paine Weber, and I don't work any more than I have to. I listen to the Wall Street doings and it sounds like a funny farm. One week this, and the next week just the opposite. It all goes back to judgment."

"Back to the Black Sheep, who were the best?"

"Bourgeois had the best eyesight. He'd call 'bogie' and it'd be five or six seconds before I could pick them up. Boyington was far ahead in mechanical knowledge. He could lean out the mixture and stay in the air longer than we could. As a farm boy, I didn't miss even though I didn't get too many shots."

"Do you think the singing helped mold the squadron?"

"Yes, that was very important. I remember they tried to teach me to sing. In the Russell Islands, remember that outhouse built on a dock? The seats were rough-hewn mahogany and full of splinters, and the rule was that when you went, you were supposed to take your knife and do some whittling to smooth it off. Mullen and Sims and I happened to go together every morning, me in the middle, and they tried to teach me harmony. The song was 'Genevieve,' and I'd be fine until we got to the second 'Genevieve.' I was the baritone. Those guys got so mad at me because I'd miss one note, and we'd do it again."

"Looking back, what would you change if you could?"

"I might have stayed in if I had been allowed to stay with the squadron instead of being shipped to China. But as far as experiences are concerned, I wouldn't change a thing. I did try for one more tour of combat duty, but Doc Reames said he'd give me a Section 8 if I put in for it. I weighed only 125 pounds when I left the Black Sheep."

Ed Harper

I visited Ed Harper at McDonnell Aircraft Company's building at Lambert–St. Louis International Airport. Security at the entrance was tight. Signs warned that no photographic or recording equipment was allowed in the building and that all briefcases were to be left at the security desk.

Had my briefcase been inspected, the two cameras and two tape recorders would have caused instant panic among the security people. Fortunately, Ed Harper had enough clout to assure them that I would be under his constant surveillance, and the guards reluctantly issued me a pass without opening the case.

Harper is vice-president, and a program manager for McDonnell Aircraft Company Division of McDonnell Douglas Corporation. Compact, alert, incisive, he was a model of the company executive as he sat behind the huge desk in his office. We talked about the way the Black Sheep Squadron was formed and how it got its name, and then about more personal things.

"Were you scared on your first combat mission, being new?"

"As I recall, I was anxious to get about it, and a bit shocked when I saw the first Zero. It got very serious very fast. It's hard to prepare anybody for the real thing.

"I give Boyington a little credit for the kind of spirit the Black Sheep had. He conducted himself well in the air; his strongest virtue was that he helped me lose any fear I had in the air. His behavior on the ground wasn't always exemplary; a few times, I wasn't exactly pleased how things went. I liked the fact that he had few rules, all of which had to do with flight safety, and tried to enforce them. When I had a squadron of my own, I tried to emulate some of that: not too many rules, but enforce those you have. The longer I flew, the safer I felt. I've always thought flying and playing basketball are similar. You've got to get to the point where you can hit the basket, comfortable and relaxed, not uptight when someone crowds you; always under control and using peripheral vision. Good coordination and good eyes."

I asked, "After the Black Sheep, you were sent to Green Island and were wounded there. How'd that happen?"

"It was the last flight of my last day of my last tour of duty. We had strafed a dozen trucks. I had only one gun firing and I decided to make one last pass. As I pulled out, I got hit. The doc said it was a 50-caliber AP [armor-piercing] clean hole so it didn't spread out as it went through me, under the arm, through the lung; it clipped my spine, and came out in the middle of my back.

"Immediately after I got hit, I couldn't move my legs. They were hanging down in the bottom of the cockpit. At first, I told the guys I'd have to go down offshore, but by the time I'd jettisoned the canopy, I decided if I didn't get home, I wasn't going to make it. I told the guys I was going home. I started having fainting spells and threw away my helmet; it had been going dark on me. The spells cleared up, and I relaxed and trimmed the airplane up, put on power. The fear was completely gone. That statement that fear brings more pain than pain brings fear is really true. I could barely breathe, and when I got to Green Island, my legs weren't working right. I got them up on the pedals with my arms helping and made a normal landing, then rolled off the runway, but I did get stopped.

"The doc was looking at me in the cockpit, wanting a crane to get me out. I told him, 'I got this airplane home and I'm not going to sit here and bleed to death. Pick me up and get me out of here!' I passed out as they did and came to about two days later.

"The G.P. type doc there, I owe my life to him. He was pumping plasma but I wasn't responding. He went out of the tent and hollered to a Seabee, looked at his dogtag for the right type of blood. He laid him down beside me, started pumping whole blood directly into me, and I began to respond.

"Back at the Russells, I was running a high fever. They thought they'd have to operate for a bone infection. That evening, a corpsman came by and asked if they'd checked me for malaria. I told him I didn't know. On his own, he stuck my thumb, got a slide, came back and said: 'You got malaria.' They canceled the operation and fed me quinine.

"I was there six weeks, then floated home on a hospital ship. I was in a hospital in San Francisco for a while, then in Farragut, Idaho—near home—for two months, and started a series of physicals. I was back on limited duty six months after I was shot.

"By the time the war was over, I was a Captain. I liked the Marine Corps, aviation, and what I was doing."

Harper went on to a fine Marine Corps career: Project Engineer at the Bureau of Aeronautics; Executive Officer of Marine Attack Squadrons; Air Group Operations Officer and Squadron Commander of a jet squadron; Chief of the Command Center, U.S. European Command in Paris; Senior Marine Corps Liaison Officer to MACV Staff in Vietnam.

He retired in 1969 as a colonel and is well into his new career at McDonnell.

"I'm happy with what I'm doing," he said. "I was promoted recently. I have a fascinating program. I could talk about it for hours. I intend to stay for several more years. I work, read a lot, jog, play bridge. I've had a hell of a lot of fun and worked with a lot of good people.

"I thought the Black Sheep were in combat at the right time, and we had an aggressive guy leading us. The aggressiveness is what I liked and carried forward. I learned a few lessons out there. Living and dealing with people. And, I guess, always aspiring to do better.

"I remember that organizationally, you held the squadron together. Someone had to get us where we had to go and back, where to eat and sleep, and you did it. I don't keep in touch regularly, and I appreciate your efforts in getting the Black Sheep back together. Give them my regards when you see them."

Estate Lawyer

Henry Miller

Henry "Notebook" Miller drove over to meet me at the hotel at Philadelphia's International Airport. I recognized his tall, square figure at once. As he strode toward the door, briefcase under his arm, he resembled a Harvard professor on the way to a lecture. True to his nickname, he brought with him an extensive file of data concerning missions, flight hours, aircraft numbers, and dates.

Miller came to us as flight officer, moved up to executive officer, and took over as squadron commander after Boyington was shot down.

"In your first aerial combat, were you scared?"

"No, I don't think so. I'd had much more training than the average, and I liked the idea of aviation because I really enjoyed flying.

"If anything, flight pay should have been *deducted* from the base pay because it was so much fun; the fact that you were shooting and

Henry Miller

Fred Losch

being shot at didn't really mean as much as the fun of flying. And I've always believed that the more you flew the safer you were, so I welcomed test hops."

Miller's record bears out that philosophy: he flew nearly twice as many missions and hours as any other pilot.

"One of the mistakes I think was made by Marine leaders in aviation at that time was that there was very little general instruction given to pilots about getting into a fight and slugging it out, dominating the enemy by your own aggressiveness. The attitude was more or less to do your own thing. Boyington's characteristic was the desire and willingness to get right in there, ride as close as he could, do a lot of shooting without regard for himself. Other people were more conservative. I guess I was probably the more conservative kind, thinking how graceful it was to be flying around in a beautiful plane and not concentrating to the extent he was on really doing what we were there to do."

"As operations officer on our second tour, you kept an outstanding set of books," I commented.

"I kept my own books on every day's flights. Who was on duty and what took place; every name, every plane's bureau, registration number, every takeoff time, landing, solo time, and so forth—it was a kind of index. The first part was each daily effort by the squadron with all the details. Then I had a section for each pilot by name as to which days he flew and what he did. I had a summary of each division's activity."

Speaking about the use of fighters for more than shooting down planes, he said: "What you're talking about is that different people contribute different things to a team; the real offensive work is the bombing, and fighters are needed to see that the bombers get to their targets. There's the role of close air support or interdicting ground movements.

"My worst experience? On Bougainville, I had the green light and was making a normal three-point landing when I suddenly felt a jar, saw something go over me. It was a damaged B-24 coming in from the opposite direction with only one main landing gear. When the pilot saw me, he used what air speed he had to pull up and over and land behind me. The strut was down and hit the nose of my plane, knocking the strut off, and he made a wheels-up landing. My plane was so badly jarred, it was junked."

Miller was later sent to Cherry Point as commander of the first Marine Corps day fighter squadron to be equipped with twin-engine planes. After the war he returned to his law practice but remained active in the Reserve Program; he was called up and served a year in the Korean War. Thereafter, he resigned his commission to concentrate on his law practice in Jenkintown, Pennsylvania, specializing in estate planning and real estate.

Henry was born and raised in Jenkintown; his roots are there. He jogs a mile each morning on his own property, spends a dozen hours a week working in his yard. He is busy in church work, too: chairman of the stewardship committee, the hunger and refugee programs; and he recently became active in prison visitation and a program for the mentally retarded, as well, and he is a driver for Meals on Wheels.

Since 1960, he has spent considerable time in legal services for the poor, and is chairman of the Hearing Board in his township.

Business Tycoon

Fred Losch

I interviewed Fred "Rope Trick" Losch in his plush home in Altadena, California, not far from plant headquarters of the building materials firm he built from scratch into a $40,000,000-a-year business. We sat at the bar in the huge Spanish-style house.

Fred has put on several pounds since the days when he weighed about 120 in his stocking feet but has kept his friendly, outgoing disposition, his love of life with a heart as big as all of California.

"When December 7th came along, I was out bow-and-arrow hunting on my folks' farm in Pennsylvania. My brother said: 'You'd better put that bow and arrow away and get yourself a gun—the Japanese have attacked Pearl Harbor.'

"We went up to Pittsburgh Monday. Everybody was planning to join the Army Air Corps, but the line was halfway around the Federal Building. A buddy said, 'This is for the birds. Why don't we try the Navy Air Corps?'

"I'd never been in an airplane and didn't know the Navy had an air corps, but in a couple of hours we were signed up. We were trained on the Corsairs, but when I joined the Black Sheep for their second tour, I looked at guys like Magee and Matheson, Bolt, Heier, and Olander— 'God, those guys are professionals! A bunch of God-damned killers.' And Boyington, he was Jesus Christ himself. I was the same age as several others, but they were six weeks ahead of me. We looked at them as if they were ten years older."

I said, "They'd aged ten years in those six weeks of combat. Were you scared on your first mission?"

"I didn't know enough to be scared. I was with Bragdon over Buka Airdrome when an AA shell burst off my wing. I asked what it was, didn't realize they were shooting at me. But I was absolutely petrified one time. I had been towing a sleeve to give some new guys altitude gunnery training. I was at 22,000, and they were at 25,000, when the weather closed under us. We started home, but I must have passed over an area with strong mineral deposits, because my compass began to spin around. I had overcast above and undercast below, and no idea where I was. Was I ever scared? I finally let down through the clouds, but it was raining right down to the deck. I started making big circles. I was almost out of gas when I spotted Espiritu Santo, 100 miles from where I was supposed to be. If someone else had been with me, both of us in the same boat, it wouldn't have been so bad.

"You know, you go through the whole thing, and all of a sudden realize you have only three weeks left on your overseas tour. You say to yourself: 'Maybe I'm going to make it home!' Up to that point, you'd put it in the back of your mind, but from then on you aren't worth a damn.

"Like after the Japanese no longer had any air operation and we flew to hunt their trucks. One day, the trucks were bait, and 20-mm guns opened up on us. I went in on the gun emplacement and came back up thinking, 'Boy, we're lucky to get out of that.' Then one of the new pilots came back for another pass, and I cut him off. I said to myself: 'My plane and I are worth $50,000 each; the beat up trucks, nothing.' When you start rationalizing this sort of stuff, you're not a good pilot anymore.

"It's the same in business. You look at a company, especially a big national company: when it was young, it was agressive—young guys running it, dynamic and going to make their mark. But when a guy is nearing retirement age, he doesn't want to rock the boat. You say, 'But look what this can do for your company.' He's not interested. I relate these two things closely.

"I'm a good example. After the war, I went to UCLA to finish up my degree, and got a job with Armstrong Cork Company.

Black Sheep Squadron members with the Corsair added to the National Air and Space Museum, 1980. *Kneeling, left to right,* Fred Losch, Harry Johnson, John Begert, Robert McClurg, Greg Boyington, Henry Bourgeois. *Standing,* Burney Tucker, Gelon Doswell, James Reames, Frank Walton, Denmark Groover, James Hill, Don Fisher, Thomas Emrich, Perry Lane, Ed Harper, Bruce Matheson, Fred Avey.

"Then I went to work in Los Angeles for an old hardwood whole-sale firm that had been started in 1884. I set up a specialty division there, and in 1961 I made arrangements to split that division off and form my own company. I was young and aggressive, and developed an innovative approach to marketing, ending up with one of the ten finest building materials companies in the United States. In another ten years, it could have been a $150,000,000 company, but by then I didn't want to work that hard.

"When you've got a going concern like that, you have three op-tions: liquidate, go public, or sell out. I'd been giving my top managers stock shares, so I sold out to them. They're all younger, and were officers in the company.

"I had a very successful business. If I were 40 years old, I could build it to $500,000,000, but I didn't have either the years left or the incentive. Now I'm enjoying life. I travel, fish, meet with my old Black Sheep buddies."

He glanced over at the wall back of the bar, decorated with Black Sheep memorabilia: squadron photos, our emblem.

"Looking back, I consider that tour one of the highlights of my life. It was a time of extreme stress and action compressed into a brief period, but in just those couple of months, I became closer to that group than anyone except perhaps my brother.

"Why was it? It was a happy combination: the stress; the dynamic leadership of Boyington; the press coverage that you were responsible for. We had a team, and we all tried to live up to it. We were the *Black Sheep* Squadron. Other squadrons were individuals—we were a *team.*

"Of course, your mind tends to block out the bad things that happened, but I'll always treasure those few weeks with the Black Sheep."

Fred Avey

Rufus Chatham

Fred Avey

Fred Avey drove out to meet me at my hotel at Detroit's Metropolitan Airport. "Lighthorse" Fred would have to be termed "Heavyhorse" Fred now. Although he appeared hale and hearty, he was no longer the slender, dapper lad; his 20-inch waist had perhaps doubled. He had been both the oldest and the smallest of the Black Sheep pilots: six weeks older than Boyington, and 10 pounds lighter than the next smallest.

"How'd you get into the Black Sheep?" I asked.

"My first squadron went home, and I was in limbo. The Black Sheep took four of us from Squadron 213.

"My worst scare was on the ground. I weighed about 110 pounds then, and I was soaped up for a shower when Boyington came staggering in and wanted to wrestle me. You recall that steel pier planking, the Marsden matting, and how sharp it was on raw flesh? I couldn't even turn the water on him to try to sober him up. I was scared, but I finally talked him into going back to his tent.

"I put in to become a regular at Cherry Point but never got a response until I went to Washington and talked to Paul Fontana in Personnel. He showed me a stack of papers, 'all officers desiring to go regular who are one day to one month too old in rank, and your name is here.'

"Later, in Korea, I tried again, and stayed on as a reserve on continuous active duty through the war; then I was at Cherry Point, training jet pilots to fly on instruments. I was finally ordered to inactive duty in 1955.

"I tried to stay in the Organized Reserves, but I was so senior in rank that there were no billets for me. I was not informed that I could have kept up my retirement points without pay, so, after 13 years, I was through. I retired with the rank of lieutenant colonel but no retirement pay.

"After that, I got a job with Ford Motor Company and worked there for 18 years, in the purchasing of special-purpose vehicles. When the 1974 oil shortage hit, it knocked out our department. I was on vacation. When I returned, my desk was gone and my phone was on the floor.

"They let me stay in another job for a few months, enough to qualify for a small pension.

"Then I got a job with a municipal golf course where I could play all the golf I wanted, free. The only trouble was that it closed in the winter, so I'd draw unemployment insurance. Each year the same. The city finally got tired of it and said: 'This won't do.' So I got a job as a bank messenger, but I can only work so many months and still get my Social Security. That leaves enough time off to play golf during the summer.

"If I had it to do over again, I'd have gone regular right off the bat, but when I left Hawaii to go overseas, I said 'Farewell to thee.' On the forms, I put 'cremate me and scatter the ashes over the sea if the body is found.' I didn't think I'd even be found, there was so much combat over water."

"Fearless" Fred, given several wrong numbers on life's wheel, was now resting on his oars, drifting comfortably with the tide before an onshore breeze.

Petroleum Engineer and Merchant

Rufus Chatham

Austin, Texas, where Rufus "Mack" Chatham lives, was the capital before Texas even became a state. The pleasant city of 350,000 lies in rolling hills about 160 miles west of Houston. Its major claim to fame, besides being the home of Chatham, is that the LBJ Library is located there on the campus of the University of Texas. I drove over from Houston and was flagged down by Mack in front of his comfortable home near the center of town.

Although minus a little hair, Chatham was still lean as a whippet, still had the dry wit and low-key, diffident approach I remembered. I asked how he happened to join the service.

"I was a bit tired of school, and a Navy recruiter said the Navy couldn't get along without me. After training, we went by ship to the South Pacific. I remember we were supposed to have 200 nurses on board but had 200 male British officers instead."

"You were in Boyington's division when he was shot down. Do you recall anything about that?"

"It was pretty messed up. A lot of Zeros below; I lost Matheson when we got scattered.

"After the war ended, I debated whether to stay in as a regular or go back to school. My father said both were great, but I'd have to make up my own mind, so I went back to school and graduated from the University of Texas in 1948. Then I went to work for Schlumberger. It's a firm that provides technical services for the oil industry, one of the largest and most profitable in the U.S. I stayed with them for 22 years, moving all over the country: Beaumont, Houston, L.A., Midland, Corpus Christi.

"I had a strong desire to make it on my own, though, so I drew out my profit sharing, about $60,000, and spent it on remodeling a Fort Worth building. I called the business Sundial, handling casual furniture, rattan, and outdoor metal furniture. I ran the business for ten years, quite successfully, but when my lease ran out, they wanted to raise my rent beyond all common sense, so I sold out.

"Now I'm building a place up in the mountains where I'm raising a few head of cattle."

"What are your thoughts as you look back?"

"It's a shame about Boyington—he was a great leader who hasn't had much success with his personal life. He betrayed his former comrades by allowing that TV show to present such a distorted image of them. I resent the characterization of us as 'misfits' and 'screwballs.' Actually, Boyington was the only one of us who ever had any trouble.

"I remember him conning bottles of whiskey out of the new pilots. One time, I saw him stoned at 2:30 in the morning and then sober enough at 4:30 to take his mission. He was an amazing man.

"The hardest thing was getting up in the morning and seeing the empty cots. You got to wondering whose cot would be vacant next; perhaps it would be yours.

"Our Black Sheep Squadron was a class operation all the way. No other squadron could come close to it in spirit."

Ned Corman

Still slim and dapper though graying at the temples, Ned Corman visited me in my apartment in Honolulu. He had recently reached mandatory retirement age with Pan Am after having flown 35 years for that airline, his last few years as Captain in 747s on the Pacific routes: Hawaii, Japan, Hong Kong, Singapore, Indonesia, Australia.

Ned's high school graduating class in Walker Township, Pennsylvania, consisted of four boys and four girls. He went on to Penn State, graduating in 1942 with a major in agronomy. The youngest son, raised on a farm, it looked as if he would come back to be a farmer. But the Civilian Pilot Training program caught his eye in the junior year. When he soloed, he found it was the first time he'd ever done anything he really enjoyed, although he had played soccer and "chased lots of girls."

"After I graduated, I went into the Navy preflight program and was in a group of pilots who got to Espiritu Santo when the Black Sheep came back from their first combat tour. Fred Losch was the only one of us who'd had any real time in the Corsair. I'd scrounged just one hour; the rest had zilch.

"We'd all heard of Pappy, and I was happy to be selected. My attitude hasn't changed to this day. I've never failed to be impressed with the Black Sheep's innovative approach to any aspect of flying or combat.

"One day, for instance, I heard this racket down by the lagoon, and here was John Bolt with a 50-caliber machine gun strapped down. He was firing into oil drums in the lagoon to determine which of the three types of ammunition we used caused them to burn. It was the incendiary, so we changed the loading to two incendiary, one armor-piercing, two incendiary, one tracer—instead of the standard one of each. When they got the results of the second tour, the Navy changed their loads to ours. It just bears out one aspect that hasn't been stressed enough: the contribution of the Black Sheep to combat out there, with no credit."

"What were your first feelings about the overall picture? Why did some get shot down? What was special about us?"

"With the little time we'd had in the Corsair, I think everyone was apprehensive. I was scared shitless. We felt better being with experienced pilots, but I recall the day after Boyington got shot down. We went into Rabaul Harbor, looking for him, and flew around the damn thing. I don't know that I've ever been more scared in my life. You know, most of the heavy AA was up on the ridges around the harbor, and they couldn't depress those guns, so we were flying *under* that fire; the tracers looked like latticework above our heads. I've often wondered what we'd have done if we had found him.

"It seems to me that in the last two weeks of that tour, we lost eight pilots, the majority experienced. I'm a great believer in fate and said: 'There but for the grace of God go I.'

"I fell for a decoy when we were patrolling Bougainville, one of my first missions. I strafed what I thought was a coastwise freighter and was ready to go up when the whole shoreline exploded at me. Strictly a trap. I kicked rudder, sprayed the shoreline, and ducked down in the trees. My division went home without me, thinking I'd been shot down. I was sure I had been hit—tracers and heavy stuff going over the cockpit and under the plane. After I landed, I looked but couldn't find one arrow [bullet hole] in the airplane.

"I knew we were outnumbered, but I think we had a very distinct reason for being in that war. I didn't think about winning or losing; I just knew damn well we'd better win! I didn't think we had any choice.

"Now I've flown a lot of soldiers on R and R out of Korea and Vietnam, and I felt that those guys in 'police actions' lacked a reason for being there. Somewhere along the line, the powers that be failed to sell the American people, especially on Vietnam."

Corman shook his head.

"The Black Sheep had the same numbers of planes and pilots as other squadrons, but the CO had his plane, and the Exec had his, and nobody touched those planes. What a difference! I remember going to our ready room and it was a recital. The Officer of the Day would assign a new plane to Boyington, and he would go and erase the number, giving it to one of the new guys, saying: 'Give me one of those old klunkers. I'll fly circles around them anyway.'

"I never ran into that anywhere else. Ours was a free-thinking, free-speaking outfit. If you had some views, you expressed them. Whether they were accepted or not was immaterial—they were heard. You never got that in other squadrons, and to me that was the greatest difference.

"If I had time, I could remember the tours to Sydney, too. God, it was like a reprieve from the electric chair. You were down there—I won't tell on you if you won't tell on me! We had a camaraderie, a wonderful group of guys.

"That was one of the most formative periods of my life. I think I

Ned Corman

Henry Allan McCartney

grew up; my sense of values changed. When I went out there, I thought I was an agnostic—there was possibly a greater power, but I felt I could pretty well control my fate. Then those eight pilots shot down; me without a scratch. One day, I asked Chaplain Paetznick if I could join his services. He said, 'That's what I'm here for,' and I went in and prayed, for one reason: I was suddenly out of control. I felt that somebody else had control of my life, and I don't believe that I have felt that way since.

"You know, Frank, it sounds awfully smug, but if I had it to do over, I'd probably have done it the same way. I've had a good life, had friendships I wouldn't trade for anything. My wartime flying led into my life as a commercial pilot. I got letters of acceptance on the same day from Pan Am and to become a career officer in the Marines Corps. I chose Pam Am and have never regretted my choice."

Citrus Grower:

Henry Allan McCartney

In order to see Hank McCartney, I drove the 100 miles from Orlando's airport to Vero Beach, a pleasant retirement community close to Florida's famous Indian River citrus industry. Vero Beach, population 16,000, has an additional claim to fame as home of the Los Angeles Dodgers' spring training camp.

Hank bought 80 acres of property at the right time, developed it over a number of years and through hard work into a profitable citrus grove, and sold out in 1979. He's a respected and active member of his community and so genteel that the information operator could find neither a "Hank" nor a "Henry" McCartney. Henry A. "Hank" Mc-Cartney had become "Allan" McCartney.

Hank owns an acre on the side of a mountain in North Carolina where he spends his summers. He is active in civic and church affairs in both states: member of his church's executive committee, chairman of the budget committee, member of the Rotary Club and the ambulance squad. And he still has time to do some woodworking.

Entering the service via the Navy V-5 program in July 1941 upon his graduation from college, Hank went overseas as a dive bomber pilot; flew a syllabus to qualify as a fighter pilot, and had two tours at Guadalcanal before joining the Black Sheep.

"Frankly, I can't recall the machinery by which I was selected. I do know there are immeasurable benefits derived from the mix of experienced with new pilots. When a kid comes on the air and says, 'Hey, they're shooting at me,' you can say, 'It's all right. It's perfectly legal for them to do that.' You can help a fellow over it.

"After the Black Sheep, I came back here to Vero Beach to join the Night Fighter Squadron. I was here for two and a half years. In May 1946 I went to Cherry Point, and later to China and Honolulu. I was in Washington for almost two years in the Division of Aviation, then in England as an exchange pilot with the RAF. That was a wonderful year, 1949 to 1950. From there to Cherry Point, then Quantico as an instructor in the Senior School, 1956—1959. Next, three years as naval attaché in Jakarta, Indonesia, to the Air War College in Maxwell; to Japan; to Willow Grove commanding the Reserve detachment until my retirement in 1966 as a colonel. I had 26 years, with never what I considered to be a bad assignment. My progression was such that with each new job came new challenges. I had a good time all the way.

"In terms of personal satisfaction, the diplomatic tour in Jakarta during the transition just prior to the removal of Sukarno was interesting, fulfilling, and really challenging. I enjoyed the RAF—a remarkable group of people.

"The service today? The biggest trouble, as I see it, is that there isn't any leadership. I was glad to retire because I was getting to the point where I was going to have some confrontations. You know there's a point where if you're going to make General Officer, you got to go along a little bit, and I was getting a little too brittle. The command had been diluted. Staffs were nameless, faceless sorts of guys sitting way off somewhere trying to tell you what to do, but they never had to answer for anything.

"It's interesting that the Commandant of the Marine Corps now [1981], Bob Barrow, was my operations officer when I was Chief of Staff of Task Force 79. He was fantastic. He was a lieutenant colonel then. If they make up their minds to turn it around, he can do it."

Marion March

Marion J. "Rusty" March was one of the older pilots in the Black Sheep Squadron. A 1938 graduate of Stanford University in mechanical engineering, he had already started on a career when a friend talked him into becoming a Marine Corps flyer. He was an instructor at Corpus Christi, Texas, when the war commenced.

Now retired after 20 years of service with Santa Clara County as a mechanical engineer, he lives in San Jose, California. He drove up to meet me in San Francisco.

Rusty had joined us just before our second tour.

"I was scared from the first flight on. We'd go on these fighter sweeps, in planes not always in top condition. I was usually on the tail end, and I'd think, 'Boyington really knows' because he'd get up there and you'd hear old Pappy say, 'Tally ho!' and see that lead plane peel off, and you knew you were in good position. He always brought those fighter sweeps in so that they had altitude advantage, coming out of the sun at the Japanese.

"With some of the other leaders you'd get a mess—planes milling around and the Zeros making runs on us instead of us on them. Not with Boyington; he had a sense—not only experience but a certain aptitude. Personally, he may not have been the greatest guy in the world, but when he got up in the air, he had real aptitude. A lot of others did, too, but I have to exclude myself. I didn't really have that knack. I'd see a Zero and get buck fever.

"After the Black Sheep, I was Duty Officer at Air Command, Northern Solomons, on Bougainville. It was a lousy tour—just strafing palm trees around Rabaul. The crash that sent me home was the result of a night flight. I landed without having my wheels locked down. They had a level with a knob you had to push all the way through the quadrant so the handle would latch—if you didn't, the thing would hang. Normally, it would have been O.K. anyway, but this plane had a bomb rack on it for bombing missions, a long pipe bolted to the underside. I started to skid on my belly, and this damn pipe snagged in the Marsden matting, jammed back and up into the fuselage, and wiped out the lower end of the gas tank. It rolled up, and the thing flamed like a big blowtorch through the cockpit. The plane finally stopped, cockpit 90 degrees, nose pointing at a bunch of guys on the embankment watching who was frying in the flames.

Marion March

Robert McClurg

"Without any knowledge of what I was doing, I flipped my safety harness and dove over the side. Chin broken, face torn up; my mustache and eyebrows burned off, burned all over my face; left wrist burned where the jacket and glove didn't meet. The funniest thing, my shoe was cooked so that the leather sole was cracked. I had a third degree burn on my left calf and up my leg. The meat wagon and fire truck found me there, trying to beat out the flames around me.

"I spent a couple of months at the Naval Hospital. They gave me a couple of skin grafts on my leg, one on my face, and shipped me home to the Naval Hospital at Seattle, where they finished the skin grafting and then sent me to Parris Island. I finished the war there and got out."

Businessman and Sportsman

Robert McClurg

Bob McClurg picked me up at the Syracuse airport and drove through a snowstorm to his magnificent estate in a wooded glen at Cedarville Ridge, New York. The pungent odor of pine needles from a brightly lighted tree in the corner of the sunken living room, and the sparkle and crackle of the log in the fireplace, emphasized that Christmas was not far away. The picture window looked over a snow-covered porch where birds were dinner guests in feeders. The living Christmas-card view continued down a slope and through the trees into a canyon, where a stream meandered through the property. Although he's a hunter and fisherman (the freezer in his garage is loaded with game: venison, pheasants, geese, ducks, grouse, trout), Bob assured me he never hunts the deer frequenting his own place.

The downstairs den walls are covered with souvenirs of his Black Sheep days, and some of his fishing expeditions.

McClurg is part owner of a highly successful agency that represents a dozen lines of plumbing and heating equipment. He is semi-retired now, concentrating on his golf, hunting, and fishing. Although graying, he still has plenty of hair; he is lean, alert, and energetic.

Already accepted by the Naval Air Corps in 1942, he left his mother to receive his college degree for him. Captain Eddie Rickenbacker was the commencement speaker. She went up to him and said: "My son Bobby is a flyer too. Do you know him?" Rickenbacker answered that oh, yes, he knew him. Bob was shipped to Hawaii with only 21 hours in fighter planes, never having made a carrier landing in a fighter.

The colonel there asked him, "How the hell did you get here?"

"I told him, 'By ship, sir,' " McClurg related.

"He said, 'You dummy, how could you get here with a logbook like that? . . . You're worth nothing to nobody. You'll have to stay here and we'll train you.'

"Two days later, I was on a plane to the South Pacific. I had my first flight in a Corsair and demolished part of a palm tree when I took off. I managed to get it down all right, but every time they'd pick up pilots from the replacement pool, they'd reject me for guys with 120 to 160 hours in fighters.

"When I was transferred, Pappy looked in my logbook and took a couple of us out to fly. He said, 'Mac, you fly like a bag of piss. You'll never get anywhere till somebody teaches you something.'

"I was grateful to him for that because I'd begun to feel like another bump on a log, and thought I'd never get home.

"The first air raid on Munda, when we were sleeping in a Quonset with mosquito nets around the four posts of each bunk, two of us got tangled up, smashed heads, and dragged the nets with us as we scrambled on all fours to the foxhole. We rolled into it, and somebody jumped on top of us.

"After the Black Sheep I went to Green Island, flew a few escort missions and strafing. I came home, did some instrument training, went to several schools, then back to the west coast to go overseas again. The colonel called me in: 'You're going to stay in when the war's over, aren't you?'

"I said 'no.' It turned out that you had to stay in a couple more years if you went overseas. But I had enough points, so I got out and went to work for a company that manufactures plumbing and bathroom fixtures.

"I worked there for 15 years, learned the business thoroughly, and struck out on my own, starting small and gradually expanding. We did about $2 million gross last year.

"In the past couple of years, I've backed off and worked my son into the business.

"Looking back, I'd say that if I hadn't been part of the Black Sheep

Squadron, my life would have been only partially fulfilled. There was camaraderie other squadrons didn't have. Tears come to my eyes now when I hear the Black Sheep song. All the ditties—Fisher, Bragdon, Bolt, Sims, and all of us singing together—nothing like it. Like that song: 'If you lose your airspeed now you'll come down from forty thou, and you'll wind up in a rowboat at Rabaul.' Paul Mullen's contribution.

"It really came back to me, Frank, at the reunion, how much you had done to help us put our squadron in the forefront—unbeknownst to us at the time because we were all playing with our airplanes. Pappy did a hell of a job; between you and Pappy and the rest, that's why people will remember the Black Sheep.

"If I should die tomorrow, I've lived a great life."

Professor

William Heier

William D. "Junior" Heier commenced his wartime service with the RCAF because he had only a high school education, and the U.S. required two years college for its airmen.

Junior retired from the U.S. Marine Corps 20 years later as a Lieutenant Colonel with a master's degree in accounting controllership. Eighteen months after that, he had his doctorate in management. Now he is a professor of management at Arizona State University in Tempe, a pleasant city of about 100,000.

Two and a half hours after I left Chicago's four-degree weather, he picked me up at the sunny Phoenix airport and drove me to his delightful home in a quiet residential area near the university. Oranges, grapefruit, and tangelos grew profusely in his back yard.

His office/den walls were covered with Black Sheep mementos. I asked why he'd joined up. "It was a matter of patriotism," he said. "My dad and mother agreed we would eventually be in the war, and I was concerned about how the British were doing, all by themselves, so I thought I'd help them, since I already had my civilian pilot's license.

William Heier

Jim Hill

"After Pearl Harbor a bunch of us Americans asked to be transferred back. After Navy training, I was introduced to the Corsair on
Espiritu Santo.

"I think everybody was nervous. You'd have to be stupid not to be
afraid of the unknown, but we were eager to get at them, to test our
skills. I was comfortable in that Corsair, never afraid of going into a
fight because it was a tremendous airplane.

"When the squadron broke up, I went to Green Island; later, I came
home but stayed in as a regular, got married, was transferred to
helicopters, and went to Korea. I finished out the Korean War in jets.
Back in the States I had a series of varied assignments: CO of a jet
squadron; TAC Squadron Commander at Cherry Point. In 1959, I went
to Washington and stayed until I retired in 1962.

"I started night school when I was in Quantico in 1949—averaging
four nights a week, year after year, taking six units every semester—
planning my career in accounting.

"Frankly, once you get your 20 years in and are eligible to retire,
you're working for half pay, because you could get the other half even if
you're not there. Besides, I was coming up a colonel, and under the
rule at the time, if you made colonel, you had to stay another five years.
I'd have been 47 by then. It's not easy to get a teaching job at a big school
at that age, even with a Ph.D. So I got out and started my second career.

"Now, I'm debating about retiring here. I've been chairman and
general manager of our credit union for over 16 years, and I was
chairman of the Arizona State Credit Union Board for six years. I could
take over and administer one of those organizations. I've been offered a
sabbatical proposal to study the shift from government financing of
pension plans back to the private sector. If I did that, it would mean a
year in foreign countries studying what's been done there, but I'd have
to stay at least another year at the university after I came back. I'd sort of
considered retiring in 1983 at age 62.

'Incidentally, you're responsible for one of my goals, Frank. Years
ago, you told me you were saving $1,000 a month. That's what I chuck
into deferred tax income."

"Fine, but one of these days you've got to plan how to spend it so
you don't end up leaving a million dollars."

"For the kids? Forget it, Frank. Our ideal has been to spend the last
nickel and drop dead."

Jim Hill

Tall, slender, energetic Jim Hill drove over from his home in Skokie to meet me at the hotel at Chicago's O'Hare Airport. Other than a slight graying at the temples, he didn't look a whole lot different from before.

"I'd originally intended to make a career of the Marine Corps. But then the war was over; I'd been overseas for a year, back in the States for six months, and back out again for another six. They were talking about adding another year to that if I became a regular. I figured that was too long to be away from my new bride."

Released from active duty, Jim went to work selling fire and safety equipment for a distributor. He is now regional sales manager for a six-state area.

"I got into aviation because my best friend was a Marine pilot. He was killed at Guadalcanal about two months before I got out to the South Pacific. I had about ten hours in the Corsair before our first combat tour. We were all charged up—scared, but looking forward to it with a certain amount of excitement.

"I saw my first Zero in my rear view mirror, and he was shooting at me. I rolled over and dove out, just as I was told to do. Coming back from my first combat hop, my engine kept cutting out. When it got so bad that I was down to 1,500 feet, I decided to bail out. I got out of my harness and had one foot up on the canopy when the engine cut back in and I stepped back into the plane.

"One time, flying cover for B-24s over Rabaul, the P-38s never showed, leaving eight Corsairs for 25 bombers. It was like a movie: some B-24s going down, guys bailing out, us spotting the nearest Zero and attempting to head it off. One B-24, one or two motors out, hit the trees on his final approach coming home.

"The Black Sheep made all the difference in the world. We got along well. Maybe it was the excitement, or being there at the right time with plenty of action. We became very close in a very short time. But we lost a lot of fellows. Like Bob Alexander—we roomed together when we first got out there, and he impressed me. I mean, he could do more things with that Corsair than I've seen anybody do. I couldn't believe we'd lost him that day.

"After the Black Sheep, I went to Green Island, then home. I took a lot of pride in the Marine Corps. I look back on those four active years, and really, with that background, any problems that I faced later in life, I thought, 'Man, this is nothing compared to what it was like in World War II.' I can remember those years and the things that happened very vividly, whereas, gee, a ten-year span after that really wasn't very interesting."

"Yes, after Guadalcanal and Munda and Bougainville and Rabaul—things get pretty dull, talking about changing the baby's diapers," I said.

"I'll never forget those days." Jim nodded as he spoke.

Business Planner

Henry Bourgeois

Henry Bourgeois met me at Newark Airport.

Hank could not only fly like an eagle; he had the eyes of an eagle. The rest of the squadron acknowledged that he could spot enemy planes many seconds before anyone else did. That capability undoubtedly saved a lot of lives, giving his flight that slight position advantage so vital in aerial combat.

His eagle eyes have dimmed now, but he is still alert and energetic, very much the business executive as Director of Business Planning for Kearfott Division of the Singer Corporation. "I'm also a farmer now," he said. "We bought 90 acres in Maryland, including a 200-year-old house and 1,800 feet of waterfront. We've planted most of it in grapes and hope to have a vineyard by the time I retire, which will be before long."

Hank was apparently born to do everything early: a flight at age seven; first plane crash at eleven; soloing at thirteen; youngest in the Navy V-5 program; and at 20 years and nine months, the youngest Marine officer ever commissioned.

"I sailed from San Diego on the *Lurline* with Pappy Boyington and six or seven other pilots as replacements. I went on up to Guadalcanal and then back to Santo, checked out in Corsairs, and went back to

Henry Bourgeois

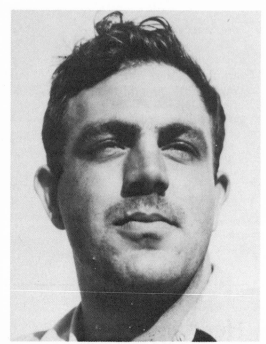

Alfred Johnson

Guadalcanal for my second combat tour. I was more scared after it was over than before, but I got more confidence as time went on and became more cautious the more men we lost. I began to see there was more to it than adventure.

"As one of the experienced Black Sheep pilots, I was a division leader responsible for training the new men. With eight experienced combat pilots and a total of 28, we had more than enough to lead each four-plane division.

"After my first and only Black Sheep tour, I trained pilots for a while in Green Cove Springs, then went to Quantico for Junior Amphibious Warfare School, then to San Diego, Coronado, and El Toro. When the war ended, I was sent to Okinawa to join the Fifth Marines. We went into China; as Forward Air Controller, I was with the Division Commander on the first jeep into Peking.

"We didn't know what the Japanese were going to do. Our job was to repatriate them to Japan: disarm them, get them out of there. We had to make sure all the people who'd been locked up, the Embassy people and so forth, got out and back into operation.

"I was there a year and a half, then went to Tientsin and took over from John Begert as Air Officer for the Division. I got involved with OSS, flying agents into Manchuria, picking them up, and other sneaky things.

"When I got back to the States, I was at El Toro for several years, then at Electronic Officers School in Memphis, where I finally got my degree in electrical engineering. I went to Korea for a year or so and came back to serve on the Marine Corps Development Center for two or three years.

"I retired in 1961 when my eyes went bad; I had three boys growing up, and decided to try my luck on the outside. I went to work for General Precision.

"Kearfott provides guidance control and navigation systems for anything: airplanes, missiles, spaceships. We do planning, short- and long-range, for new products and business areas, deciding where we should invest our funds in developing new products and trying to forecast where the Defense Department is going and where we fit into that picture.

"In 1973, Mildred and I went to Japan. Our company, Singer, owns part of Mitsubishi Precision, and I went to do some work on strategic planning. The director of marketing, Suwo, was a retired major general of the Japanese Air Force. We got to talking one night, and it turned out that he'd been a squadron commander on Bougainville. We had long talks that resumed when he came to the States later. He'd brought his logbook and I got mine out. Comparing flights and dates, we found we'd been shooting at each other! He got transferred back to Japan, and became head of training the Kamikaze pilots. He claimed to have shot down 27 or 28 American planes. He said they wondered where all the American planes were coming from.

"He was quite a man. He was a hunter, and so am I, so I took him to my place in Maryland. We had a great day of duck shooting; it was lousy weather, and the ducks were flying. I took him to dinner that night, and he said, 'Hank-san, I'm sure glad I didn't shoot you down!'

Travel Agent

Alfred Johnson

Al "Shorty" Johnson drove from his office through the snow to talk to me at Bob McClurg's home in Syracuse, New York. Al owns a successful travel agency which, in addition to making him a comfortable living, has afforded him the opportunity to travel over most of the world. Al is still alert, energetic, and as quip-tongued as he was with the Black Sheep.

"The day after Pearl Harbor, I went across the street from where I worked to sign up for the Army Air Corps. I filled out quite a few piles of papers. I thought I was another Lindbergh: I already had a private pilot's license for a seaplane, so I kept asking about flying and trying to tell them about my seaplane experience, but they kept ignoring my remarks. Some little corporal with a big cigar kept handing me more papers. I thought, 'I don't like this outfit,' and I rolled the papers in a ball and popped him right in the face and walked out.

"Up the street I saw a sign: 'Navy.' I think it was 181 Broadway in New York City. I told them I had a seaplane license, and they said: 'My God, just a minute,' and called a chief over: 'This gentleman has a seaplane license!' I thought they'd give me a plane that night!

"They gave me a physical, and a lieutenant said, 'You have everything, except you need a tooth filled.'

"I said, 'O.K., I'll get it filled.'

"He said, 'How would you like to do it now?'

"I said, 'Good,' and we took an elevator to the next floor. There was a dentist. The Lieutenant said, 'Doc, I have a great prospect here.'

"Whambo, the next thing I know, I'm downstairs again, holding my jaw. 'Raise your hand,' and that was it!

"Then they said: 'We're going to let you finish your semester at New York University; then you'll have your two full years of college, and you can go in June. We're going to send you to preflight training.' The first preflight battalion was sent to the University of North Carolina at Chapel Hill. We were on Movietone News. But first, we got off the train at Greensboro, and there're these guys looking like my Uncle Mose, a forest ranger, with those funny hats.

"One of them was screaming and cussing bloody blue, and they seemed madder than hell about something. A guy from Syracuse and I were good buddies, still are. I asked, 'Hey, what the hell is he so mad about?'

"He said, 'I don't know who he's yelling at.'

"So we looked around behind us on the train. That set off the second stage, and the guy told us in no uncertain terms: *we* were the objects of his affection; he was a Marine drill instructor. I thought they'd been sent to drive the bus or pick up the luggage or something. He marched us to the buses, and when we got to Chapel Hill, there was a big open field with a desk at one end, guys signing up. It started to rain.

"They said to put down our gear, formed us into what they called platoons, and gave us close-order drill—and we still had civilian clothes on.

"Some guy said, 'We've had it. There's only so many openings. We're gonna be the grunts, gravel crunchers, or jungle bunnies. We're gonna get a rifle and be on our way.'

"That set off the DIs again, but they finally signed us. Preflight was three months of nothing but physical activity, Navy regulations, and hikes, hikes, hikes. We got sent to New Orleans for Elimination Flight Training with two strikes on us because of all the publicity. They called us the 'supermen.'

"I got to Espiritu Santo the end of September and saw my first Corsair. I didn't know how to get in it, since I'm so short; I thought you had to run and jump and climb up the side. Then one of the mechs showed me how you push this thing and the flap drops, put your foot here, your hand here, and that's it. I asked him, 'Where's the pilot's manual?' He thought that was funny.

"The first week, we had two killed out of our 15, mostly ferrying planes back and forth to Guadalcanal. One rainy night somebody came to our hut and said: 'You guys are now in the Black Sheep.' We figured this is it; we'd heard all those wild stories. There's $10,000 going home to mama. If they needed us, then half the squadron must have been wiped out.

"We reported to the Dallas hut in the rain. Standing there in our ponchos, we saw this big red-headed guy that had this other guy by the belt—it was you handling Pappy. You'd caught him outside in the rain, and his hands were swinging back and forth. We said, 'Uh-oh, that's the skipper. We're dead!'

"I'd come back from a hop and ask the mech, 'What's that switch for?'

"He'd say, 'Come on, Lieutenant, you're kidding me.'

"I'd say, 'I'm not gonna touch it. Maybe it jettisons the engine.'

"We'd touch something, and they'd say, 'Forget that, that's only in cold weather.' That's how we learned.

"I went back to the States and was released from active duty, but stayed in the Reserves. I had a job with Goodyear, traveling in 29 states, and got in my drill wherever I happened to be. But they stopped that and transferred me to the Volunteer Reserves, throwing me out of my home squadron. About four months later, they got called to Korea, so I guess they did me a favor.

"I joined Colonial Airlines, and they merged with Eastern Airlines; I was with them for 11 years. In 1962, I bought a rundown travel agency. I thought I'd bought a hobby, but after a hairy six months I got it back on its feet, and now it's doing well.

"It's been pleasant, but I wouldn't trade the Black Sheep experience for anything. It was an extension of what they say in the Marine Corps: 'I always wanted to be a Marine' and 'there's nothing as good as a Marine or even close to it.'

"We were a band of brothers. I've never seen another service that will get together and stick together, even if we don't know each other. Once a Marine, always a Marine."

Tom Emrich

W. T. "Long Tom" Emrich is an internationalist. A commercial airline pilot (a Captain with TWA), he had better than a girl in every port: he had property in every port—or at least in Spain, Arizona, and Hawaii. He's been flitting from one to the other since he retired from TWA in 1981 and is now president of Global Enterprises, a firm that's developing an area in Colorado.

Tom talked to me in my apartment in Honolulu. He has lost most of the beautiful head of hair that was his pride and joy, but he is still erect and alert. Tom had wanted to be a pilot from his high school days. He'd spent two years at Wentworth Military Academy in Lexington, Missouri, then joined the Navy V-5 program, graduating as Aviation Cadet.

After another year of training, he was shipped to the South Pacific in mid-1943.

"I considered myself lucky to be assigned to a squadron with experienced people in it. I'd never flown a Corsair before, and there, I got only 20 or 30 hours.

"Late one afternoon Fisher and I were sent on an alert; we'd never flown at night. Pretty soon it's getting darker and darker. He called me: 'Do you know where the light switches are?'

"I said, 'It beats me, Lieutenant.' We had to fish around, and you didn't have much room to maneuver, but we finally found all the lights.

"When we landed, Fisher said, 'Well, I guess we checked out the airplane for night flying.'

"In the beginning, I didn't know enough to be scared—later on, I could get dry-mouthed. Sometimes, you could tell that the land-based pilots had limited experience. Like the Japanese Zeros doing slow rolls while they were escorting their bombers. It seemed pretty stupid to me, doing slow rolls when somebody was likely to be shooting them down. Maybe it was their way of impressing us with their ability to fly, like two Samurai prancing around waving their swords. But it didn't impress us.

"Afterward, I went to Green Island, back to Cherry Point, to Parris Island, and then to Congaree Field in Columbia, South Carolina. By that time, the war was about over. It was there I met a fellow who knew the Chief Pilot of TWA. We took an SNJ [training plane] and flew to Washington, D.C., for an interview, and I had a job.

Tom Emrich

Chris Magee

"On 16 October 1945 when I got out, I called him, and he explained how the seniority system worked. I told him to put me in the first class, and I drove straight through from Columbia to Wichita, spent the night at my mother's, and arrived in Kansas City in time to report for class that morning. That way, I got a lot of seniority on the guys who took time off before looking for a job. As it was, a lot got in ahead of me because the Army Air Corps released them earlier.

"I stayed in the Organized Reserves and got called up for Korea. Because of my airline experience, I was sent to Honolulu to fly transport, moving supplies to Korea; then to Japan supporting the First Marine Air Wing over Korea. I was released after 14 months, stayed in the Reserves. I started getting checked out for Captain with TWA and had to move to New York. It was difficult to make the schedule commuting to Anacostia [District of Columbia]; one day the squadron CO made an example of me for needing to leave the weekend drill early for a flight. I was transferred to the inactive reserve."

By 1955, Emrich was a TWA Captain, then worked his way up to flying the 747. As a respected senior pilot, he took a lot of flak over the TV Black Sheep show.

"I was disappointed in that show; it made us all out to be dumbbells, somebody nobody wanted, and through the grace of God and Greg Boyington, he took us over and saved us. That wasn't the case at all. It was just that everything fell together—the command in the right place at the right time. We were very fortunate in winding up where we were for that particular job."

Free Spirit

Chris Magee

Chris "Wildman" Magee was perhaps the ultimate combat fighter pilot. Utterly fearless and totally aggressive, he had the knack of knowing where the action was, plus complete mastery of the airplane; he could make it do things no other pilot could. His record of nine Zeros was exceeded in our squadron only by Boyington's total.

Maggie turned out to be one of the most difficult Black Sheep to locate. When I finally found him, I understood why. He'd had a most colorful career.

After the war, he'd joined the Israeli Air Force during their war of independence. Following that service and his return to the States, he had run into some difficulty with the law; as a result, it took the assistance of my friend, the Chief of Police of Los Angeles, and the FBI to locate him. Finally, I received a letter from Maggie.

Greetings, Frank,

Strange how a few words can do more to reveal something of the nature of time than all the equations a team of Einsteins could formulate in a lifetime of blackboard gymnastics. It isn't so much that words throw a bridge across a considerable gulf between "now" and "then" events as it is that they collapse all intervening activities below consciousness, and unite the "now" with the "then" as if by some alchemical implosion, some magic infusion.

Such, somehow dramatized, was the effect of your letters, which I picked up recently when I dropped by my former pad in Chicago Southside to check the possibility that mail may have strayed that way.

I've been to Florida a couple of times this year, roving the Gulf Coast, into the Everglades, and down through the Keys. And Westward Ho! too. Colorado, etc.

A change of pace after six years as editor/writer/reporter for a Chicago community newspaper of approximately 30,000 circulation.

Aside from two days and nights of intense involvement every week, I was free to set my own pace, so there was some compensation in terms of freedom, which I needed.

There was further compensation in the form of a discipline imposed by the ever-present demand of the next deadline. But once a week for six years is a bit too much of that kind of compensation for me.

The paper was sold and the new owner brought in his own editor, so I'm free of the printer's ink mold, and have spent a number of months recuperating from a bad case of brainlock, induced by overexposure to journalese.

Before that job, I edited another community newspaper for a couple of years.

Previous to these forays into the legitimate, I was a house guest of J. Edgar Hoover at his resorts in Atlanta and Leavenworth, where due to SNAFU bureaucratic behavior in the manner of record keeping, teamed with a paranoiac penchant for secrecy, my durance vile went considerably beyond what had evidently been intended.

During my sojourn, I taught a wide variety of high school classes, picked up some 80 college credits via extension courses, and became editor of Leavenworth's quarterly magazine, "New Era," a slick, 50-plus-page organ with pretensions to literary excellence. In fact, it was included in a survey and index of literary "Little Magazines." We also had close and friendly ties with Engel's famed Writers' Workshop at the State University of Iowa.

Some of my work was reprinted in other publications around the world that are oriented to more esoteric fare. For instance, the Sai Aurobino Ashram in Pondicherry, India. I was deep into the psycho-spiritual thing long before the recent boom began. And I *don't* mean the Tim Leary, Baba Ram Das, Allen Ginsberg, Holy Man circuit bit, or any of this swooning over Eastern mysticism. The West has its own tradition, only touched upon by C.G. Jung.

Anyway, retreating further yet, timewise, I was active in the Caribbean area in the mid-1950s, and before that was working with construction crews in Greenland, above the Arctic Circle, setting up the air warning network. Earlier, in 1949, I was in Aspen, Colorado, tape recording highlights of the Goethe Bicentennial Celebration, the event that kicked off Aspen's ascent to an off-the-beaten-path cultural center. Albert Schweitzer ('Reverence for Life') was guest of honor; his first absence from Africa in 25 years.

In 1948, I was flying ME-109-Gs for the Hagannah in Israel (while Herr Hitler did snap rolls in his Nazi hell. Must have been a blowtorch on the bollocks to hear about Jews in Messerschmitts!). But that wasn't until I went through a cloak-and-dagger underground smuggling operation in New York and Europe.

So, that's a fair abbreviation of my post–Black Sheep days. Although there are those who would say, cynically, of course, that for me they never ended, that they in fact became more than an upside down euphemism, more than a play-name adopted by a bunch of great guys whom it would be almost miraculous to reminisce with over a vat of milk punch.

Well, Frank, it was a high, hearing from you. I'd enjoy being on the receiving end of any other information you seine from the stream of years.

Chris enclosed one of his own published poems, entitled "Postscript from One Who, Like His Age, Died Young" and prefaced by the following note: "Several years after World War II, the wreck of a U.S. Marine Corps fighter plane was discovered in the interior jungle of New Ireland, in the Solomons, by a former Royal Australian Navy Coast Watcher. A jungle kit was recovered from the cockpit of the Corsair; among its items of survival gear was a wax-sealed, fungus-resistant plastic folder containing a box of ammunition for a .45 automatic and a sheet of paper with these lines."

> I have skimmed the ragged edge of lightning death
> And torn from bloody flesh of sky a thunder song.
> Across the nakedness of virgin space
> I've blistered my frozen hand in feathered ice
> And dared angelic wrath to smash
> The snarling will of my demon steed.

Far above sun-glint on winded spume,
High executor of laws no man has made,
I've welded Samurai knights into fiery tombs
And hurled them down like the plumed Minoan
Far down the searing heights to punch
Their livid crates in the sea.

'Enemies,' you say. They were not mine.
More than blood brothers, I swear,
With tawny skin and warrior eye.
Bushido-bred for hell-strife joy.
Much closer my kin, my race than those
Who cud-chew their lives can ever be.

'War-lover,' you say, 'sadist, psychotic'—
That sick cycle of canned clichés masking
Your lust for eternity fettered to time.
Go, epigonic pygmies, make peace with hell,
Drag the myths of our ancient might
Through the miserable muck of a cringer's dream.

What could you know
Who have never heard
The soaring song of the Valkyries,
Felt thunder-gods jousting with livid peaks:
You who have never dared to walk the razor
Across the zenith of your peevish soul?"

Subsequent letters to Chris's address have come back marked
"Return to Sender—Unable to Forward." Possibilities as to where he is
and what he's doing are endless. He may be in Central America; he
may be involved in another secret mission somewhere in the world; in
view of the Middle East situation, he could very well be back with the
Israeli Air Force; he may be in Africa. Like Kipling's Cat Who Walked by
Himself, "He went through the wet, wild woods, waving his wild tail,
and walking his wild lone. But he never told anybody."

He may have passed on to Fighter Pilot's Heaven. I certainly hope
not. The world has desperate need for free spirits, even those who
suffer occasional aberrations.

Rollie Rinabarger

To reach Rollie Rinabarger's home in Tulelake, California, I drove north from San Francisco almost to the Oregon border, then turned east through a national wildlife refuge, home of some two million waterfowl. I passed thousands of ducks, geese, swans, and other water species, as well as quail, pheasant, and deer.

Tulelake, population 900, is situated in the center of a major rice-growing area, where the clean air is cooled by the 4,000-foot altitude. Hunting and fishing are excellent; local residents usually have a side of venison in their freezers. Nearby is the hundreds-of-years-old Lava Beds National Monument containing ancient petroglyphs and Indian pictographs. Rollie's directions led me to his home in the middle of this relatively unspoiled mountain utopia.

I talked to him in the garage/office from which he runs his active electrical contracting business. During the season, he also flies a crop-dusting plane over the ricefields. The walls displayed memorabilia of Black Sheep days, which for him had ended in a hospital. On 26 September 1943 he had been attacked by a swarm of Zeros over Kahili and his plane severely shot up. A fire in the cockpit and a shell that hit him in the back, shattered on a knife at his hip, and lodged fragments in his back and left leg did not prevent his getting back to us—but only temporarily—for our Sydney trip.

"I was sent to the States on a hospital ship, and in Schumacher Hospital they were still picking pieces of metal out of me months later. Afterward, I was sent to El Toro, then Santa Barbara. I was there when the war ended; I was released from active duty then but stayed in the reserves.

"In 1946 my father and I bought an existing electrical contracting business. Now, though, I'm getting to the point where I can't do some of the heavy lifting and crawling required, so I'm taking just the work I want. I've been doing the crop dusting for over 30 years, since 1951.

"The Black Sheep were a fine group of people. I thought we had a tremendous combat leader. I tried to emulate him when I had my own squadron. I didn't like the way some of the other squadrons were handled; you couldn't find the CO, or the CO would put the best people on his wing instead of having them lead divisions where they'd do the most good.

Rollie Rinabarger

Gelon Doswell

"It was a hell of an experience. Of course, I'd rather not have been hit. I'm sorry I wasn't around with the guys longer; it damn near broke my heart when Doc sent me out of there."

Contract Negotiator

Gelon Doswell

Gelon H. "Corpuscle" Doswell, still looking as though he could use some plasma, might benefit from some of Rinabarger's invigorating mountain climate. Instead, he lives in a town where the altitude is only 22 feet: Ocean Springs, Mississippi, an almost 200-year-old Gulf Coast resort that has become an artists' colony.

I interviewed Doswell in my hotel room in New Orleans during the Marine Corps Aviation Convention. He'd put on some weight, was still pasty-faced, and wore his hair in a Marine Corps brush cut.

"The Black Sheep were pretty much the same as other squadrons except that they seemed closer knit. It was a gung-ho situation, and everybody seemed to pull together very well. I got more enemy contact, and Dustin and I were convinced we were going to paint some Japanese flags on our airplanes, but it never happened.

"Afterward, I returned to the States by ship and was assigned as a Corsair test pilot after training at Patuxent. I applied for a regular commission that came through in Hawaii, and I was sent to multi-engine school and became a transport pilot.

"I was at the Bureau of Aeronautics for a couple of years, commanded a Night Fighter squadron, and had the usual tours: Armed Forces Staff College; Fleet Marine Force, Atlantic; Iwakuni, Japan. I commanded the Reserve Training Detachment at the Naval Air Station in New Orleans and was assigned to the International Secretary of the NATO Standing Group in Washington—and selected for colonel there.

"One interesting assignment was at Quantico, heading up a small task group working on the Marine Corps Fighter Study. At that time, it appeared the Defense Department was going to cram the F-111 down

Ed Olander

Harry Johnson

our throats. The thing had grown from about 40,000 pounds up to about 70,000 pounds, and during its first carrier trials, I think, it buckled the deck of one. Then we were testing all kinds of ideas, like a one-man helicopter.

"In 1965 my back began to bother me. At Bethesda, they told me they could do surgery but couldn't guarantee anything, so they wrote me up for a disability retirement, and I retired in 1966.

"I sent out résumés and interviewed with several companies. Colt Industries in Hartford wanted me to sell weapons to the Army, Navy, and Marines; for a retired regular officer, that's illegal, of course. I told them that. So I messed around awhile and finally came to Ingalls Shipbuilding Division of Litton Industries. I'm in subcontracting management, negotiating and administering major subcontracts. Been here 14 years, like the work, and expect to stay till I'm 65.

"We like living in Ocean Springs, too—we like to fish.

"I've had many outstanding times: a joint exercise with the Thai Marines in Bangkok, where we called on the King and the Ambassador; meeting Lord Mountbatten in Paris with the NATO Standing Group. And there were close calls, like Christmas Day of 1943, when I had to limp into Torokina just as the plane quit on me.

"The Black Sheep experience was great. I consider it an honor to have been a part—a hell of a squadron. I know Greg had his problems, but he was a fine combat pilot and a good combat commander. A little rough for a peacetime Marine Corps—actually, his own worst enemy."

Politician and Entrepreneur

Ed Olander

"Big Old Fat Old Ed" Olander has slimmed down considerably since his days with the Black Sheep. He was on vacation in Hawaii, and I interviewed him in my Honolulu apartment.

After being released from active duty, Ed went back to his home town of Northhampton, Massachusetts, and carved out a distinguished career. He started a building materials business, which he still owns. He served two terms as Northhampton's mayor; he was a member of his Community Hospital board for 18 years, nine of them as president; and he is now on the board of directors of a national bank.

About four years younger than Boyington, Ed was the oldest of the pilots who served both tours.

"It turned out to be a good mix, having new pilots with the experienced ones. We didn't have the opportunity, like the other squadrons, to become familiar with each other's moves before we went into combat. I don't think I was scared, the first flight, but I remember it because I was confused—didn't know which was east or west, or what the islands were going to look like. If we'd had enemy contact that day, I don't think I could have found my way home. Later, we were confident because we had good leadership in the air, and the right airplane. I've had a love affair with the Corsair for 40 years. Yet after 40 years, the missions are a blur; I recall some misses more than I recall any hits.

"After we broke up, I went to dull Green Island, then to El Toro and trained in field carrier landings for the invasion of Japan that never happened. When the war ended, I was released from active duty, just before Thanksgiving 1945.

"The Black Sheep were a very special squadron, and not only because we were at the right place at the right time and compiled a good combat record. I can recall no group I served with that had such esprit. Part of that may have been the good feeling generated by success and by combat; part was a confidence maybe instilled by Boyington. It was a good-times squadron. Everyone knows Greg's affinity for drink, and we all seemed to have a little, and we had some parties. But I think by the luck of the draw we had some damn nice guys who would have had this kindred spirit any place they happened to congregate. I've said many times that I spent six months with a total of 50 people and felt closer to them than people I lived with for four years at Amherst College.

"I let the Black Sheep experience all lie fallow until you organized that first reunion; then it all came alive again as though there had been no interim period at all. It was a very special group. It occupies a very special niche in my life."

Harry Johnson

Harry "Skinny" Johnson drove the nearly 400-mile round trip from his home in Birmingham to meet me in Nashville. Like Yankee Doodle Dandy, Harry was born on the fourth of July. At six feet, two inches, he was one of the taller Black Sheep, and he was still distinguished looking. He might have been a banker.

I asked why he had chosen the Marines after he received his commission.

"There was this Marine Captain with all the ribbons. He said, 'If you want to have tea at three o'clock and lace on your drawers, you stay in the Navy. But if you want to be the sorriest son of a bitch in the world, get in the Marines.'

"I said, 'Well, I'd like to get into fighters.'

"He looked at me and said, 'We have a new fighter, the Corsair, and its big enough for a 300-pounder.'

"I said, 'Thank you, Sir,' and that's how I got in, but the first time I flew a Corsair was in Espiritu Santo. I was real hepped up to get assigned to the Black Sheep. I thought Boyington knew what he was doing, and if I listened to him and the others who'd already had the first tour, I could learn a lot.

"I don't recall ever being real scared until later, in Korea. That's because I was older, and we had to work under the flares at night, 4,000,000-candlepower parachute flares. There, most of the roads are river beds, so you have to get down below the mountains to see anything, then corkscrew yourself out.

"When I got back from Korea, I stayed on extended active duty as a Reserve for a couple of years, and on Organized Reserve until 1961. By then I was 40 years old, and they were trying to put us in ground school, so I was through with it. I had a wonderful time in the Marine Corps; I just wanted to get out and make some money, and that's exactly what I did.

"I started to work on a commission basis, then decided to go into manufacturing. Now I have a small plant, the Harry C. Johnson Company, manufacturing electrical connectors. Every power company uses them. We thought about expanding like the *Wall Street Journal* says, but I decided to keep it small and dirty. I have anywhere from four to ten employees.

"When somebody talks about recession, I say, 'We don't have a problem.' We have orders for all of next year. Don't get me wrong. It's not a big outfit because I don't want it to be, but I can do my boating and fishing. I have six boats. At the lake south of Birmingham, I have what they call a 'deck boat'; there's a stereo on it where I play my favorite, Frank Sinatra's 'I Did It My Way.' Then I have a bass boat that'll go 54 miles an hour; a pontoon boat; a small aluminum boat; and at the yacht club I'm a member of, a 47-foot Swannee with all the deals on it. It's slick. And I own a 42-foot antique, all-mahogany boat that I'm having refinished now. It's beautiful—18,000 pounds of good stuff.

"But I've never been in any group like the Black Sheep since then that would even approach it. It was fun. It was a feeling that we were the best and we'd take any job. I liked the singing; I just liked it. You don't see the same loyalty now that we had—I don't believe I knew a one who wouldn't risk his life to save another.

"Getting married and having a family, and the Black Sheep experience were the high points in my life.

"I agree with football coach Bear Bryant; what he preached and what we had was pride. When you have pride, you have class. When the crunch comes, you're in there in your formation; you want to be a winner.

"In the Black Sheep, we had pride; we had class; and we were winners."

Professional Marine and Accountant

Bruce Matheson

After serving 30 years in the Marine Corps, Bruce Matheson has retired to a comfortable life in Kailua, Hawaii, on the other side of the island of Oahu from Waikiki. Daily runs on the beach have kept his weight about the same as in our Black Sheep days; he still has his hair, with a few flecks of gray. One of the original members of our choral society, he is still musically inclined: he has an organ in his home, and he sings with a choral group and in the chorus of both the Honolulu Opera Company and the Honolulu Symphony Orchestra.

Named outstanding freshman in his University of Illinois ROTC unit, he joined the regular Marines the day after Pearl Harbor. He had no thought of aviation but was tested in boot camp in San Diego and selected to go to aviation electronics school in Florida. Commissioned in January, he arrived in Espiritu Santo in July 1943.

"When Boyington introduced himself with a bit about his Flying Tiger tour, I was impressed. He had seen combat and could tell us that the Japanese were not really ten feet tall. We felt we were there purely to fly. No such things as electronics officer, oxygen officer, parachute officer; when we weren't flying, we had nothing else to do.

"I felt I knew what I was supposed to do; I had confidence in the people I flew with and thought the missions were certainly within our capability.

"My first aerial combat taught me about as much as I learned previously or subsequently: you can't afford to get a fixation on anything. I was devoting so much attention to shooting at a plane that I became a target myself, and didn't realize it till I heard something like hail on a tin roof. I went into a split S and lost the Zero. The action moved like a swarm of bees in the general direction of the bombers, but it didn't seem so much an overall movement as split-second glimpses of happenings you had to evaluate in a fraction of a second.

"I got my last Zero on the mission when Boyington went down. I wish, for our sake, that we had not been split up. It would have been wonderful to continue with that group of people. However, by the time we came back from R and R in Australia, for all practical purposes the air war in the Solomons was finished.

"By the time the war was over, I was a Captain, with a wife. I found I enjoyed flying very, very much, and we could fly in first-line airplanes. We traveled a lot. I liked the people. My college had been interrupted, so when I was asked if I wanted a regular commission, I cast my lot with the Marine Corps.

"When the Korean War started, there were no Marines in China, Guam, Philippines; none even in Hawaii. Had it not been for the Korean War, there might not have been any Marines, period."

Matheson had a distinguished career: service in Guam with John Glenn, a Marine pilot before he became an astronaut and then U.S. senator. After Korea, Mat was in Hawaii three years; commanded the Marine Air Reserve Training Detachment at Norfolk for two years; was head of Shore Development Branch of the Division of Aviation at headquarters for three years; trained to fly helicopters; spent one year in Japan and then three years as Deputy Chief of Staff, G-4, Pacific

Bruce Matheson

Glenn Bowers

Marine Corps Headquarters in Hawaii. In 1968 he went to Vietnam as commander of Marine Air Group 36, the largest Marine Air Group ever sent overseas; it consisted of 12 helicopter squadrons at two locations.

His final year of active duty was spent as Chief of Staff of the Development Center at Marine Corps Schools. After retiring with the rank of colonel, he took a position as head of general accounting services for a data processing firm; most recently, he has become an income tax specialist with H&R Block.

As Mat thumbed through my musty War Diary, I asked him what set the Black Sheep apart from other squadrons.

"One thing that seemed to set us apart and also draw us together was the fact that the squadron comprised a number of college students, all bringing their own lore from various parts of the country. Entertainment was pretty much what you could make of it. Many of us liked to sing barbershop harmony, and we each brought with us songs the others didn't know. Our songfests became sort of impromptu get-togethers—it didn't even make any difference if you couldn't carry a tune; we still learned the words. And despite the TV show, very little hard liquor was available on combat tours; it wasn't the drinking. The relationship among the pilots was extremely good; we felt we were part of a group we had confidence in, and I think that is possibly the reason for the success we achieved.

"I don't think I've ever seen people as motivated to go again and again without question and hang it out as much as the Black Sheep and some in the other Solomons' squadrons. I think the shock of Pearl Harbor literally carried me to and through V-J Day, through years of effort to try not only to survive it but to right the wrong that was done there. There was no such impetus for Korea, and you might say there was negative impetus for Vietnam.

"The youngsters who came through flight training just prior to Vietnam were given much better training, both on the ground and in the air, with better equipment, more sophisticated equipment. Their basic education was much better than we had, so they were a lot more capable.

"I don't think we get the draft-card burners in the military now, but we got them in Vietnam because we were at the head end of the 'me' generation. In Vietnam we began to have trouble with drugs, and found drugs in flight crews. The obvious difference was motivation. I had hundreds of young pilots and thousands of enlisted men. I had to do the best I could to convince them that what they were doing on a daily basis was right, that it was productive and in the country's best interest. At the same time, we were being visited by correspondents from U.S. newspapers who would tend to ask all the wrong questions and draw all the wrong answers, and go back and paint a wrong picture.

"The highlight of my entire 30 years was those two tours with the Black Sheep. As I look back, never before or since have I been in a situation that was a literal life-and-death effort, where you would knowingly place yourself repeatedly and routinely in these remote air battles hundreds of miles from your base and really think nothing of it. I don't believe it was a matter of stupidity; we had reliance on each other and the airplane. I never found anything subsequent to those two six-week tours that was nearly as challenging or completely demanding of me as a person. Other things were colorful and enjoyable, but in that crucible I made friendships and attachments and long relationships such as I've never again experienced.

"Never since that time have I been given the opportunity to achieve or attain or do anything as notable or noteworthy as I was able to do in those few short weeks with the Black Sheep Squadron."

Wildlife Manager

Glenn Bowers

Glenn Bowers is one of those rare persons who had his sights fixed on his career goal early in life and managed to achieve that goal. He had completed three years as a zoology and biology major at Penn State when he enlisted in the Marine Corps. After his release from active duty, he returned to Penn State to obtain both his bachelor's and master's degrees, and then started to work for the Pennsylvania Game Commission. Commencing as a wildlife biologist, he worked his way up to the Division of Research, then to Deputy Director, and for the past 18 years Executive Director of the commission.

At his home in Dillsburg, Pennsylvania, Glenn talked forcefully and enthusiastically about the work he and his people in wildlife management are doing in the state. He runs an outfit with over 700 employees and an annual budget of $32 million. The state owns a million and a quarter acres of land used by some 1,300,000 hunters. His regular staff is augmented by 1,500 deputy game protectors who donate most of their time.

"I don't want to break my arm patting myself on the back, Frank, but I think we have one of the best deer management programs in the country, and our waterfowl management is far better off today than it was some years back.

"One of the real drawbacks has been the loss of habitat through development: housing developments, shopping centers, roads, factories, and modern agricultural practices that destroy small game habitat on the farms. Without favorable living conditions, these animals cannot survive, any more than you and I could out in the desert without anything to help us.

"We've taken steps to help some of the species that are most threatened. We've got a fine turkey management program: we do a lot of trapping and transfer to move wild birds into areas that are not now occupied but have the potential for self-sustaining populations.

"As to our deer program, Pennsylvania is about thirty-third in deer population and maybe fourth in human population, but I expect we have about the third highest harvest of white-tailed deer. We have an excellent hunter education program, too; it's mandatory for all new hunters and has substantially reduced the number of hunting accidents, actually by some 90 percent."

"Let's think back to another kind of shooting. Can you recall joining the Black Sheep? What else do you remember?" I asked.

"I joined not long after I arrived in the South Pacific in October 1943, and it was my first chance to fly the Corsair.

"I remember Boyington was confined to quarters and not released till we went up in combat, the squadron's second tour. A number of us younger guys smuggled whiskey in a coke bottle to him in his hut. We'd rap on the shutter and stuff it in through the opening there.

"I think everybody had some misgivings, flying a plane we weren't all that familiar with. One of the first flights I remember was Torokina on Bougainville, following those big muslin banners—arrows—as to where to glide across the jungle and strafe. The ground Marines reported we killed 106 of the enemy. The thing I recall most vividly was that when we went across the trees, the jungle erupted with thousands of white birds."

"I also remember New Year's Day, 1944, escorting bombers to Rabaul, and there were Zeros stacked practically from the ground to

Herb Holden

Sandy Sims

36,000 feet. The antiaircraft had crippled a number of bombers, and we kept hovering as long as we could to keep those hordes of Zeros from making final kills.

"There was a lot more camaraderie and leadership in the Black Sheep than other squadrons I was in. The leaders wouldn't ask you to do anything they wouldn't go into themselves. In other squadrons, they apparently didn't give a shit if you got lost or not; all they wanted to do was save their ass. A lot of men were lost for just that reason.

"The whole thing comes down to leadership and that we all got along well. We were all sort of one, and that made for a really good outfit—team effort, everybody working together to make sure that things were going to go right. I think that was the secret of our success.

"Looking back on my military career, the only regret I have is that the squadrons I was in following the Black Sheep could not have been the same kind of outfit. They just didn't have the leadership or teamwork. It all stems from the fact that the Black Sheep wanted to work together, and nobody tried to push anything on anybody that he wouldn't do himself."

Banker

Herb Holden

To meet Herb Holden, I drove some 500 miles from Dillsburg, Pennsylvania, to Pipe Stem Resort State Park, West Virginia, where he was spending the weekend with his family and some friends.

Herb entered the Navy V-5 program in the spring of 1942, after graduation from Williams College, and was shipped to Espiritu Santo in time to join our second combat tour.

"I'd heard what the Black Sheep and Boyington were doing and was glad to join, but mainly, I wanted to get started on the combat tour. My first flight? Damn right I was scared. I was looking for Japanese all over the place, and there weren't any. After a while I got more confident, and my only concern was the airplane—mechanical troubles.

"After we were broken up, I went to Emirau for two tours, then back to the States to instrument school because I realized that the problems of combat were more weather than Japanese. But when the war ended, I got out in December 1945.

"Looking for a job wasn't easy—who wants a fighter pilot with a B.A. degree in history? After a lot of interviews, I decided on National City Bank, as it was called then. (now it's Citibank—not only international but global). My intention was to get their training, find out what the business was like, and give it a five-year stint; then, knowing something, I'd be able to make a better selection. I ended up staying there for the next 37 years, winding up as senior credit officer and head of the Petroleum Department, which is a national organization.

"I decided it would be a good time to retire. I was over 60, healthy, and happy; I'd made a little money, so we could get by without worrying."

Herb is now working part time as a director and member of the executive committee of an investment company in New York; acts as an expert witness in banking cases; plays golf. He has recently moved to Columbus, North Carolina.

"My worst experience? When I got an oil leak and the engine quit, 10,000 feet off the other side of Espiritu Santo, at 7:30 in the morning. When I hit the water, the chute *and* the boat sank, tangled in the shroud lines. I could see land, but it took me all day to swim ashore. I found a couple of Army Coast Watchers with a broken radio. Anyway, they had the planes out looking for me, and I got picked up.

"The Black Sheep Squadron was a unique operation. I knew the fellows were trying to live up to our reputation; they were very proud, interested in being sure we maintained this aura. There were no cliques—we were one group. The character of Boyington was unique, too; he was a warrior and a fighter and a leader. He knew what he was doing and how to do it, and got the job done.

"My association with the squadron was one tour, about six to eight weeks overall. It's been 37, 38 years. A very short episode in a life, but one that's as vivid as it could be for something that short and that long ago."

Sandy Sims

Sanders S. "Sandy" Sims drove out to talk to me at my hotel at Philadelphia's International Airport. Sandy and his wife had recently moved to Philadelphia after spending the bulk of the previous 25 years in Europe.

His has been a fascinating career. At war's end, he returned to Philadelphia where he had been born and raised. A fine athlete, he was a member of the 1948 U.S. Olympic Field Hockey Team. He worked for a time in a savings bank and then, finding it boring, went to work for a friend who had a hosiery business, which was still extremely restricted—along with butter, meat, gasoline, sugar, and other luxury items. Quality nylon stockings were about as easy to obtain then as tickets to the Superbowl today.

"It was a lovely time, a seller's market, and all the buyers were pretty girls in New York making $50,000 a year. They would take me out to lunch and ask, 'How many hundred dozens can I have this week?'

"I'd say, 'Well, it all depends.' So I'd have a little bonus.

"After a couple of years I went to work for an arms manufacturer, Oerlikon, the biggest in the world and, among other things, the only company that ever made its own guided missile. Theirs was the most famous 20-mm cannon in World War II. Their factory was in Zurich; then they built a plant in Asheville, North Carolina. About this time, I got married, and we moved there.

"I decided I wasn't going to get rich that way, so I quit and went to Washington with the CIA for two or three years. I resigned in 1953, a hard thing to do in those days, and went back to the painting I'd done off and on all my life. At the same time, I took a job with the U.S. Information Service as a cultural officer for almost eight years before deciding to paint full time. We lived in London for about ten years, then divided our time between France and our place in Maine. Eventually, we sold the Maine house and lived full time in France until last June, when we came back to the United States.

"What kind of painting do you do?"

"Depends on the day. Sometimes it's good, sometimes it stinks, but anything for money—objective, not abstract. Sometimes portraits, flowers, mostly landscapes; and if I work, I'm successful. There are a few good 'Simses' around that may have appreciated in value. There are a lot of bad ones. Anyway, I like it; it keeps me out of trouble.

"We took a trip to Africa in 1963. I did a lot of sketches of some of the little villages in the Sudan. I painted those things for a long time, and people kept asking me for them. I finally had to say I couldn't do anymore; you start repeating yourself, and it's not healthy.

"Right now, I'm supposed to be doing a lot of things for a gallery in Santa Fe, New Mexico: Indian villages, Hopis, Navajo. I'll have to go out there soon; so far I've been working from some sketches.

"As for the South Pacific, I was too stupid the first time to be scared. By the second time, it began to sink in that those were real bullets.

"The whole emphasis had shifted from defensive to offensive, sometimes as much as 300 miles from our base over water. Not like Guadalcanal; if you lost an engine you could go down and land there or Bougainville.

"It's complicated as to why some got shot down and others not. The rates of contact varied for each pilot; some divisions got worked harder than others. And there's basic coordination; you had to be fairly agile up there, and you had to keep the fighter plane absolutely on a straight line or the rounds would go off line. Sometimes you could see the Zero going around, its nose going from side to side; that's not the guy to worry about. And it's a question of luck, too.

"The Black Sheep were a great deal of fun, an extraordinary group of different characters. I had the great fortune to room with the flight surgeon for a while; all the medicinal brandy was in our foxhole, and that was pleasant. We had more sense of unity than I found in any other squadron, more esprit de corps. I'm sure that was partly due to Pappy, and partly due to the vile treatment from the colonel he called 'Colonel Lard.'

"The other thing was that it was a period of going forward on the offensive. My first tour, Guadalcanal, was mild; before that, they were hanging on by their fingernails. With the Black Sheep, you had a lot of water; if your plane went bad, you were stuck. I realize what a great job the crew did to keep those old beasts flying.

"Taking it all together, we had good people with great spirit, aggressive leadership, and a dependable airplane—at a time when we had moved to the offensive: an outstanding team."

Perry Lane

Perry Lane lives in Nashua, New Hampshire, a city of some 70,000, not far from the Massachusetts border. It took me about two hours to drive there from Logan International Airport in Boston.

Big, easygoing Perry had put on some weight and lost some hair but was as friendly as ever; his welcoming smile was wide, his hand-shake firm. He had been born and raised in Rutland, Vermont, scarcely a sleeper-jump west; his accent signals his Down East heritage. We sat in comfortable chairs in his living room as I turned his thoughts back to those Black Sheep days when he joined us shortly before our second tour.

"I had my first flights in the Corsair in the South Pacific, about 35 hours by the time we went up. My combat flights are all sort of a blur. I was a little nervous at first, not knowing just what was going to happen. Back in the States, they wouldn't have let some of those planes off the ground. After the Black Sheep, I spent time at Guadalcanal, Green Island, Bougainville, and finally got sent home after I fell off a coconut log and broke my leg on the way to the movie one night. I stayed in California till my leg healed, then went to Quantico; to Air/Infantry School; back to Cherry Point for training again in a fighter squadron. I was released from active duty in January 1946 but stayed in the Reserve program.

"I went back to Vermont, returned to college for my degree in electrical engineering. The GI Bill helped some, but I was married, so I painted buildings, dug ditches—anything to make a few dollars to pay our way.

"I was called up for Korea, primarily a Reserves war, in September 1950. Our squadron had 51 pilots; about 30 were Reserves. We lost quite a few people there; we'd fly interdiction hops at about 1,000 feet. A tentmate was shot down in the first two weeks. I flew 54 missions, then was sent up as a Forward Air Controller for about six weeks.

"After Korea, I came back to work for General Electric. They treated me very well, and I spent 19 years with them before resigning to go to Sanders, here in Nashua, in order to be near home. After a year, I went to work at Federal Aviation Administration—been there ever since about 1970. (I've now retired from the Reserve program.)

"I'm in communications: when information comes in about any

Perry Lane

Burney Tucker

problems that occur, I keep people advised about what's happened. I enjoy the work and expect to stay at least till I'm 65."

"You've been pretty faithful about making our Black Sheep reunions, and seem to get along great with all of them," I said.

"Yes, we were a close-knit group, much closer than any other I've ever been in. The squadron had tremendous morale. We had a leader who was experienced, and we had faith in him. He was one of the boys on the ground, but he knew what he was doing in the air, and we knew he was on the level with the rest of us. If you got a lousy aircraft, you figured, well, he's got one, too."

Architect

Burney Tucker

Nashville, Tennessee, dates back to 1779, when a band of pioneers cleared an area along the Cumberland River and built a stockade for a fort. A few months later, several families arrived by boat to settle the area. Now, Nashville is a thriving metropolis of some half a million people; its Grand Ole Opry is world famous; about an hour's drive south is Lynchburg, home of the best sipping whiskey in the world: Jack Daniels. Famous Tennesseeans include Andrew Jackson, Davy Crockett, David Farragut, and Sam Houston.

To these can be added Black Sheep Burney Tucker, with four Japanese planes to his credit, 105 missions, five Battle Stars, Air Medal, Distinguished Flying Cross, Japan Occupation and Presidential Unit Citation.

Burney was born in Nashville and reared in Murfreesboro; he'd had two and a half years at Middle Tennessee State College when he went into the Marine Corps. I interviewed him in a Nashville hospital room. During the course of a routine physical, the doctors had discovered an arrhythmia in his heart and insisted on an immediate angiogram—which was negative. I arrived the next day and found him in excellent spirits although still under observation.

"I saw a lot of places: I was at E Base in Atlanta and then Jacksonville for basic training, where I got my wings in January 1943; up to Great Lakes to qualify on the carrier *Wolverine*; San Diego and overseas on the U.S.S. *Wharton*—somebody told us it was Admiral Byrd's Southern Cross; New Caledonia in July 1943; then Espiritu Santo. There we bounced from one squadron to another; they said we were in the pool. I had several hundred hours in the Corsair when all of a sudden, in September, I was transferred to 214 and went into combat a week later. I was scared, the first mission. If anyone says he wasn't, he's a liar. The only thing that saved us was our training.

"On the second or third hop out of Munda, when I was flying on Boyington's wing, a Zero made a pass at him and was on his tail. I shot that one down; then I got a hot feeling on my neck, looked around, and I'm being attacked. I did the right thing: turned in to him and went under. If I hadn't, I probably wouldn't have gotten away. But I'd saved Boyington's neck. I always said that Pappy Boyington wouldn't be here if it wasn't for Burney Tucker. I also was one of a four plane division who later searched Blanche Channel for Pappy after he was lost in January 1944.

"After the war I decided to stay in and make a career in the Marines, but after I was accepted, I began to have second thoughts. I'd read a lot about architecture while I was in Japan and liked the idea of it, so I got out and went back to college. When the Korean War came along, I was at Georgia Tech working on my master's degree, and perhaps that's why I was one of the two (out of 34) in my Reserve squadron who did not go.

"I got my degreee and spent five years as an architect's apprentice in Phoenix. In May 1956 I came back to Nashville and opened my own office."

Tucker is a member of the National American Institute of Architects, the Tennessee Society of Architects, and the National Council of Architectural Registration Boards. He has also served as member and chairman of the Brentwood, Tennessee, Planning Commission.

"Black Sheep success? I think we were at the right place at the right time; we had a great airplane, Boyington's leadership, and experience. By that, I mean we had more experienced pilots than a brand-new squadron commissioned in the States. As time went on, we became more honed and a better and better team. That's the real reason for our success: we were a team. Others had just one man. Of course, we had Boyington, but the whole squadron shared in the work and in the record. After all, the other pilots, besides Boyington, shot down 75 of the 97 planes we scored.

"It was easy to be misunderstood by the folks back home. When I was overseas, my grandmother turned over some of my letters to a local newspaper, which published some articles based on them. I'd written that I'd found some 'cats eyes,' and evidently the girl who wrote the article didn't know they were a type of seashell. She wrote that I killed jungle cats and liked to keep their eyes. I thought I'd never hear the last of that.

"My practice keeps me busy now, but I'm trying to slow down. I do a lot of reading. I enjoy life, and I tell others to enjoy life. I enjoy my work, my family, and my fond memories of those days with the Black Sheep."

Printer and Humanitarian

Al Marker

Sonoma, where Al Marker has his lovely home, is steeped in tradition. The town of some 6,000 is the site of the flag raising in June 1846 that proclaimed California a republic. The Stars and Stripes replaced it in July of that year.

Sonoma is in the heart of wine country; there's one high-quality winery just up the road, and nearby is the Sonoma State Historic Park containing the well-preserved home of General Vallejo, the city's founder. Close by are the home of macho author Jack London, and the Jack London State Historic Park.

Although one of the youngest Black Sheep, Al's gray hair and shaggy gray beard make him appear the oldest, but he is energetic, vigorous, and active in civic and philanthropic affairs in his city.

His tour with the Black Sheep was shortlived. Joining us for our second combat tour, he was injured in a crash at Bougainville not long afterward, evacuated, and hospitalized; he did not rejoin us until we returned to Espiritu Santo. He completed his overseas duty at Green Island, came back to the States, retrained, and immediately volunteered to return overseas.

"I felt I hadn't done anything toward the war. The senior officer at

Al Marker

James M. Reames

San Diego said, 'What the hell are you doing here? You just got back a few months ago. You don't have to go overseas.'

"I said, 'Hey, I know, but I'm going.' At the same time, I had this gut feeling, Frank, that I wouldn't live through a second tour of duty overseas.

"They sent me to the Marshalls, where we spent all our time bombing a little rock. I was totally frustrated; it was extremely disappointing. I came home assigned to Norfolk, giving out jackets to Marines who were coming back from overseas. By this time, the war was over, and I had enough points to get out, so I did, staying in the Volunteer Reserves.

"By the time the Korean War came along, I had been married about two years, had a child and a good job, but I still wanted desperately to get into the war. I remember vividly: I was on the phone with Bill O'Brien, who had a responsible position in a squadron forming up. He said, 'Do you really want to get in?'

"I said, 'Hell, yes, Bill, what do I do?'

"About this time, my wife came into the room, and she went *swissssh*, right through the ceiling. It was the first time I'd seen her mad. She said, 'You're not volunteering for anything! You have responsibilities; you have a wife and child.' And I had to agree with her, Frank.

"But I suspect I'm still not over the disappointment, the embarrassment, the feeling that I just didn't do my job. As far as I was concerned, my job was to shoot down planes, not to strafe barges or blow up bridges or anything like that, however successful. And I had done everything possible to get into position where, somehow, some way, I could do my job."

I reminded him, "Some guys never left the U.S., and others hung onto their civilian jobs and got promoted. Tell me about your life after the war."

"I worked for a couple of printing firms for about 20 years, then bought my own company. I specialized in a very narrow area of the business, focusing on service. As a result, I was grossing a million three when I sold out.

"I just ran out of gas. I'm not a good delegator—tried to do everything myself. I lost my partner; there was too much entertaining to do, and I got tired of that. So, I got lucky. I sold the place and expect to live happily ever after.

"I figured I'd play a lot of golf, and we've been doing some traveling. But I've always thought I was fortunate and wanted in some way to 'repay my debt to society.' So all of a sudden, I found I was a board member of Sonoma Valley Family Center, a counseling organization with a 24-hour crisis line we call Help Line. It may be wife- or child-beating, or a lonely person, or a life-threatening situation. Our volunteers make recommendations. Usually, the people come and talk, and pay what they can afford. I became chairman of fund raising and spent a couple of years at that. I also spent a year on the county grand jury, two or three days a week.

"I guess I'm still trying to do my job."

Doctor

James M. Reames

Doctor James M. "Happy Jack" Reames drove up to Altadena from his home in Whittier to meet me at Fred Losch's place.

At the time Doc was tapped to become Flight Surgeon for the Black Sheep, he had been attending casualties being evacuated from Guadalcanal on hospital planes. He was a natural for the squadron position. He had graduated from Navy Flight Training and Aviation Medicine courses at Pensacola, so he was both a doctor and a pilot; at 26 he was barely older than most of the pilots so they could understand one another.

Reames possessed a gentle, compassionate, nonabrasive spirit that enabled him to get along with absolutely everyone. Everybody loved him, and not because he had a footlocker full of medicinal brandy. It was his southern charm, his wide-eyed college-boy enthusiasm over the performances of our young combat eagles, the optimistic outlook that enabled him to find something cheerful in everything.

His soft accent sounded as though his throat had been bathed in olive oil; we called him "King of the Yamheads." But his easy talk disguised a quick mind, as his poker opponents paid dearly to learn. Because of his slow, slightly bumbling style of play, it was a while before we learned enough about his game to call him "Diamond Jim."

Sitting in Losch's den, Jim didn't appear to have changed very much. Older, yes, with glasses and gray hair—he looked like what he was: a solid, respectable family physician. Even so, it was not hard to visualize him, sleepy eyed, at the poker table, asking, "What y'all gonna do?" Or exuberantly passing out tiny bottles of brandy, shouting, "Eleven Zeros!" Or holding onto an upright at 3:00 A.M., saying incredulously: "Strafe Kahili?"

"I'll never forget those Black Sheep days," he said. "Those wild rides down the hill to the airstrip when we came under bombing attack, and jumped off the truck, and crawled into that muddy culvert for safety, to find out the next day it was a bomb storage dump we'd huddled in.

"Or Kolombangara, collecting Japanese rifles, and I picked up what I thought was a nice brass souvenir and stuck it in my pocket, then knocked around the jungle a couple of hours before I went back onto the boat. I was showing it around when an ordnance man said, 'Hey, that's a live detonator off a 90-mm shell!'

"And the foxhole full of rats we swore we wouldn't get into.

"The strangest was on Munda when they found a Japanese soldier in our chow lines. He'd scrounged a Marine's fatigues and had been a regular customer.

"And the flight surgeon who circumcised the colonel and saved the shriveled foreskin. He used it as bait a few days later, and landed a 150-pound marlin."

"That sounds like an old-time ditty," I chuckled. "Perhaps that bait was specially attractive to marlin. In any case, not too easy to come by— colonels' foreskins, I mean, not fish."

"Or when we were in Sydney," Jim went on, "I was afraid Boyington was going to cause an international incident. We were in the bar at the Australian Hotel, and Boyington somehow got into an argument with two Australian enlisted men. I followed them outside, and they were squared away about to tangle. I rushed inside and found the highest-ranking Australian officer; he went out and told those enlisted men to beat it.

"The thing about the Black Sheep was that they were, with few exceptions, all eager to go, gung ho. None of them had any combat fatigue. The British had already discovered that the younger men are more eager than the older men. They're more daring."

After his two Black Sheep tours, Reames returned to the States and was assigned to the Marine Corps Air Station at Mojave, California, where it sometimes cools down to 100 degrees in the evenings. Scheduled to go out on the carrier *Franklin,* he was grounded because of his eyes. His replacement was killed when the *Franklin* was bombed and heavily damaged.

Medically retired in July 1946 because of his eyes, Jim opened a general medical practice in East Los Angeles, where he has been extremely successful.

One of his patients was Pappy Boyington. During the course of a physical examination, X-rays disclosed a spot on Boyington's lung; lab tests proved it to be cancerous. Reames assisted at the operation, which took place a number of years ago.

Beyond Social Security retirement age now, Jim works a slower pace; he gets in regular fishing and bird-hunting trips, with an occasional junket to Las Vegas to keep his hand in at poker and dice. And he attends our Black Sheep reunions.

Real Estate Appraiser and Bon Vivant

Don Fisher

Don "Mo" Fisher picked us up at Savannah's airport and drove my wife and me to Beaufort, South Carolina, a lovely old city of 14,000. The Fishers live just outside of town in Port Royal, a community of 2,000. Their plush Spanish-style home, a two iron shot from Parris Island, is built over the remains of an old fort, overlooking Spanish Point and the scenic waterway leading into Beaufort's waterfront area. There's a steady stream of boats drifting past his patio window.

Fisher's hair is grayer and his forehead higher, but he is still big, vigorous, affable, friendly, and outgoing, and he still loves to arrange everything for a get-together.

He insisted on putting together a party: he picked up a couple of bushels of oysters; Lou Markey, the Chance Vought technical rep who'd been with us at Vella Lavella, brought a huge package of venison from a deer he'd bagged; a retired Marine general brought a rum cake he'd baked; my wife, Carol, helped Mo's wife, Bette, prepare a batch of eggplant from the Fisher garden. It was a feast, with Fisher his typical hospitable self.

I asked him why he left college to join the Marines, what he remembered.

"I don't mean to sound patriotic. It was something the majority were doing. I had a civilian pilot's license and had gone through the CPT program in 1940, so I joined up.

"After training I went to Glenview and checked out on the carrier *Wolverine*, then to San Diego and overseas. On Espiritu Santo, we got checked out in Corsairs: somebody showed you how to start it, you sat in the cockpit, and they pointed out a few things.

"When we first started going to Rabaul, there was tremendous air opposition—I saw my only Japanese carrier in Rabaul Harbor—but toward the end of our tour, there was no air opposition.

"After the Black Sheep were broken up, I went to Green Island, back to Cherry Point, then to Congaree. I put in my letter to become a regular. I flew off a carrier with a stunt team to represent the Marines—sort of like the Navy's Blue Angels except that we flew in a group of 16; they fly in fours.

"I went out to China in 1948, assigned to the ground forces in Tsing Tao; I was the Air Officer for what they called the Fleet Marine Force of the Western Pacific.

"A year in China, then back to the States, then out to Korea on a jeep carrier flying close support. Back in the States, I commanded an attack squadron for a year; went on a Mediterranean cruise; saw Japan for a year; went to Quantico for four years on the Senior School staff.

"In 1964, I came to Beaufort as CO of MAG 31. My wife had an operation and needed to stay near the hospital, so when it came time to leave, I retired. That was 1966.

"I read in the paper that the Beaufort city manager had resigned. Playing golf with the mayor, I asked, 'What is this city manager job?'

"He said, 'Do you want it?'

"Later, while I was in Tampa, the mayor called and asked me to come up for an interview. I took the job and stayed for five years. I resigned to try construction work, and that evolved into real estate, and that into appraising. Now I have so much work I'm thinking about expanding, renting a building, and hiring a couple of assistants."

Don has also served as a member of the city council, as mayor for

Don Fisher

Denmark Groover

two years, and as president of the Rotary Club. As we walked along the streets, it was obvious that everybody knew and liked him, pausing to exchange a few friendly words.

Some things don't change.

Trial Lawyer

Denmark Groover

Denmark "Quill Skull" Groover drove 400 miles round trip from Macon to Savannah, Georgia, to meet me for dinner. A busy trial lawyer, he had to be in court the next morning to defend a woman who had stabbed her husband. Groover's hair is no longer coal black; he has less of it and it no longer sticks out. Today he looks distinguished.

He became a flyer, he said, because "I got seasick if I rode in a boat, and I didn't want to wander through the mud."

Commissioned in December 1942, he was shipped overseas in mid-1943. I asked how he felt on his first mission.

"I was wondering whether the hell I was going to get back or not. There's no substitute for experience—I realized the only reason I got shot up was that I had extraneous matter in my mind.

"When I got shot up my right arm and leg were paralyzed, my right aileron cable was severed, and I had no rudder control. My instruments were all out, but I made the best landing I ever made—rolled to the end of the strip where I just kept going around in a circle until they got me out. At the emergency room, Doc wanted to give me a shot, but for some reason I was afraid of it. He gave me one of those bottles of brandy, and I got as high as three tall pines. They took me to Guadalcanal, and after a week I started to come back, but they caught me and operated on my right arm and ankle. I was there for a month before I came back for the second combat tour.

"The Black Sheep were different; we had a strong feeling of camaraderie. Boyington was a motivating factor; you were a stabilizing factor; and Doc Reames had a knitting, cohesive effect on the group. It was a maturing experience. I came from a section of the country where prejudice was the order of the day, and it knocked a lot of that prejudice out of me. I remember selling some whiskey to the mess boys, who were black, for $60. Boyington found out about it and made me give the $60 back *and* let them keep the whiskey, which was a damn good lesson to me."

After the war, Groover went back to the University of Georgia, got his law degree, and commenced practice in Macon, Georgia, 41 years ago. He served as a member of the state legislature for three terms and then as general counsel for the Georgia Farm Bureau, which owns an insurance company that does some $70 million a year in premiums. In 1984, Groover was reelected to the state legislature.

He also has a broad general law practice, handling everything from criminal cases to contests of wills—anything that has to do with trial work, where he has earned the reputation of being a master. Law classes make it a point to adjourn to the courtroom to listen when Groover sums up for a jury.

One of the swiftest ways to get his temper boiling is to mention the TV series about the Black Sheep. "It amounted to mass character assassination. I thought of suing them when it came out, but that would have just given it more publicity. The show brought down and deprecated men of considerable bravery and valor, and for them, by God, I resent it.

"I feel some compassion for Greg; I am sure he participated because he needed the money. I am delighted, of course, that he is able to get something of a financial reward based on his combat record. It does seem a shame, however, for the others who contributed so much to the squadron's record, and indeed made possible Greg's record, to have been vilified—that was unnecessary, as well as completely ridiculous."

"As for today, there's a disturbing difference in the young people. The problem is having too much of everything; they're used to getting all they want with little or no effort. It's the 'government will look after me' syndrome. We were raised in the Depression, when a dime was a dime and we had to work for it. Even those with money recognized what it was all about, and there was still pride in your country, pride in being a part of it.

"When I listen to the radio on the way to work, half the telephone calls coming in to this talk show disc jockey are from people employed in the biggest air materiel area in the country. They're at work, sitting around calling in on some damn show instead of doing their jobs.

"What happened to that pride?"

Bill Case

Bill "Casey" Case picked me up at the Seattle/Tacoma International Airport. Although his hair is now graying and has receded somewhat, he is still alert and energetic, his frame compact and well maintained. We took the ferry to Bainbridge Island where Bill lives, a small bedroom community lying in Puget Sound between Seattle and Bremerton. We talked of old times, sitting in the den of his comfortable home.

"I'd taken Civilian Pilot Training in college, and went into flight training a couple of months before Pearl Harbor. My first combat tour was at Guadalcanal with Marine Fighter Squadron 122. I saw no enemy planes in the air.

"About the time we were ready for another tour, Boyington was reassigned from the Operations Office to us. We did some training in June; then Ed Schiflett, a pilot in 122, broke Boyington's leg in a Saturday night 'wrestling match,' and Greg got shipped to New Zealand while we went up to combat. At the end of that tour, the squadron number was sent back to the States. Several of us needed a third combat tour before we were eligible for home leave, so we were part of the beginning of the Black Sheep.

"I was naive about combat, never thought that I was going to be hurt or could be shot down. I took it for granted that nobody in our outfit was dragging his heels. It was a chance to get out and be productive at the game of fighter pilot we were playing. The Corsair was a superior airplane, would get us out of any trouble we might get into. We had a strong sense of cohesion, of challenge, and not a sense of doom.

"I give Pappy credit for a lot of our difference. He was an aggressive person and a lot of that rubbed off. And we had the opportunity. I didn't see any planes the first three-quarters of my South Pacific experience. After that I probably shot at 100 and if I'd been a good shot, could have had 20 or 30 birds, instead of eight. You have to have the talent for shooting, and the guts.

"I'd applied to go regular before I left the South Pacific. I liked the people I was with, liked the Marine Corps, and had some fine assignments. I was at headquarters; flew in Korea; had a great tour in Italy and another in Japan. Along the way, I earned a master's degree in business, and retired in 1969 as a colonel.

Bill Case

Gregory Boyington

"I worked for two years as a business consultant; then as assistant to the president of Western Farmers, a multi-million dollar farmers' cooperative. In 1972, I went to Alaska to become business manager of the Fairbanks School District System and later budget director for the University of Alaska Statewide System.

"After I had a heart attack, I moved to a job with less tension and stayed with it until I had open heart surgery. Then I retired and came here. Now, I swim to keep healthy. I've been both president and maintenance officer for the Water Corporation, of which our home is a part; and I've been commodore of our local yacht club. I've been racing competitively with a sailboat the past three years."

He paused. "Remember the bullet that split my helmet and scratched the top of my scalp? The only time my seat was lower than usual—just two inches!—otherwise, I'd have been drilled right through the back of my skull. If it had missed me altogether, I'd probably have been dead, too, because the round hit the bulletproof windshield, ricocheted down my gunsight, and made powdered glass spatter across my forehead. There was enough of the 7.7 bullet going through my helmet to yank my head down; otherwise, I'd have had my eyeballs full of powdered glass, and we were 300 miles out. I'd never have made it back.

"I attribute my narrow escape to the fact that the Lord said 'Today is not your day to go.' It gives me a higher sense of responsibility for making my life more useful. I've been given an extra run, and it's colored every move along the way. I call it a religious experience, and it happened."

Gregory Boyington

Gregory "Pappy" Boyington has traveled a rocky, roller-coaster road since those days when he made Marine Corps and aerial combat history with the Black Sheep in the South Pacific.

He'd been picked up by a Japanese submarine after he was shot down on 3 January 1944, and spent the remaining 20 months of the war in Japanese prison camps.

Released by U.S. forces, he was an international hero, acclaimed all over the world. He had an opportunity to grab life's brass ring.

I recall sitting with him in the steam room of the St. Francis Hotel in San Francisco during our fabulous party after his release.

"Greg," I told him, "you can be or do anything you want. Your name is a household word. Your picture has been in every paper in the country. Your story has been told and retold. You can be a congressman; you can be governor of your home state; you have your choice of positions in a dozen corporations—everyone wants you. But you absolutely *must* control the booze. Liquor has been your major problem to date. If you don't solve it, this will all turn to ashes."

"I know it, Frank, you're absolutely right. But I want you to know that I had a chance to do a lot of thinking while I was in that prison camp. I'm going to be able to handle the liquor. You don't have to worry about me on that score."

Later, when he was staying at our home, he told my wife, "You know, Carol, the happiest time of my life was when I was in that Japanese prison camp. I was told what to do. Everything was arranged. I had no decisions to make."

Then again, during his media-hyped courtship with two women vying for his affections at the same time in a story reminiscent of today's soap operas, he once told me, as we sat quietly at Marine Corps Camp Miramar: "You know, Frank, I don't want to marry anybody."

"You certainly don't have to, Greg. You're not hooked till they say the words over you. If you don't want to get married, then, for Christ's sake, tell them both, 'no'."

But, while one, who was getting a divorce so she could marry him, waited vainly in Reno, he married the other one in Las Vegas.

Unfortunately, his resolve regarding the liquor didn't last long, either. While another Marine Corps war ace and Medal of Honor winner, Joe Foss, became governor of his home state, Boyington went through a series of lurid, broken marriages and bounced from one job to another: beer salesman; stock salesman; jewelry salesman; wrestling referee. Liquor was always present.

More recently, Alcoholics Anonymous has given him a measure of help.

In 1958 he published *Baa, Baa, Black Sheep*, a best-selling book based on his wartime experiences. In 1976–77 he was listed as "technical adviser" for a television series of the same name. It was the usual Hollywood hokum, featuring drunken brawls and jiggly nurses, and depicting Black Sheep pilots as fugitives from courts-martial. When some of the Black Sheep protested Boyington's connection with the show, he said, "I only did it for the money."

In 1980, he stood before us at our Washington meeting, no longer the barrel-chested, swashbuckling terror of the skies. His deeply lined face showed every mile of the tortuous road he'd traveled over the years: "Enough booze to float a battleship" as he often said; the stress of combat flying; the ravages of 20 months of Japanese prison camps; the strains of multiple marriages and divorces; brushes with the law; bouncing from one job to another; medical problems, including the lung cancer operation; sessions with psychiatrists—a classic picture of a man driven toward self-destruction.

He looked around the auditorium: "Whaddya looking so funny for, lady? I'm Robert Conrad with wrinkles."

The TV show had not been true to life, he said, because "no one ever wanted to make a movie about the Boy Scouts." At the time the Black Sheep Squadron was formed, the members thought the idea of being different was great, he continued. "That's why they picked the name and insignia. I explained in my book that they were not outcasts and misfits."

He said that when he speaks in a town where members of his old squadron live, he tells the audience that these boys were "young, unmarried, red-blooded Americans" and that he never saw any of them swear, fight, drink, or chase women. "I did all these things. The only thing I ask is that when they come to my town, they lie about me, too."

He admitted that the TV program was embellished, but no more than others: "I've been thrown into enough jails in this country and abroad to know that TV police shows, for example, are not more than 10 percent accurate."

The TV show was successful, especially with kids, he claimed: "We got more mail than any series that's been on the air. We weren't cancelled for any lack of having a good show—there were too many letters from teenagers who said they were going to join one of the services when they finished school. The networks are very left-wing in policy, all three of them; they don't like promoting recruiting for nothing."

He went on, more seriously, "It takes more than one guy to make a squadron. It takes everybody.

"My job was like a coach. Most of our training was word of mouth. Sometimes on a rainy day when there was no flying, I'd tell them to try to think of all the possible problems or situations they might get into, and then think what they'd do. I was trying to get them to act by reflex. You don't have time to think what to do; you have to act, sometimes in a split second. My purpose was to get rid of unnecessary fear.

"Actually, you're safer in the air than you are on the freeway. The enemy can't shoot at you beyond 1,000 yards, and he can only shoot straight ahead, so he usually has to be directly behind you.

"Another thing, you can't afford the luxury of anger in the air; you have to think."

He then volunteered to answer questions, saying that he was an expert on many subjects besides the Corsair. For example:

"Medicine—I've had three major surgeries; four, if you count the one in Japan without anesthetic.

"Marriage—I've had several; I can tell you what not to do."

He was asked about a Japanese pilot who claims to have shot him down and is now in the United States.

"I gave up on that character. I tried to help him, but I was already in POW camp the day he says he shot me down. He wrote a book titled, *The Road To Conquest*. He gives me half a page. He makes a living going around to air shows peddling his book."

Boyington now lives in Fresno with his current wife. He is seen at various air shows and aviation conferences, peddling autographed copies of his own book.

"I'm an entertainer," he said recently. "Say you're at a convention of medical people. Hell, they don't want to listen to some boob with a bunch of charts talking about upper sinus tubes. They want to be entertained."

And that's what this combat pilot who had been the scourge of the Japanese in the South Pacific has come to. Like a dancing bear, he's an entertainer.

For Gregory "Pappy" Boyington, war hero, F. Scott Fitzgerald said it best: "Show me a hero and I'll write you a tragedy."

Epilogue

These were the Black Sheep, a cross section of America. In response to our country's call, the 51 young men came from 23 states across the nation, from Vermont to California, and from Washington to Florida. From a variety of backgrounds, they meshed into a smooth, deadly combat team that wrote a glorious page in Marine Corps and American history.

It was a time of high adventure. The Black Sheep had the support of the American people. No janefondas or ramseyclarks carped in the background or gnawed, ratlike, at that support.

The key word that keeps coming up in all our recollections about those days is "camaraderie": loyalty and warm, friendly feeling among comrades. Founded on our unique beginning, forged in the crucible of battle, our loyalties were firm; our desire to achieve intense. Friendships formed during those 84 days of combat, when the Black Sheep spearheaded the drive that broke the back of Japanese aerial opposition in the Solomons, have remained steady for 40 years. Black Sheep memorabilia adorn the walls of most of our homes or offices.

Some of the Black Sheep gave their lives; others their blood.

All gave something of themselves.

The survivors became a part of the warp and woof of our country. They became doctor, lawyer, merchant, chief, airline pilot, printer, architect, banker, artist, professor.

Today, they have blended into the fabric of America.

But once they were eagles.

Appendixes

Roster, Boyington's Black Sheep

Both Combat Tours

ASHMUN, George M.
  Far Hills, N.J.
BOLT, John F.
  Sanford, Fla.
BOYINGTON, Gregory
  Okanogan, Wash.
BRAGDON, Robert M.
  Pittsburg, Pa.
EMRICH, Warren T.
  Wichita, Kan.
FISHER, Don H.
  Miami, Fla.
GROOVER, Denmark, Jr.
  Quitman, Ga.
HARPER, Edwin A.
  Wallace, Idaho
HEIER, William D.
  Kansas City, Mo.
HILL, James J.
  Chicago, Ill.

MAGEE, Christopher L.
  Chicago, Ill.
MATHESON, Bruce J.
  Chicago, Ill.
MCCLURG, Robert W.
  New Castle, Pa.
MOORE, Donald J.
  Amarillo, Tex.
MULLEN, Paul A.
  Pittsburg, Pa.
OLANDER, Edwin L.
  Northampton, Mass.
REAMES, James M.
  Hughes, Ark.
SIMS, Sanders S.
  Philadelphia, Pa.
TUCKER, Burney L.
  Murfreesboro, Tenn.
WALTON, Frank E.
  Los Angeles, Calif.

First Combat Tour Only

ALEXANDER, Robert A.
  Davenport, Iowa
BAILEY, Stanley R.
  Thetford, Vt.
BEGERT, John F.
  Topeka, Kan.
BOURGEOIS, Henry M.
  New Orleans, La.
CASE, William N.
  Vancouver, Wash.

EWING, Robert T.
  Lafayette, Ind.
HARRIS, Walter R.
  Sterling, Neb.
McCARTNEY, Henry A.
  Long Island, N.Y.
RAY, Virgil G.
  Hallsboro, N.C.
RINABARGER, Rolland N.
  Medford, Ore.

Second Combat Tour Only

AVEY, Fred V.
  Portland, Ore.

FFOULKES, Bruce J.
  San Mateo, Calif.

BARTL, Harry R.
  Sacramento, Calif.
BOWERS, Glenn L.
  York, Pa.
BROWN, John S.
  Indianapolis, Ind.
BRUBAKER, James E.
  Clearwater, Fla.
CARNAGEY, Pierre
  Corpus Christi, Tex.
CHATHAM, Rufus M., Jr.
  Beaumont, Tex.
CORMAN, J. Ned
  Bellefonte, Pa.
CROCKER, William L.
  Worchester, Mass.
DOSWELL, Gelon H.
  New Orleans, La.
DUSTIN, J. Cameron
  Bellevue, Neb.

HOBBS, William A., Jr.
  Webster Groves, Mo.
HOLDEN, Herbert, Jr.
  Elizabeth, N.J.
JOHNSON, Alfred L.
  Utica, N.Y.
JOHNSON, Harry C.
  Birmingham, Ala.
LANE, Perry T.
  Rutland, Vt.
LOSCH, Fred S.
  Larryville, Pa.
MARCH, Marion J.
  Seattle, Wash.
MARKER, Alan D.
  Park Ridge, Ill.
MILLER, Henry S.
  Jenkintown, Pa.

Boyington's Black Sheep consisted of 49 pilots, one Flight Surgeon, one Intelligence Officer.

Four pilots lost during first combat tour:
    Captain Robert T. Ewing   16 September 1943
        Missing in action over Ballale, Solomon Islands
    First Lieutenant Walter R. Harris   27 September 1943
        Missing in action over the Shortlands, Solomon Islands
    First Lieutenant Robert A. Alexander   30 September 1943
        Killed in strafing run over Kolombangara, Solomon Islands
    Second Lieutenant Virgil G. Ray   13 October 1943
        Missing on flight from Russell Islands, Solomon Islands

Eight pilots lost on second combat tour:
    Major Pierre Carnagey   23 December 1943
        Missing in action over Rabaul, Bismarck Archipelago
    First Lieutenant James E. Brubaker   23 December 1943
        Missing in action over Rabaul
    First Lieutenant Bruce Ffoulkes   23 December 1943
        Missing in action over Rabaul
    Captain J. Cameron Dustin   28 December 1943
        Missing in action over Rabaul

Second Lieutenant Harry R. Bartl   28 December 1943
   Missing in action over Rabaul
First Lieutenant Donald J. Moore   28 December 1943
   Missing in action over Rabaul
Captain George M. Ashmun   3 January 1944
   Missing in action over Rabaul
Major Gregory Boyington   3 January 1944
   Imprisoned by the Japanese; released in 1945

Two Black Sheep lost on later missions with other squadrons:
   First Lieutenant William L. Crocker, Jr.
   First Lieutenant William H. Hobbs, Jr.

Two Black Sheep lost in operational aircraft accidents after the war:
   First Lieutenant Paul A. Mullen
   Major Stanley R. Bailey

Two Black Sheep died of natural causes after the war:
   First Lieutenant Robert M. Bragdon
   First Lieutenant John S. Brown

As of May 1985, 34 of the original Black Sheep survived;
   Burney Tucker died 10 June 1986.

Appendix B

Marine Fighting Squadron 214— Information for the Duty Officer

FIVE DIVISIONS ON DUTY PER DAY:

Since we are assigned 20 planes, 5 divisions will be sufficient to man all our planes at any particular time even in the unusual case where all are in commission at the same time. Some divisions may fly more than one flight a day but it is believed better to have pilots fly hard when they are on duty, and then have a day off, than to have those same pilots on duty for two light days successively with no days off.

ROTATION OF DIVISIONS:

The five divisions on duty will always be consecutively numbered divisions, and will fly in the order of their numbers. Thus, beginning at the top of the list, numbers 1 through 5 would be together and would fly in that order. On the next day, numbers 6 through 1 would be on duty. When more than one division is on the same flight, the senior division leader will lead the flight and take the lower call.

TIME FOR REPORTING:

(1) When no early takeoff is planned. Enough divisions will be called (awakened at 0430; breakfast at 0445; at the Ready Room at 0515) to man all the available planes at 0515. If an odd number of planes is available, Operations requires that another division be called. For example, if 13 planes are in, four divisions must be called.

(2) When an early takeoff is planned. Divisions as required will be awakened one hour and 45 minutes before takeoff time, will have breakfast one hour and 30 minutes before takeoff time, and will be at the Ready Room one hour before takeoff time.

(3) Other divisions. Divisions on duty but not required for manning the available planes, or for an early takeoff, will get themselves up, and will report not later than 0800.

TIME FOR SECURING:

About 1600, the Duty Officer should secure any division not needed to man the planes available, for the rest of the day. For example, if any eight-plane flight has just gone out, and seven planes on the ground are available, he should keep on duty the two divisions next to fly and secure the fifth division. But if an eighth plane flight is due to come in about 1600, and the same seven planes on the ground are available, the Duty Officer must wait until those eight planes have landed. He can then secure the division last to fly (which will ordinarily be one of the divisions which has just landed). Everything on the ground secures at 1815.

SCRAMBLE STANDBY:

Every third day, the squadron will provide for the scramble standby which is usually four planes but may be more. Beginning at 0530, each division should be on duty once for two and a half hours; the last division two and three quarters hours which carries it through to 1815. The duty should follow the regular rotation, but normally it should begin with the division reporting last on the early call (so as not to conflict with the rotation flying, which always comes first, and which so far, at least, seems to involve about five divisions flying one hop a day). This idea of starting the scramble alert with the division reporting last on the early call will have to be modified as the situation requires. It will take a certain amount of juggling to get every division on duty into the scramble alert at some time during the day, without interfering with their flying (which must go on in the routine order). Correction of the above: The scramble alert begins at 0515 (the division involved must be called as if for a takeoff at 0515 also) so that the division taking it first will stand it for two hours and three quarters like the last division.

CHOW ROTATION:

On each day's schedule will be listed three divisions which may be called upon for relief for noon chow. They will be called upon in the order listed. Unless otherwise directed by the Duty Officer (who should give them their instructions about 1030), they should eat early, at 1100. All planes available on the ground must be manned continuously through the noon chow period.

CALLING FOR THE DOPE:

Every evening someone from the Flight Department will go to Operations with the next day's Duty Officer to get the next day's operations schedule. This operations schedule is usually ready by 1930 and should be called for as near that time as possible in order to protect our interests. The Duty Officer will then stop by Major Boyington's tent and mark briefly on the schedule posted there what will be going on early in the morning. If Lieutenant Walton is available, the same dope should be given him so that he can brief the early flights as may be necessary.

SQUADRON AND TOWER DUTY OFFICERS:

At the present time, in order to give the spare pilots an opportunity to fly, the squadron and tower duty officers are taken from the division on duty which is fifth to fly. They are named as much as possible giving credit for similar duties performed at Buttons since the Sydney trip.

TAKEOFFS ON TIME:

Above everything else, flights must go out on time. This means that the last plane be airborne by the time scheduled. The time requirements as for pre-dawn takeoffs are listed above. For ordinary takeoffs the pilots must be out at the planes at least half an hour before the takeoff time. In all cases the Duty Officer will go out to the planes in the truck with the pilots, making sure that the planes are in and ready. After dropping off and assigning all the pilots, he should make a run back to check up.

ASSIGNMENT OF PLANES:

The Duty Officer will assign planes to cover all flights. The planes at the top of the board are Marine maintained; those below are Navy maintained. Marine planes are nearer the strip and are listed in order of their respective nearness to the strip. All planes will be assigned so that the division leader will have the plane nearest the strip so that there will be a minimum of confusion in taxiing out. As a check when we have a scramble alert, the planes should be marked: "Scramble 1, Scramble 2, Scramble 3, and Scramble 4" and the scramble pilots will take them accordingly.

TEST PILOT RECORDS AND TROUBLE REPORTS:

In Lieutenant Walton's desk are kept test flight and trouble report forms. In assigning test hops, the Duty Officer will provide a test flight form and see that it is properly made out. When flights come in, the Duty Officer will see that any pilot downing a plane makes out a trouble report and turns it in to him. The Flight Clerk will see that these forms reach the appropriate engineering departments.

Appendix C

Marine Fighting Squadron 214— Notice to Pilots (to be added to from time to time)

MAPS AND NATIVE LANGUAGE SHEET:

Along with maps appropriate to the area, carry at all times the sheet of paper bearing instructions to the natives in their language and in our own.

TAXIING:

A crewman should always be on the wing. The pilot will observe his signals and taxi slowly, avoiding abrupt turns and stops which might throw him off the wing. In the vicinity of the strip, watch the tower for directions by the light.

CLEANING OUT ENGINE AND TESTING MAGNETOS:

In cleaning out the engine and testing the mags prior to takeoff, in every possible case turn the tail of the plane toward the water. In every other case, place the plane so that the slipstream will have a minimum annoying effect upon tents, personnel, engineering work, etc.

CROSS WIND:

In deciding in which direction to land, do not consider merely the convenience of taxiing directly into our revetment area but consider also the direction and force of the wind. If necessary, call Eskimo Base and ask advice.

TAKEOFFS TO THE NORTH:

In taking off toward the North, follow the coast line in a right turn, keeping a bit low until outside the traffic circle, and join up over the water in a right turn back toward the South.

CHECKING GAS:

Before all flights, check the gas in all three tanks by actually removing the caps.

YELLOW SHEETS, TROUBLE REPORTS, AND TEST FLIGHT RECORDS:

On all flights fill out the yellow sheet carefully and completely. When downing a plane for a cause which is not obvious, such as vibration, rough running, etc., fill out a trouble report form (obtained from Frank Walton) and turn it in. Likewise, before a test flight, obtain a test flight record form (also obtained from Frank Walton), fill it out during the test, and turn it in to Sergeant Ledyard.

PRE-DAWN TAKEOFFS:

In the absence of express arrangements to the contrary, agreed upon by the pilots concerned prior to takeoff, the following provisions will be observed for the sake of safety and smoothness:

(1) The leader for the takeoff will wait for the members of the flight to gather behind him at the point where the taxiway meets the strip, but he will not wait later than 15 minutes before takeoff time. At 15 minutes before takeoff time, if not sooner, he and all planes then ready will taxi together (with mechs still riding the wings, preferably the left wings) to the North end of the strip for takeoff. Anyone not then ready will not be permitted to take off. Someone from

the Flight Department will be at the mouth of the taxiway to see to this. Having exactly four or eight planes on an early patrol is not important enough to make it worthwhile to take chances in taxiing or delay planes already airborne.

(2) The planes will rendezvous either by divisions or as one whole flight, as indicated by the leader prior to takeoff. In either case, the leading pilot will go straight out from the strip for a long enough time to permit the planes rendezvousing on him to get into the air. He will then make a shallow 180-degree turn to the left. If his planes have not joined up by the time he is abeam the strip, he will make a left circle just offshore from the strip. In the rendezvous, the leader or leaders may profitably leave their landing light on.

(3) It is not necessary that the planes fly out to their mission in the order in which the pilots usually fly. The important thing is to get joined up with someone, to get away from this area and then later, by daylight, to shift back to the desired positions. Of course, each pilot should figure out beforehand what heading he will fly if he turns out to be leading another plane or planes.

PARKING IN THE REVETMENTS:

Bear in mind the following considerations:

(1) The revetments at this base are somewhat narrow for F-4-Us. At one time, in an effort to prevent avoidable damage to elevators and wingtips, it was required that the plane be parked by the pilot in front of the revetment and pushed back into place by the crew.

(2) F-4-Us are heavy and hard to push, particularly into revetments which slope up hill. Also, the taxiways may be blocked if the planes are left by the pilots in front of the revetments.

(3) The revetments vary somewhat in width and the plane crews vary in experience.

Therefore, it will be left to the judgement of the pilot whether the particular revetment is sufficiently wide and the plane crew sufficiently experienced for the pilot to be able to bring the plane in successfully under power. He will use extreme caution to avoid damage of any kind. When it is getting close, it is better to shut off the engine and have the plane pushed or towed into place than to do something which may even mean a wing change.

Air Intelligence Fighter Command Barakoma—Strafing and Searches

GENERAL REGULATIONS REGARDING STRAFING:

From time to time special restrictions on strafing will be issued but unless specifically notified, strafing will normally be governed as follows:

(1) *Permissible only* in hatched areas as shown on posted map (dated 11-22-43). In unhatched areas there will be *no strafing* of shipping or shore installations. At night there will be *no strafing* in areas of PT operations.

(2) *Not advisable* to make more than one strafing run over an area where AA positions are known or reported to exist. There is recent evidence that some enemy AA batteries are not using tracer ammunition.

(3) *No jousting* attacks shall be made on AA positions or concentrations.

(4) Unless ordered otherwise, there will be *no strafing* on escort missions.

SPECIAL SEARCHES:

(1) *Charlie search:* Search coast at Laruna River, up the Laruna River, and over the Numa Numa Trail to Numa Numa; then proceed down the northeast coast of Bougainville strafing any surface vessels sighted. Shore installations within one mile of the coast are legitimate targets.

(2) *Able Search:* Search and strafe Matchin Bay and Chabai.

(3) *Southern Cross Search:* Search and strafe area south of a line from Mupeka Village (immediately northeast of Motupena Point) to Moila Point.

(4) *Plan Baker-Oboe:* Primary targets are enemy shipping. Search and attack enemy shipping west and northwest of Bougainville. In the event no shipping is found, the southern Bougainville airfields will be secondary targets. This operation combines SBDs, TBFs, and PV-1s. See ComAirSols instructions. *No strafing* by fighters unless specifically ordered to do so.

RECENT SPECIFIC STRAFING INSTRUCTIONS: Do not strafe Kieta Harbor and airfield area unless specifically ordered. *Do not strafe ANY* native canoes *ANYWHERE.*

Briefing for Rabaul Fighter Sweep (17 December 1943)

1) Mission:
   (a) Strip maps everyone
   (b) Rabaul Harbor everyone
   (c) 8 x 8 target maps, Division leaders
2) Makeup of strike and radio calls:
   * VMF 222— 8 F-4-Us—Crystal 20, 21   (26,000 feet)
   * VMF 223— 8 F-4-Us—Crystal 22, 23   (23,000 feet)
   * VMF 214— 8 F-4-Us—Crystal 24, 25   (20,000 feet)
   * VMF 216— 8 F-4-Us—Ruby 4, 5   (20–25,000 feet)
   * VF   40 — 8 F-6-Fs—Crystal 66, 67) (15–20,000 feet)
   * VF   33 —16 F-6-Fs—Gem 60-63   )
   * NZAF   —24 P-40s —Gem 40, 45   (10–15,000 feet)
               80 aircraft (32 Marine F-4-Us,
                  24 Navy F-6-Fs, 24 New Zealand P-40s)
3) Takeoff schedules:
   04:45—8 F-4-Us (Crystal 20, 21)
   05:00—8 F-4-Us (Crystal 22, 23)
   05:15—8 F-4-Us (Crystal 24, 25)
   05:30—8 F-4-Us (Ruby 4, 5   )
   05:45—8 F-6-Fs (Crystal 66, 67)
   06:00—16 F-6-Fs (Gem 60, 63   )
   06:15—24 P-40s (Gen 40, 45   )
   All F-4-Us pancake Cherry Blossom (Bougainville) by 0600; all F-6-Fs by 0645. P-40s will probably pancake after 0700.
4) Bougainville landing instructions: Three ball—East to West; One ball—West to East. All turns to be made over the water.
5) Strike:
   0830—First fighters take off Cherry Blossom for strike.
   0900—Last fighters take off Cherry Blossom.
   1020—Over Rabaul (1 F-5-A over Rabaul at 35,000).
   1045—Leave Rabaul (Rally at Cape St. George).
   1200—Over Cherry Blossom. (All planes low on gas, pancake Cherry Blossom; others return to Vella Lavella or to Ondonga).
6) Rabaul strength (5 December 1943):
   Lakunai 100 (65 fighters; 35 others)
   Tobera 22 (fighters)
   Vunakanu 31 (4 fighters; 27 others)
   Rapopo 7 (bombers)
   Keravit 0

Other: New Britain—45

TOTALS: 205 (91 fighters; 114 others)

7) Antiaircraft:

Rabaul is ringed with it as is each air strip.

8) Forced landings:

Two PVs will patrol between Rabaul and Cherry Blossom between 1000 and 1200.

Two Dumbos will be on alert at Cherry Blossom between 0730 and 1500. Pilots will call Dane Base for Dumbos.

9) Coast Watchers:

New Britain: On a stretch of land running North and South from near Jacquinot Bay toward Open Bay.

DO NOT, REPEAT, DO NOT GO ON GAZELLE PENINSULA

New Ireland: Look for a native named Boski.

His hiding place is "Place Mamboo." It is near Weilan River, several miles inland. Boski's village is named Pukton, 15 miles above Cape St. George. It is located between Cape Siar and Cape Bun Bun.

Bougainville: Northeast—Teaposina and Tinputs.

Northwest—Sarime Plantation.

10) Currents:

Always paddle with the currents unless using sail. Go into water on Northwest side of Bougainville; you'll drift along the West coast.

11) Weather:

Generally Southeast.

12) Diversion:

Nine B-25s over Cherry Blossom at 0905 for 10 minutes and then on course for 10 minutes to their targets. Purpose: deception.

13) In the event of bad weather, the call is: "Dagwood, I am returning."

Request That Black Sheep Squadron Be Kept Intact

HEADQUARTERS, MARINE AIRCRAFT GROUP ELEVEN
FIRST MARINE AIRCRAFT WING, NAVY NO. 140 (ONE FOUR ZERO)
C/O FLEET POST OFFICE, SAN FRANCISCO, CALIFORNIA

12 January 1944

From: Major Henry Miller, U.S. Marine Corps Reserve
To: The Commanding General, First Marine Aircraft Wing
Via: The Commanding General, Marine Aircraft Group Eleven

Subject: Flight echelon known until recently as VMF 214, disposition of.

1) The flight echelon known until recently as VMF 214 has just completed its second tour of combat duty under the command of Major Gregory Boyington.

2) The number 214 has gone back to the United States with the ground echelon, so that the flight echelon of VMF 214 is without a number and therefore is attached at present to Headquarters Squadron, Marine Aircraft Group Eleven.

3) The flight echelon referred to is concerned about the possible division of its personnel among other squadrons.

4) The flight echelon referred to, known as the "Black Sheep," wishes to urge strongly that it be maintained as a unit in order not to destroy its high morale and its smooth operation as an aggressive squadron of the type which we believe of the most value to the Marine Corps. We wish to present the following reasons for preserving the "Black Sheep" as a unit:
(a) It is generally realized that a combat team should be kept together. About 1 October 1943, the flight echelon of the original VMF 214 was broken up after two successful tours. We believe that it is recognized that the effects of that breakup were unfortunate.
(b) Under the aggressive leadership of Major Boyington, the Black Sheep put into successful practice his ideas of combat operations. The record speaks for itself. Now Major Boyington is missing in action and we believe that his ideas of strategy and tactics should be perpetuated. We know them, we believe in them and feel that we as a unit are in the best position to carry them on.
(c) Our unit is practically intact at the present time. Our Intelligence Officer had made the two tours with us and is available for a third. We would be seriously handicapped without him. We need only a Flight

Surgeon and thirteen first-tour pilots to make up a full squadron divided equally among first-tour pilots, second-tour pilots, and third-tour pilots. This combination will permit the perpetuation and development of Major Boyington's ideas through the three different levels of pilot experience included.

(d) We have trained together and fought together for a long period of time. Twelve of our thirteen pilots who have had two tours have been together for these two tours. The thirteen pilots who have had one tour not only trained together here for seven weeks before making that tour but trained together in the United States and came overseas together.

(e) Finally, under Major Boyington, the Black Sheep developed an esprit de corps we believe unparalleled in this area. This spirit will be lost if the unit is broken up.

(5) For these reasons it is urged that this unit be kept intact.

Henry S. Miller

Appendix G

Accomplishment Record of Boyington's Black Sheep Squadron

Combat tours: 12 September 1943–24 October 1943
                27 November 1943–8 January 1944

97*	Enemy planes shot down in aerial combat: 95 of them fighter planes; 94 over enemy territory
35	Enemy planes probably shot down in aerial combat
50	Enemy planes damaged in aerial combat
21	Enemy planes destroyed on the ground
203	Total enemy planes destroyed, probably destroyed, or damaged

*Upon Boyington's release from Japanese prison, he reported that he had shot down three Zeros instead of the one we had reported and that Ashmun (who was lost) had also shot down one. These raised the Black Sheep total from 94 to 97.

  1 100-foot transport vessel destroyed
  1 50-foot transport vessel destroyed
  1 70-foot Japanese-operated Chinese junk destroyed
  1 70-foot steam launch destroyed
 20 barges destroyed
  3 barges loaded with enemy troops destroyed
  1 raft loaded with enemy troops destroyed
 15 other craft probably destroyed
125 Japanese bivouac and concentration areas and antiaircraft positions in
     New Ireland, New Britain, Buka, Bougainville, and the Shortlands
     strafed.
  4 Japanese airfields strafed: Kahili, Kara, Ballale, Borpop.

Successfully intercepted enemy aerial formation attempting to attack U.S. Task
Force reinforcing Barokoma.

Relieved Bougainville ground Marines in an untenable position by strafing
enemy mortar positions.

Participated in 1,776 individual combat missions and flew a total of 4,195
combat hours.

Black Sheep aces and their scores:

Major Gregory Boyington	28
Lieutenant Christopher Magee	9
Lieutenant William Case	8
Lieutenant Robert McClurg	7
Lieutenant Paul Mullen	6½
Lieutenant John Bolt	6
Lieutenant Don Fisher	6
Lieutenant Edwin L. Olander	5

The Squadron Presidential Unit Citation reads, in part:

In some of the most bitterly contested Air Combats on record, contributed
substantially to the establishment of an aerial beachhead over Rabaul . . .
frequently outnumbered but never outfought, Marine Fighting Squadron 214
achieved an outstanding combat record.

Index

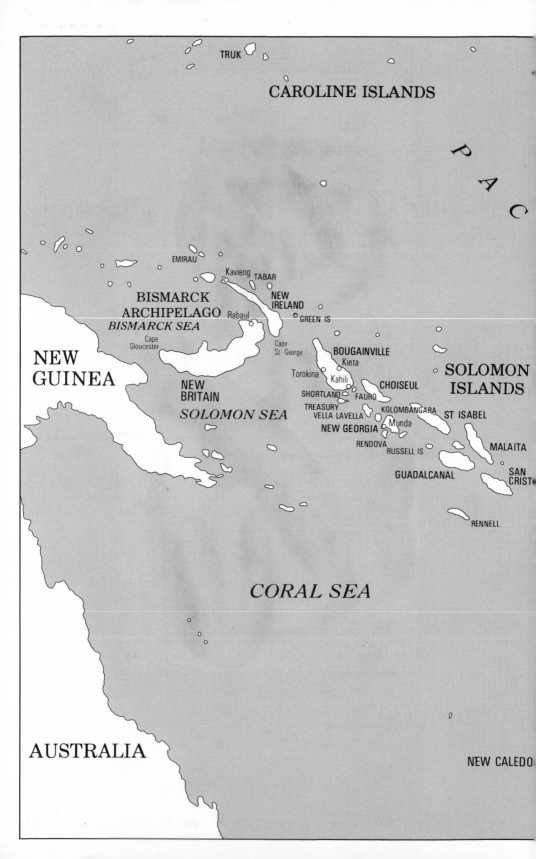